PEAKY
BLINDERS

Professor Carl Chinn MBE Ph.D. is a social historian with a national profile; he is a writer, public speaker and teacher. An off-course bookmaker himself until 1984, he is the son and grandson of illegal bookmakers in Sparkbrook, and the great-grandson of a peaky blinder, whilst his mother's family were factory workers in Aston. His writings are deeply affected by his family's working-class background and life in the back-to-backs of Birmingham and he believes passionately that history must be democratised because each and every person has made their mark upon history and has a story to tell.

PEAKY BLINDERS

THE REAL GANGS AND GANGSTERS

The true story of Britain's most notorious street gangs

CARL CHINN

First published in the UK in 2025 by Blink Publishing
An imprint of Bonnier Books UK
5th Floor, HYLO, 105 Bunhill Row,
London, EC1Y 8LZ

A CIP catalogue record for this book is available from the British Library.

Paperback ISBN: 9781789467291

Also available as an ebook and an audiobook

1 3 5 7 9 10 8 6 4 2

Design and Typeset by Envy Design Ltd
Printed and bound in Great Britain by Clays Ltd, Elcograf S.p.A.

MIX
Paper | Supporting
responsible forestry
FSC
www.fsc.org
FSC® C018072

The authorised representative in the EEA is
Bonnier Books UK (Ireland) Limited.
Registered office address: Floor 3, Block 3, Miesian Plaza,
Dublin 2, D02 Y754, Ireland
compliance@bonnierbooks.ie

www.bonnierbooks.co.uk

This book is dedicated to the hard-working and honest poor of backstreet Victorian and Edwardian Birmingham. They suffered from both the class prejudice of an unequal and unfair society and the violence and bullying of the peaky blinders who lived amongst them. Poorer women especially had it rough and it's they who should be admired for their fortitude and selflessness, not the thugs of the street gangs. Treated as second-class citizens legally, politically, socially and culturally, they were subjected not only to misogyny but also to sexual assaults and abuse by peaky blinders. Yet it was these poor women who were on the front line of the unrelenting war against a ruthless enemy: poverty. They knew that today would be like yesterday and tomorrow like today: an endless struggle to stay clean and respectable whilst battling bad housing, insanitary conditions, hunger and hardship aplenty. Fully aware that their lives would never change, still many hoped that one day through their toil and sweat, one of their own would have something denied to themselves: a better life. There's still much to do to make that better life for all our citizens.

CONTENTS

ABBREVIATIONS

Unless otherwise stated, all prison sentences are for hard labour.

Money is given as pre-decimal. With 20 shillings to the pound and 12 pence to the shilling, a shilling was the equivalent of 5p.
s – shilling/shillings
d – penny/pence

A dash (–) in newspaper reports indicated a swear word.

ABG	*Aris's Birmingham Gazette*
B&AC	*Birmingham & Aston Chronicle*
BCP	Calendar of Prisoners, 1870–1935
BQS	Birmingham Quarter Sessions, 1839–1971
BG	*Birmingham Gazette*
BJ	*Birmingham Journal*
BM	*Birmingham Mail*
BP	*Birmingham Post*
BST	*Birmingham Suburban Times*
BWM	*Birmingham Weekly Mercury*

BWP	*Birmingham Weekly Post*
ED	*Evening Despatch*
HO 140	Home Office: Calendar of Prisoners
ILP	*Illustrated Police News*
MEPO6	Metropolitan Police: criminal record office, habitual criminals' registers and miscellaneous papers
PCOM 2	1770–1951 Home Office and Prison Commission: Prisons Records, Series 1
TNA	The National Archives
WH	*Warwickshire Herald*
WMPM	West Midlands Police Museum

TIMELINE

1838   The Bull Ring Riots.

1839   The Birmingham Police Force formed.

1867   The Murphy Riots & the crusade against pitch and toss are catalysts for the emergence of street gangs. Both the Liberals and Conservatives employed gangs of roughs to disrupt each other's meetings.

1868   Irish Park Street Gang and English Barr Street and Barford Street gangs emerge.
A murder by one of the Harding Street Black Band was the first gang murder in Birmingham.

1872   The term slogging gang was first used in the press.

1873   Joseph Chamberlain elected mayor of Birmingham.
Rioting by the Navigation Street Gang.

1874   John Kirkham of the Milk Street Gang killed by 'Jacky' Joyce of the Park Street Gang. Both were young teenagers.
Bordesley Street Riot.

1875   Navigation Street Riot and PC Lines murdered.

1876   Joseph Chamberlain elected an MP for Birmingham. Lionel Street Riot of the Livery Street Gang.

1878   Savage Attack on PC Copestake by the Navigation Street Gang.

1884   The Aston Riots: the Harding Street, Barr Street, Lench Street and Cecil Street Gangs named in Parliament as paid by the Liberals to violently disrupt a large Conservative meeting.

1886   Weekly battles between the Whitehouse Street Gang and the Nechells sloggers.

1888   The Highgate Street Gang's ruffianism in Balsall Heath.

1890   Birmingham pronounced as the best-governed city in the world. First mention of peaky blinders in the press.
        The Deritend Riot by the Milk Street Gang.
        Murder of the manager of the Mucker music hall by the Park Street Gang.
        James 'Big Jonah' Jones kills a man in Summer Lane – his description is the first detailing the peaky blinders' fashion.
        Police baiting by the Sparkbrook Slogging Gang.

1894   The Bromsgrove Street Disturbance & Watery Lane Affray.
        Murder of John Metcalfe of the Park Street Gang by John Cherry of the Barford Street Gang.

1897   Murder of PC Snipe by the peaky blinder George 'Cloggy' Williams.

1898   Killing of Emily Pimm by a supposed peaky blinder. PC Leach savagely attacked by peaky blinders.

TIMELINE

1899 Charles Haughton Rafter appointed Chief Constable.

1900 Serious affray in Barford Street with its peaky blinders/slogging gang.

1901 Murder of PC Gunter by peaky blinders.

1902 Brutal assault on PC Blinko by peaky blinders.

1905 Frederick 'Satan' Timbrell of the Summer Hill Gang killed in a gang fight by William 'Young Brush' Lacey. It was the last report of a peaky blinders/slogging gang feud.
The *Birmingham Mail* reported that the palmy days of the peaky blinders were over.

1908 The *Birmingham Mail* rejoiced that the peaky blinders were disappearing.
The Garrison Lane Vendetta erupts between the Sheldon Gang of older criminals, formerly in the Barr Street Gang, and the Beach Gang of local hard men.

1909 The last mention of the Ten Arches Gang.

1912 Garrison Lane Vendetta ended with severe sentencing. The Birmingham press writes about the peaky blinders and slogging gangs in the past tense.

1915 The *Birmingham Mail* reported that former peaky blinders were in the Army or employed as unskilled workers in factories.

1921 Former peaky blinder Billy Kimber leads the infamous Birmingham Gang in a bloody war with the Sabini Gang of North London for control of the racketeering on southern racecourses.
Britain's first gang war between gangs from separate cities: it was the catalyst for organised crime gangs in London.

ACKNOWLEDGEMENTS

Born in 1956, I grew up belonging to two big extended families proud of the tough working-class streets they came from. As a youngster, various grandparents and great-aunts and uncles used to gather at Our Mom's on a Sunday afternoon, and I would listen raptly as the chat turned to the goings-on down 'the old end'. The Chinns were from Studley Street off The Lane, the Ladypool Road part of Sparkbrook, and the Woods/ Perrys from Whitehouse Street, Aston. I was fascinated by the often-rumbustious stories of my families, their streets and neighbourhoods. Told in the vigorous speech of Brummies from poorer working-class backgrounds, they were stories about people and places that weren't found in history books. Those stories inspired me and instilled in me a loyalty both to the streets my families belonged to and to those like them. Although those relatives are all gone, they are with me still and I pay tribute to their deep effect on me, my research and my writing. I also thank all those many other working-class Brummies who've shared their memories with me.

Growing up, and like others of my generation in

Birmingham, I'd heard about the peaky blinders, but I first researched and wrote about them in my doctoral thesis in 1986. The next year, when gathering evidence for a study of bookmaking, I interviewed Simeon Solomon, the younger brother of the real Alfie Solomon, portrayed as Alfie Solomons in the *Peaky Blinders* television drama. I also spoke with the son of George Langham, real name Angelo Gianicoli, a close friend of and enforcer for London gang leader Darby Sabini, another character depicted in the TV series. Old racecourse bookies I spoke with told me about Billy Kimber, the leader of the Birmingham Gang and a Brummie who's given as a Londoner in the show. The knowledge I gained from those bookmakers and others was invaluable. I thank not only them but also the Birmingham descendants of Billy Kimber who contacted me in 2013 before the television series was aired and shared family stories and photographs with me.[1]

This book is based overwhelmingly on primary evidence through family stories, recollections, rare memoirs, newspapers articles, censuses, police and criminal records, and military service holdings. In bringing to life real peaky blinders, another vital source is photographs, especially those from the West Midlands Police Museum. Started by the forward-thinking Charlie Elworthy, it was later based at Sparkhill Police Station, where it was expanded due to the indefatigable efforts of Dave Cross, who introduced me to its priceless collection of prisoners' photographs. Now it's an award-winning museum at the late Victorian Lock Up in Steelhouse Lane, where many peaky blinders spent nights in the cells. The development of the museum owes much to the vision and determination of Corinne Brazier, its Heritage Manager, and her staff and enthusiastic volunteers. I thank her,

ACKNOWLEDGEMENTS

Bernard May who sourced some material for me, and all those concerned with this outstanding museum. For other photos, I appreciate the following: the Library of Birmingham; Juliet Banyard, the great-granddaughter of Billy Kimber; Edward Becker, the great-grandson of Edward Emanuel, the *éminence grise* of the Sabini Gang; and Michael King, the great-great-great-grandson of the slogger Thomas Joyce.

For her confidence in my work and her support, my appreciation goes to Ciara Lloyd, publishing editor at Blink, Bonnier Books UK. I also thank Saira Nabi, Assistant Editor, Bonnier Books UK, and all those involved in editing, typesetting, proof reading, printing, and sales for this book. Confidence is a fragile, intangible yet powerful thing and for the confidence to write about the people I belong to I acknowledge the role of the noted historian and my doctoral supervisor, the late Dorothy Thompson. I would not have become a writer without her encouragement. And without the people I belong to, I would never have had the chance to have an education past the age of fifteen and nor would I have been instilled with a passion for working-class history. For those gifts, I pay tribute to Our Mom, Sylvie Chinn née Perry, Our Dad, Alf 'Buck' Chinn, Our Nan, Lily Perry née Wood, Our Granddad Arthur Perry, and great aunts and uncles Our Winnie Martin née Wood, Georgie Wood, Billy Wood, Bill Chinn, and Wal Chinn. Finally, but never least, my deep gratitude goes to my Irish wife, Kay, for her constant support over forty-seven years of marriage since we met in Benidorm in 1977, for her understanding of my passion for the history of Birmingham and the urban working class, and for her compelling insights into growing up in the tightly knit council estate of Finglas West in north Dublin.

INTRODUCTION:

BEST-GOVERNED CITY IN THE WORLD & CITY OF PEAKY BLINDERS

BIRMINGHAM: BEST-GOVERNED CITY IN THE WORLD?

Proudly sitting in the grandeur of their newly built Council House inspired by a medieval Venetian palace, the late nineteenth-century political elite of Birmingham were convinced they could do deeds as great as those of Renaissance Pisa, Florence and Venice. This was no matter of mere local pride for they gloried in controlling 'the best governed city in the world', an accolade bestowed in 1890 by the American journalist Julian Ralph in the prestigious *Harper's Magazine*. Though renowned as one the most wonderful workshops of the world, he pronounced that Birmingham now commanded the greatest interest abroad for developing the science of municipal government to the highest standards. A model for the burgeoning towns of North America, it built its own trams, made and sold its own gas, collected and sold its own water, provided its people with a free museum, art gallery

1

and art school, and gave them swimming and Turkish baths at less than cost. All these and other services were possible because Birmingham was a business city run by businessmen on business principles. So it was.

Previously dominated by a raggle-taggle assortment of small-minded men bent on keeping the rates for property owners as low as possible, Ralph attributed the council's transformation into a municipal ideal to one man: Joseph Chamberlain. Wealthy through his partnership in Britain's biggest wood screw making business, in 1873 he led like-minded Liberals into a sweeping electoral victory locally. Appointed mayor, he used this traditionally honorary position as if he were the chief executive of a business, boldly directing a rapid and far-reaching policy of municipal socialism through sewerage and drainage schemes and the municipalisation of the private gas and water companies. Council ownership of the facilities for the welfare and well-being of the people was deeply influenced by local ministers preaching a Civic Gospel, encapsulated by the charismatic George Dawson proclaiming that 'A great town is a solemn organism through which should flow, and in which should be shaped, all the highest, loftiest and truest ends of man's intellectual and moral nature.' Chamberlain also pushed for the building of the Council House. Deliberately located in a prominent position on one of the highest points of the town centre, it was an imposing display of the importance of both Birmingham and its leading councillors.[2]

Chamberlain's whirlwind of change ended with his election to Parliament in 1876. With his customary assertiveness and pride, he declared he left Birmingham 'parked, paved, assized, marketed, gas and watered, and <u>improved</u>'. He himself underlined the word improved, stressing the significance of the Birmingham Improvement Scheme, a project he launched and drove forward and regarded by many as his crowning glory. Praised by Ralph as amongst the most stupendous, courageous and wise acts ever performed by a municipality, some of the worst and most unhealthy housing in a clump of run-down streets was compulsorily purchased and cleared. Set amidst the central business and civic district, they'd affronted forward-looking Birmingham, and their disappearance enabled the development of a wide Parisian-style boulevard. Flanked by fancy modern shops and striking terracotta public buildings such as the Victoria Law Courts, this aptly named Corporation Street reflected the council's prestige and Birmingham's status as the metropolis of the Midlands. Chamberlain, though, emphasised another reason for such a great town improvement: the reconstruction of this unwholesome district would physically and morally advance the lives of the poor who'd lived there. In supporting his proposals, he told the council that:

We bring up a population in the dank, dark, dreary, filthy courts and alleys such as are to be found throughout the area which we have selected; we surround them with noxious influences of every kind, and place them under conditions in which the observance of even ordinary decency is impossible; and what is the result?... The fact is, it is no more the fault of these people that they are vicious and intemperate than it is their fault that they are stunted, deformed, debilitated, and diseased. The one is due to the physical atmosphere – the moral atmosphere as necessarily and surely produces the other. Let us remove the conditions, and we may hope to see disease and crime removed.[3]

Chamberlain's speech captured the arrogance and prejudice of the fortunate wealthy. Too many of the poor did suffer from diseases and were physically less well developed than the well-fed, well-housed middle class in their pleasant districts, but these were not self-induced problems. They were the glaring consequences of an unfair and uncaring economic system beating down the incomes of the poorest and forcing them to live in a vile environment. Though denigrated, the people of the Improvement Scheme area weren't vicious degenerates. Although some were criminals and drunkards, the majority were widows, abandoned wives, children, the aged, disabled people and the infirm. Still, damning their neighbourhood as a rookery, a criminal district, made it easier to gain support for the Scheme, which far from improving the lives of the poor, made them worse. The dignity of Birmingham was enhanced by the removal of hundreds of unhealthy dwellings and the development of the splendid Corporation Street, but no provision was made for rehousing the poor whilst compensation went to their landlords.

In the purportedly best-governed city in the world, the bitter cry of the outcast poor went unheard. Those made homeless had no option but to move into nearby poverty-stricken neighbourhoods. Profiting from the high demand, landlords put up rents, meaning families had to take in lodgers. The resultant overcrowding of dwellings and areas exacerbated the spread of communicable diseases and pushed up death rates. Late nineteenth-century Birmingham was a tale of two cities. The growing central civic, business and shopping district, projecting an image of prosperity, pride and progress, was surrounded by a collar of life-destroying neighbourhoods. About 200,000 people, almost half the population, lived in this ring of hardship equivalent in size to Cardiff, Bolton or Salford. This city of poverty was hidden from the middle class travelling on main roads to work and shop in the town centre. They never saw the deprivation in the back streets where want rampaged: want of regular work, want of a reasonable income, want of good housing and health, want of warmth, want of food and want of hope.

Out of sight was out of mind. Few were concerned with the struggles of the mostly unskilled men and women and street traders scratching a precarious income below the poverty line and packed into over 44,000 back-to-back houses. Their construction was banned from 1876, but previously unhindered by planning regulations, jerry builders threw them up as quickly as possible on impure foundations with inferior materials. Having more dirt than sand for the mortar and too little lime in the horsehair plaster, back-to-backs were infested with stinking bugs, big black beetles and other verminous creatures. Arranged in a terrace of six to eight houses at the back of which was another terrace, they shared dividing walls merely a brick deep. Having no back doors or windows, they were dark with no through ventilation. Many back-to-backs were two storeys high, having two small bedrooms reached by steep stairs above the one room below. Others of three storeys had a little more space with an attic above the one bedroom. Usually just fifteen feet square, they were claustrophobic. One of eight children, Vero W. Garratt's household was 'pressed into one small living room, where we jostled each other with the restless abandon of children, while in the same atmosphere was done the cooking, the bathing, the eating, and the clothes-mending to the never-ending din of voices'.

The only furniture was perhaps a squab (a hard bench-like sofa), table, a couple of chairs and two or three shelves over a cupboard. Cooking was on an open fire or range, and the often-damp flooring was either beaten earth or porous quarry tiles covered by peg rugs made by women bodging (stitching) old rags on to urden (hessian) sacking. Sometimes there was an often-flooded cellar where coke and wood for fuel were stored if there was enough money to buy it. That was rare and instead, as Kathleen Dayus recalled of her Edwardian childhood, 'There was always some rubbish tipped in the cellar ready to put on the fire for warmth or for cooking. I don't suppose this habit would be regarded as altogether healthy today but then it was essential.'

The streets of Birmingham's poor were fronted by back-to-backs with a narrow entry between four or more leading into one of about 6,000 unpaved and usually sodden courts, colloquially called yards. The houses backing on to those on the street faced into the yard, and usually so did a terrace running at right angles to the entry and backing on to another terrace in the adjacent yard. A shared space, the yard had communal facilities including a brew'us (washhouse) with a copper (boiler) set in brick and below which a fire was lit. It took fifty gallons of water to fill it, with women drawing bucket after bucket from one standpipe in the yard. By contrast, each house in middle-class Edgbaston boasted its own tap. Close to the brew'us was the miskin, a foul-smelling and overflowing ash and rubbish pit; a reeking and often blocked suff (drain); and the lavatories. One of Chamberlain's few positive actions for the poor was the closing of filthy communal privies or cesspits from which offensive matter seeped. Yet to save costs, they weren't replaced by more hygienic water closets but by cheaper and repellent dry pan privies of the slimmest construction. Shared by two or more families, they were emptied irregularly and broken easily. Dayus remembered that 'each consisted of a square box with a large round hole in the middle. Us children had to hold the sides, otherwise we could have fallen in. You can imagine the stench in the summer!'[4]

Built hard and fast by factories and innumerable works, industrial pollution worsened the pernicious smells of yard life. In 1901, in a series of hard-hitting articles about 'the blackspots in Birmingham', the local journalist J. Cuming Walters railed that their atmosphere was heavy with a sooty smoke and acid vapours: 'You can veritably taste the pestilential air, stagnant and mephitic, which finds no outlet in the prison-like house of the courts; and yet here, where there is breathing-space for so few, the many are herded together, and overcrowding is the rule not the exception.' The poor had nowhere else to go for it was amid the 'rank and rotting garbage, in the filthy alleys and within the time-blackened old-fashioned dwellings, near the ill-smelling canal, or in the vicinage of factories which pour out their fumes in billowing masses from the throat of giant stacks – here it is they must come for shelter.' Three years later, the Reverend T. J. Bass, vicar of a deprived parish bordering the Improvement Scheme and plagued by peaky blinders, was incredulous that it included an Oxygen Street: 'Ye gods, what a name for a street where the atmosphere polluted by neighbouring works made my throat and nose smart and my eyes run.' Cut through by a canal, its basins and wharves, his parish of fourteen acres was covered with a brewery, flour mill, timber yard, malthouses, vinegar brewery, several large workplaces and much 'shopping' – small workshops. Housing was packed on to only eight acres, meaning that 2,429 people crowded into 589 decrepit houses. This resulted in a population density of 272 persons per acre, six times as great as the average for the city.[5]

Following the so-called 'rediscovery of poverty' in England in the 1880s, a plethora of writers and commentators closed in on the East End of London as 'Povertyopolis', unsettling the middle class with vivid descriptions of its wretched housing and squalid environment. Bass strove to alert a wide audience that Birmingham too had its East End, but sadly failed. However, in December 1903, a rare account of the misfortunes of Birmingham's poor was brought to a national audience by Edgar Wallace in the *Daily Mail*. Later a prolific writer of 'thrillers' featuring criminals, gangsters and detectives, he told his readers that:

If you have never seen a Birmingham slum, you have never seen abject misery at all. There is something in the air that makes it different from other slums – the reek of strange acid fumes, the pungent odour of unsymbolised gases. Wedged between high grim factories, their blank walls are an epitome of the life the people live beneath their shadows. Overlooked by great dirty stacks that belch black clouds of smoke unceasingly, the wretched hovels of the poor of Birmingham stand typical of the misery of their tenants. Up narrow lanes and grimy courts, away from the sunlight of God or the pitying glance of man, live the men and women for whom there is no work and consequently no hope. Honest, decent poverty elbows vice and the 'peaky blinder'.[6]

Venturing behind the facade of the best-governed city in the world, an investigation into conditions in St Bartholomew's Ward by Birmingham's Medical Officer of Health in 1898 emphasised the deadly link between back-to-backs and ill health. Now the lively Digbeth quarter, named by the *Sunday Times* in 2018 as one of the 'coolest places to live in the UK', then it was a desperately poor locality. Over half of its housing was back-to-back, rented weekly at 3s 6d. This amounted to a fifth of the income of an unskilled man if in regular work. Most weren't that fortunate and to stave off hunger and the rent man, everybody in the family had to pull in something. Wives earned pitiful amounts taking in washing, charring and carding buttons, pins and hooks and eyes, and so did children selling firewood, local evening newspapers, and horse manure for the gardens of the middle class.

Overall, the annual death rate in St Bartholomew's was 37.6 per 1,000 people compared with 17.1 in wards where there were no back-to-backs – meaning that each year, 3,000 people died who would have survived if they'd lived in better housing. Poverty killed, a dismal conclusion substantiated five years later when Dr Robertson reported on the 10,000 people in the twenty-five streets of the Floodgate Street area within St Bartholomew's Ward. Just a few hundred yards below the Bull Ring markets, it was one of the city's most impoverished localities. Dominated by the high-level blue-brick viaduct of the Great Western Railway, a great engineering achievement of the Victorian age, it was filled with canal wharves, factories, workshops, warehouses and small shops, between which an unplanned muddle of back-to-backs were confined. The inquiry revealed that measles, scarlet fever, diphtheria, diarrhoea, enteritis, tuberculosis, bronchitis, pneumonia and pleurisy were decidedly more fatal there than in Birmingham as a whole. This caused a general death rate 60 per cent higher than the average and a massive 90 per cent greater than a district where skilled men and their families lived. Differences in the infant mortality rate were as stark. The city's annual average per 1,000 live births was 195, dropping to 173 in affluent Edgbaston but soaring to 263 in St Bartholomew's as a whole.[7]

BIRMINGHAM: CITY OF PEAKY BLINDERS

Unhappily, the people of back-to-back Birmingham were scourged not only with bad housing, an insanitary environment, ill health and high death rates but also with the relentless bullying and violence of the real peaky blinders. These late Victorian and Edwardian back-street thugs were nothing like the glamorised gangsters of the hit BBC television series *Peaky Blinders* set during the 1920s and '30s and revolving around the magnetic anti-hero Tommy Shelby. With a calm demeanour, 'he doesn't get crazy, he doesn't fly off the handle' and, according to former New York mafia kingpin Michael Franzese, Shelby is 'what a real mob guy should be'. Bolstered by his brothers, his Peaky Blinders are a tight neighbourhood gang operating from the Garrison pub, Small Heath. Infused with dread, they're named after their favoured weapon: the peak of their flat cap into which safety razor blades are sewn and which is slashed across the eyes of their enemies to blind them. Shelby's position of authority amongst them is derived from both his reputation as a fearsome fighter and his leadership qualities. Able to think quickly and strategically, he cleverly manoeuvres his Peaky Blinders into becoming a major organised crime force nationally, victoriously taking on the top London gangsters and even the Mafia. And though his hands are bloodied by murder and maiming, Shelby has positive qualities shown by his loyalty to his family and concern for children and orphans especially.[8]

With its compelling characters, powerful storyline, inspirational acting, pulsating modern soundtrack and eye-catching fashion, the drama has captured an international audience. Soldiers in a Ukrainian Army drone unit fighting the Russians have called themselves 'Peaky Blinders' whilst Sligo Racecourse, amongst other racing venues, has featured a 'Peaky Blinders Day', 'where fashion and festivity converge, as attendees are encouraged to don their finest Peaky Blinders-inspired attire and immerse themselves in the spirit of the 1920s'. In spotlighting the allure of 'Shelby-chic' for Australian racegoers, sports and lifestyle writer Brad Nash recognised that 'Tommy Shelby's smouldering gaze has kicked off an entirely new era in menswear.' It has. Stylishly dressed in long overcoats, tailored three-piece suits with high-cropped trousers, penny-collar shirts, leather boots, and wool tweed Newsboy and Bakerboy caps, the Peaky Blinders sport distinctive hair styles with aggressively cut short back and sides. Tommy Shelby tops his with long hair brought forward and swept to one side, whilst his brother Arthur's top hair is slicked back.

The real peaky blinders looked very different as depicted by Bertram Hildick, who was confronted by one of them as a teenager in the early 1890s:

> His coat had an exaggerated flare and his hat – a sort of bowler but higher in the crown with a narrow brim bent in front and back to form peaks – partly covered the eye. It was because of these odd hats which gave them such a threatening look at times that they were called Peaky Blinders.
>
> His trousers were the 'bell bottoms' his crowd wore: close-fitting about the hip, thighs and knees, and then spreading out to cover the widest 'Oxford bags' . . .
>
> Sometimes they would cock their hats at a slant over their heads to display a strip of hair pasted on their foreheads as flat, shiny and trim as peacock feathers. The rest of their hair was cropped close to the scalp revealing, perhaps, a bulge or white scar or two, results of past boot-and-buckle battles.[9]

This strip of hair was like a quiff or curl grown long on one side of the head and soaped down obliquely across the forehead. As for the odd hat recalled by Hildick, it was the billycock, a type of bowler hat, adapted so that the brim fitted the sides whilst the front was brought to a point, almost like the spout of a jug. This was done either by wetting the brim, warming it by the fire and moulding it to the peaky shape required, or by pulling and stretching the brims over the knee. Another contemporary noted that by wearing their hats low down over the left eye and exposing the lock of hair over the right forehead, peaky blinders had a quite sinister look. Though a much less dramatic reason for the name peaky blinder, this style of 'blinding' their eyes is historically accurate. The name carried on after billycocks were mostly replaced as the headgear of fashion by flat caps, the peaks of which were also drawn down over one of the wearers' eyes. This style continued after the donkey fringe across the forehead replaced the quiff as one of the visible signs of peakies.[10]

Before arriving in court in 1897, a judge visiting Birmingham noticed a very ill-favoured youth with a great patch of hair plastered down in a broad band upon the forehead, and wearing certain clothes. Enquiring if there was any meaning to these features, he was told they indicated that the youth belonged to a gang. Predominantly unskilled and poor, peaky blinders couldn't afford expensive clothes but still managed to 'dress up in an outrageous fashion' because of their bell-bottom trousers like those of sailors. So noticeable was this appearance that they were also called the 'bell-bottomed crew'. Fifteen inches round the knee and twenty-two round the bottom of the leg, these trousers were sometimes adorned with a ring of pearl buttons. Born in 1911 just after the end of the peaky blinders, Tom Golding was told by his father of the havoc they caused and how eventually they were overwhelmed by the police.

He also recounted that their corduroy or moleskin bell-bottoms were named Harry Barnes, after the tailor whose shop in Stafford Street was on the edge of the new Corporation Street and the deprived areas of the Gun Quarter and Gosta Green, where Golding's father grew up. In 1890 and off the peg, Barnes sold men's very fine black, brown and drab corduroy trousers for 5s 6d. This was within reach of unskilled men and hawkers who would earn no more than

17s 6d a week. Though dearer with cords at 7s 9d and moleskin at 9s 6d, made to measure trousers were just about affordable for single men. Boasting that he'd the largest stock of cords in the Midlands with upwards of 3,000 pairs, Barnes advertised himself as the 'People's Tailor' and 'Working Man's Tailor' and had a catchy slogan in the 1890s: 'Trousers cut spanky to suit the ikey'. Although 'ikey' was also a racist and derogatory term for a Jewish person, in Birmingham it related to a youth well turned out in the peaky fashion as indicated in 1898 by a mocking poem about a peaky blinder's wedding: 'Billy looked quite ikey, and was got up rather smart.' Interestingly, ikey was another term given to the hooligans of Manchester and Salford, the successors of the scuttlers who also wore a peaked cap pulled over an eye and bell-bottoms, although theirs were cut of fustian, not corduroy or moleskin.[11]

The peaky blinder style was taken for granted in reports in the Birmingham newspapers, usually with the phrase 'distinctive characteristics', but an unusual account from 1906 was fuller. Once a 'Brummagem Tyke' himself, Sam Allen transformed his life by moving away from the gangs and setting up an adult school in a poor neighbourhood to elevate the peaky blinders. He noted that each week, the barber clipped their hair as close to the skin as possible and shaved their chins so closely that it was as if they were rubbed with sandpaper. Allen drew attention to another essential feature of the peaky blinder look, a silk muffler tied so tightly around their necks that they bulged. F. Atkins recalled that this was called a daff and when twisted twice round the neck it was a 'choker'. Hobnailed boots for kicking enemies finished off the peaky's clothing. Photographs from the West Midlands Police Museum bring to life the peaky blinder fashion of billycocks, quiffs and daffs, although as they were shots only of the face they don't show the bell-bottom trousers and hobnailed boots.[12]

Ex-superintendent W. J. May went into more detail in his reminiscences. Joining the Birmingham Police in 1894, he felt that to an extent, the peaky blinder was like his prototype, the London costermonger:

He almost invariably wore his hair short at the back and sides but with a well-greased forelock plastered over the forehead nearly to the eyebrows and upwards towards the left, the whole surmounted by a cap worn at a jaunty angle besprinkled with pearl buttons.

When rigged in her best the girl friend usually wore velvet, or velveteen, generally of some bright colour also very plentifully bespangled with pearl buttons, and a large hat covered with ostrich feathers. She usually walked with very short steps and that walk she rarely got rid of.

The peaky blinder almost invariably wore a heavily buckled belt – and this was his weapon of offence and defence.

Most of them belonged to a 'slogging gang' and when another gang or individuals had incurred displeasure the belts were used freely upon their heads. Every time a battle or isolated slogging took place it was pretty certain that some had to go to the hospital for attention. Sometimes the injuries were pretty severe and necessitated detention in the institution.

Sometimes knives were used and sometimes that

heavy metal covering for the knuckles (with a solid piece of smooth metal to hold in the palm) which was known as a 'knuckleduster' was brought into the fray.

Very ugly wounds were inflicted by means of these weapons. Bottles, half-bricks and missiles of that sort were also pressed into service with very effective results.[13]

Named not after an imaginary weapon but a documented fashion, peaky blinders were universally acknowledged as the equivalent of London's hooligans, Manchester and Salford's scuttlers, and often with New York's Bowery Boys and Australia's larrikins. First mentioned in the Birmingham press in March 1890, following a brutal assault on an inoffensive victim, it's likely that the generic label peaky blinder was used on the street before that. However, the slogging gangs to which most belonged emerged a generation earlier in the late 1860s, although they were not so called until a shocking outbreak of street ruffianism in April 1872. To 'slog' was a pugilistic term to hit with a heavy blow and the sloggers did so with fists, belts, boots, stones, brickbats (half bricks), coshes, knives and any other weapon they could grab. As related in *Peaky Blinders: The Real Story*, the catalyst for their appearance was a crackdown on the large gatherings of youths and men on waste ground on Sundays. On this, their only day off in an exhausting week of toil and moil, they played rough sports, gambled at pitch and toss and other coin games, and too often swore and cursed. In a period when the working class and those under thirty were by far the most numerous sections of the population, this unruly behaviour disturbed the middle class. Frightened by the coming together of large numbers of boisterous men and teenagers unfettered by social control, they were outraged at the lack of respect for the Lord's Day and by activities that were the antithesis of rational recreation. Stirred into action, in Birmingham clergymen and other influential figures led a 'crusade' against pitch and toss, pressurising the police to put it down. That campaign precipitated a violent reaction, with young men forming street and neighbourhood gangs to repulse detachments of police when pitch and toss meetings were targeted.[14]

With back-to-backs districts having neither gardens nor parks, the playground of the poor was the street, and the police were hated for interfering and trying to control street life. Quickly, lone constables patrolling their beats were increasingly subjected to assaults from the numerous slogging gangs erupting across poorer Birmingham and Aston, a separate authority until 1911 but effectively part of the city. Rampant in the back streets, as well as baiting the police, these 'roughs' battled each other in ferocious clashes and tormented the decent folk amongst whom they lived. In a society which didn't value poor men economically, socially or politically, the only way many asserted themselves was through their hardness in fighting. Infused with what might now be called toxic masculinity and impelled by a fierce loyalty to their street and gang, the only things completely belonging to them, sloggers revelled in their brawls, flaunting their manliness to their pals and girlfriends with the scars on their heads inflicted by truncheons and 'the dreadful buckle'. Made of brass and about three inches across, the buckle was the most dangerous part of the belt and in a clash, it was fastened to one end. Most of the belt was then wrapped round

17

the slogger's wrist so that he could grasp it in his clenched hand. With the buckle at the top, about eight or ten inches of the belt was left loose to slash, strike and wound an opponent.

Birmingham's escalating street rows drew national notoriety in 1875 when PC Lines was murdered in a riot by the Navigation Street Gang. Two years later, a leading judge commented that night after night, the city's streets became the setting of an almost irrepressible violence and brutality. Sarcastically, *The Times* observed that such a scenario was a stark contrast to the 'speeches in which eminent men bestow no qualified praise on the inhabitants of Birmingham for the perfection of their municipal institutions and the unrivalled interest and intelligence they display in their devotion to political progress'. Indeed, strangers to Birmingham failed to understand how high political and municipal development existed side by side with almost open lawlessness and barbarism and why there was no explanation from civic leaders for such discordancy. Outraged at what they perceived as a slur to the town's honour, its civic leaders didn't explain but instead vehemently refuted the accusations.[15]

The depredations of the slogging gangs in back-to-back Birmingham didn't seem to matter to councillors as they had no regard for those who suffered – the poor. Their attitude was more positive towards skilled and regularly employed working men who'd been enfranchised in 1867 and whose votes they needed. Praised as intelligent and honest by John Bright, one of Birmingham's MPs and a celebrated Liberal politician, they differed from those whom he decried as the 'residuum' – the residue or waste of the population. It was a branding as distasteful as its meaning of the underclass. Bright's unsavoury views were reflected in the dominant civic ideology of Birmingham which excluded the poor from citizenship. Unable to vote, they had no political influence and unskilled and unorganised, they had no economic leverage. Demeaned as lesser, uncivilised beings, they were ignored in a city praised as the pinnacle of municipal achievement. So too were the slogging gangs and peaky blinders. Safely ensconced in fashionable Edgbaston or agreeable rural outskirts, the civic elite, including its magistrates, were well away from the violence. They had no understanding of the misery wreaked by the gangs and showed little concern.[16]

There is no evidence of Chamberlain at any time addressing the severe problem of thuggery in the back streets. In the official history of the Corporation of Birmingham, which he initiated, the volume covering the years until 1884 said nothing of the slogging gangs even though they'd arisen, thrived and drawn national opprobrium in this period. The author was John Thackray Bunce, the editor of the Chamberlain-supporting *Birmingham Post*, whilst the subsequent volume for 1885–99 was written by Charles Anthony Vince, a leader writer for the newspaper and Chamberlain's political organiser. Though Vince included a detailed chapter of forty-one pages on the judicial system and the police, he made merely a brief reference to the serious increase of crimes of violence during the latter years, resulting in the popular demand 'for more drastic measures for the repression of this evil'. For all their ill repute, the peaky blinders received no mention.[17]

The local press differed, regularly reporting on gang fights, assaults on the police and the beatings of innocent people. Unhappily for the city's reputation, these reports attracted widespread publicity. In 1882, the *Sheffield Daily*

Telegraph mockingly commented that Birmingham's latest gift to the country's institutions was the slogging gang. Fifteen years later, and under the scornful headline 'Brummagem Beauties', it explained that the recent murder of a constable and the disablement of two or three more preservers of peace by peaky blinders was a humiliation for Birmingham when it considered itself to be the best-governed city in the world. 'The reign of the rough' was a theme picked up by numerous other publications, with Birmingham increasingly dismissed as 'the city of the peaky blinders'. Thankfully, their reign was soon to end.[18]

As the nineteenth century waned, calls to stamp out 'peaky blindism' grew louder, with *The Globe*, a literary paper for London's 'educated class', announcing that the people of Birmingham made bitter complaints of the brutal tyranny exercised by street ruffians. Amid this epidemic of brutality, the chief constable resigned in 1899. His successor was Charles Haughton Rafter, formerly an officer in the Royal Irish Constabulary and a Protestant from Belfast. In the television series, Major Campbell has the same background. Brought in to put down the fictional Peaky Blinders led by the Roman Catholic Shelbys (of Irish descent), he's a sectarian bigot. Unlike him, Rafter wasn't. His application for the post in Birmingham was supported by Count Arthur Moore, a Catholic and Irish Nationalist MP, and Rafter's deputy was Michael McManus, a Catholic from County Mayo who'd risen from the ranks. Realising that the Birmingham Police was seriously undermanned, Rafter launched the rapid recruitment of tall and fit young men who could fight. Their training included vigorous physical instruction and when ready, they and older constables were sent into the toughest areas in pairs. In the battle of the streets raging since the late 1860s, the police were on the back foot, but now they took on the peaky blinders to wrest back control. In this violent struggle, they were supported by the magistrates and judges imposing more severe sentences for assaults on officers and by most of the poor, assured that in coming forward as witnesses they'd be protected from retribution. There were also social forces at work pulling teenage boys away from the streets and from becoming peaky blinders. A few concerned clergymen and women provided the equivalent of youth clubs in poor neighbourhoods and a growing number of lads were keener on playing football, boxing and going to the pictures (cinema) than in joining gangs.[19]

In 1905, just six years after Rafter took office, the *Birmingham Gazette* announced that the palmy days of the peaky blinder were over. No longer did he flourish in triumph and disgrace the city with his outrages. Instead, he was living upon his past reputation and thanks mainly to the exertions and vigilance of the police, he'd retired from active service. Despite such confidence, the peakies were not quite defeated, but three years later, the *Birmingham Mail* rejoiced that the peaky blinder was fast disappearing from the city: 'We no longer see gangs of men with the donkey fringe adorning their foreheads, and their legs encased in bell-bottomed trousers . . . who delighted themselves in organised acts of crime.' By 1912, the local press was writing about the peaky blinders and slogging gangs in the past tense. They'd disappeared. What happened to them? In 1915, during the First World War, the *Birmingham Mail* reported that many had joined the Army and made good soldiers, whilst others were in respectable jobs with employers prepared to engage unskilled workers. It was a perceptive observation as reflected in the life of Henry Lightfoot, the only individual to be called a peaky blinder in court. Seemingly an incorrigible rogue with dozens of convictions for violence and petty theft, he was wounded in 1916 in the Battle of the Somme.[20]

Billy Kimber took a different path. Depicted in the drama as a London mobster in charge of the racecourse rackets, as made clear in *Peaky Blinders: The Legacy*, he was a burly Brummie from the Summer Lane neighbourhood. Along with other vicious peaky blinders, he moved from the back streets and petty criminality to head one of the many small packs of Birmingham rogues pickpocketing and black-mailing bookmakers at horse race meetings in the Midlands and North. A fearsome fighter, he was smart and succeeded in bringing these crews together into a powerful force called the Brummagem Boys. A deserter in the First World War, afterwards he teamed up this Birmingham Gang, as it became known, with the Elephant Boys of South London and the Camden Town mob of North London to take over the rackets on the lucrative racecourses of southern England. In so doing, he propelled himself from peaky blinder to leader of the first major semi-organised crime gang in England.

Infected with racism, Kimber's alliance took especial pleasure in intimidating Jewish bookies, one of whom was Alfie Solomon. A secular Jew from North London, he was nothing like the Alfie Solomons of the series with a Yiddish, Orthodox Jewish background. After he was brutally beaten by a member of the Birmingham Gang, the real Alfie Solomon was bent upon revenge and turned to Edward Emanuel, the guv'nor of the East End Jewish underworld and reputed to have senior policemen in his pocket. Though a menacing figure protected by other Anglo-Jewish hard men, he was much more than a tough and through shrewdly forging a relationship with a rich bookmaker, he made big sums running spielers – illegal gambling dens. Now Emanuel sensed an opportunity to oust Kimber's combination from the southern racecourses and reap the rich rewards, but he knew that Solomon and his own men weren't strong enough without back-up. Emanuel found that in Darby Sabini and his gang of Anglo-Italians and men of solely English heritage from in and around Clerkenwell, the capital's Little Italy. Britain's first war between gangs from two different cities exploded in the spring and summer of 1921. It was won by Emanuel, a cunning operator who outwitted Kimber through forming the Bookmakers' Protection Association. A legitimate body gaining the support of southern bookies, the racing authorities and the police, it then employed Sabini and his associates as 'stewards' at race meetings, making it impossible for Kimber's men to operate.

Having lost out, Kimber shifted away from gangsterism, changing into a prosperous bookie living in Torquay. Shorn of his leadership talents, the Birmingham Gang disintegrated and disappeared like the peaky blinders they'd once been. That story is recounted in *Peaky Blinders: The Aftermath*, as is Emanuel's move into legitimacy by setting up a printing company supplying bookmakers and sporting concerns. Waxing wealthy, he bought a splendid house in Golders Green, a far cry from when he'd been living in the East End and working as a fruit porter. For all his new-found respectability, Emanuel remained the *éminence grise* of the Sabinis. Unlike the conglomeration of bands that made up the Birmingham Gang, Darby Sabini tightly controlled his

23

gang. Backed by a clique of childhood friends and two of his brothers, he oversaw a loyal hardcore of 'soldiers' that could be reinforced by other villains as and when needed. Highly organised, the Sabinis expanded away from the racecourse, oppressing small businesses in and about their north London stronghold and dominating extortion in Soho's burgeoning clubland. Their activities ensured that the Sabini Gang became the prototype for London's organised crime gangs that followed, including the Krays. Similarly, their chief, Darby Sabini, was the exemplar of a gang boss. A formidable fighter with a commanding personality, he instilled loyalty in his men whilst striking fear in his enemies.

But unlike the Krays, Sabini neither courted publicity nor flaunted his power, basing himself in local pubs and dressing like a working man with a flat cap and collarless shirt. The son of an Englishwoman and a northern Italian who'd been brought to London as a child, Sabini often used his mother's surname of Handley, didn't speak or understand Italian, married an Englishwoman, and saw himself as an Englishman. He is startlingly different from the fictional Darby Sabini in the drama *Peaky Blinders*. Arrogant and impeccably dressed, he speaks English with an Italian accent and is portrayed as a Sicilian-type don in the style of classical mafia fiction. Though not Italian, Tommy Shelby shares some of the characteristics of such a glamorised gangland boss. An aspirational anti-hero undermining society's codes, whilst an outlaw who gains wealth, possessions and respect, yet is he a Robin Hood figure helping those in need.[21]

In series one of *Peaky Blinders*, a character says of the Shelbys and their gang, 'They're bad people but they're our bad people. They do bad things for us.' The real peaky blinders were bad people, but they didn't do bad things for the poor amongst whom they lived. They did bad things to them. Neither glamorised gangsters nor big-time criminals, they were back-street bully boys glorying in their violence. Annie Church knew that. In late 1898, having given evidence against two violent youths, she was targeted by them after their release and finally stoned. Each was handed merely two months as the missiles hadn't struck her. That intimidation prompted a local newspaper to call for the police protection of witnesses. Church was just one of many poorer Brummies suffering the violence of the peaky blinders.[22]

The back-street gangs of Birmingham baited the police, maiming many and killing several in mob-handed attacks. They were responsible for nationally notorious riots that wracked Birmingham, with four gangs named in Parliament, and they launched racist attacks on Italians and Jews. Terrorising their neighbourhoods, they committed unprovoked assaults, levied blackmail and inflicted injuries on their neighbours, shopkeepers, publicans and concert-hall-goers and managers. Battling with each other, gangs from Park Street, Barford Street, Charles Henry Street and elsewhere caused mayhem and murder, with the Bloxwich brothers of the Milk Street Gang, the Sheldons of the Barr Street Gang, the Butterworths of the Highgate Street Gang, and the Simpsons of the Whitehouse Street Gang, amongst others, causing horrible injuries. Boiling with violence, peaky blinders indiscriminately attacked women and savagely battered their girlfriends and wives, as did my peaky great-grandfather, Edward Derrick, who abused my great-grandmother, Ada. Like him, many peaky blinders were petty thieves and became habitual criminals. A few like Billy

Kimber joined the Birmingham Gang, but others turned their lives around, serving honourably in the First World War. Those who survived returned to a Birmingham liberated from the peaky blinders. So complete was their disappearance that in 1929, a local newspaper confidently wrote that 'in a few decades the memory of "the peaky blinder" will have gone from Birmingham, and even old men will no longer be able to tell tales of street terrorism in quarters which once even the police dare not patrol singly.' Memories of street terrorism did fade away, but the myth of the peaky blinders and the razor blades in their caps lingered on, sparking the drama and a fascination with all things Peaky Blinder. The real peaky blinders were not fascinating. They were nothing like their fictional counterparts and the fear and injuries they inflicted should neither be ignored nor forgotten.[23]

Chapter 1

CONSTABLE BAITING

PREYING ON LONE OFFICERS

Venturing into Birmingham's gloomy back streets in 1901 for the first of his disturbing newspaper articles revealing the desperate lives of the respectable, hard-toiling poor living in infernos of poverty, J. Cuming Walters swiftly realised he was out of place. A stranger, he filled the residents with dire foreboding and dismay. From every window, he dimly saw all sorts of brows and faces snooping at him from behind curtains of brown calico and bits of brown bluish muslin. Almost as quickly, he was made aware of the pervasive threat of the peaky blinders when approached by three hard-headed youths in their costume. Taking matters seriously in hand, they queried, 'Who might you be a-wantin?' Cautiously, Walters made his excuses and walked away. Carrying on down the greasy and malodorous street, he noticed that at the ends of the entries and at each corner there was 'inevitably a collection of typical "peakies", hands thrust low in the pockets of their bell-bottomed trousers, caps aslant on their closely cropped heads'. They watched him furtively, now and then seeming about to accost him, but instead spat and cursed as he passed by.

Peaky blinders slouching in the city's many less frequented streets were a menace not to be disregarded. Although policemen weren't rare, Walters thought they might be more readily encountered, and when they were it struck him that almost always, they were in pairs. Where constables were regarded as a natural enemy and their mere presence an affront to the mob, they couldn't be too careful. Constable baiting was an exciting pastime and pelted with bricks and slashed with buckled belts, lonely officers had been half-murdered or maimed for life in revenge for arresting an offender. One of those unfortunate policemen was Herbert Leach and the savage attack on him in 1898 was described graphically by the Reverend Bass:

> Instantly the bottles loaded with stout (beer) were flung with full violence at the copper's head. One of them struck him on the forehead, crushed in the skull and made a wound five inches long. The constable reeled and fell, that was the opportunity for the brave men who were slogging him. The buckle belts flew, the crowd closed on the unfortunate constable, they hit him and kicked him all over the body.[24]

From a poor family living around Cheltenham, the unskilled Leach couldn't get a permanent job and after working as a haulier, gardener's labourer and milkman, he applied to the Birmingham Police. A more secure position with a regular wage, it would allow him to support his widowed and disabled mother eking out a living taking in washing for the better off. At just under six foot tall, Leach was well qualified physically and his application was backed by excellent testimonials from clergymen and previous employers. He was accepted in November 1896, but within two years, the *Cheltenham Chronicle* bemoaned that in attacking him, Birmingham's ruffians again had shown their callousness by preying on a single policeman in large numbers. At about 11.30 on the evening of Saturday 23 April, he'd taken William Astle into custody for disorderly conduct outside the 'Fox and Dogs' in Love Lane, Gosta Green. Bordering the city centre and now covered by Aston University and Birmingham City University, it was amongst the city's poorest localities. One newspaper was outraged that with names reminiscent of the country it was 'the home of the "peaky blinder", the Birmingham hooligan, and the worst member of his class in the kingdom'. From here, he waged war on society, and 'if he be pursued, he only has to make a rapid retreat to the courts with which he is familiar to render all search for him unavailing.'[25]

As usual when a peaky was arrested, a crowd gathered and there was a struggle as Leach strove to march Astle to the nearest police station in Duke Street. A general attack was launched, with Jonathan Jones urging, 'Let's have a go for him, we've got porter-bottles.' Throwing one, he knocked off Leach's helmet. As it rolled on the floor, a woman picked it up and put it back on. Astle's brother, John, then tried to rescue his brother, twice striking the beleaguered constable on his head with his buckled belt. Worse was to come. Albert Medlicott hurled a brick, James Shaw threw stones, and his brother, William, flung a bottle that hit Leach full on, disabling him. As the roughs ran off, a boatman called

Charles Bond bathed the stricken constable's head before helping take him to the General Hospital in a horse-drawn cab. Leach's injuries were serious and having a fractured skull, the surgeons had to perform trepanning – the drilling out of a circular piece of bone. In court, it was stated that it was almost a marvel and entirely due to the great surgical skill in Birmingham that he was still alive, and that William Shaw was not charged with murder.

Thanks to evidence given by Bond and his wife, most of the attackers were handed long sentences of penal servitude. Found guilty of grievous bodily harm, Shaw was given five years, the most severe stretch for such an offence. Aged nineteen, he was a grinder with convictions for burglary and gambling and would be fined in 1908 for being drunk and disorderly when another policeman was assaulted by the group he was with. Jonathan Jones, also nineteen and a gun screwer, started the 'murderous attack' and was imprisoned for four years. A year younger and a tube drawer with two convictions for gambling, James Shaw was sent down for three years. So too was Albert Medlicott. Aged twenty-one and another tube drawer, he'd previously assaulted a constable and in 1895 was named as a member of a dangerous slogging gang when sentenced to two years for wounding with intent.[26]

Despite having struck Leach with his belt, John Astle was treated more leniently, receiving nine months for assaulting a constable. The oldest at twenty-three, he was also a grinder and lived in the Oxygen Street described by the Reverend Bass. As a youngster, he'd been sent to an industrial school in the hope of steering him away from criminality. That hope was dashed, and he went on to accumulate convictions for assaults on the police, drunkenness and obstruction. He didn't change and three years after the attack on Leach, Astle served another four months for wilfully breaking four plate glass windows at a pub. As for Charles Bond who'd helped Leach and provided valuable assistance to the police in identifying the attackers, he paid a heavy price. Six nights after the affray, he was in Oxygen Street when Henry Stokes came up to him. Saying, 'This is for my pal who you put away,' he knocked Bond down, kicking him severely and inflicting a scalp wound. A police officer was also kicked when arresting Stokes, who was given four months. Bond's involvement as a witness is intriguing. Notorious and with convictions for malicious wounding and assaulting a policeman, he'd been in the Whitehouse Street Slogging Gang with Medlicott's older brother. It seems there must have been a fallout, or else Bond had changed his ways.[27]

SHOWERS OF STONES

Fortunately, PC Leach recovered, retiring in 1922 with an exemplary record, but the savage assault on him moved the Reverend Bass to write to Birmingham's Watch Committee, the councillors responsible for the city's police. Emphasising that there were too few policemen to cope with the disorder locally, he appealed for constables not to patrol singly as they were considered fair game for peaky blinders. Sadly, lone constables had been considered fair game for the back-street gangs for a generation, as a long-serving officer made clear. He joined the force in the 1870s, when it was positively dangerous for people to walk along certain streets unattended, and the slogging gangs led ruffianism of the worst kind. Almost every

Saturday night, surgeons at local hospitals dressed scalp and other wounds caused by knives, buckled belts or by the throwing of bricks and stones. Rife in central Birmingham, Aston and Ladywood, the slogging gangs fought each other most violently, attacked the public and made the lives of constables anything but rosy. Each week, there were always several injured officers and the policeman who could not fight himself, or use his staff effectively, had a poor chance. Invariably the police were resisted when making arrests, and prisoners were taken to the lock-ups amid perfect showers of stones. Called 'petrified kidneys' because of their shape, these large stones covering back-street footpaths were often loose and easily pulled up by women to carry in their aprons as supplies for the sloggers.[28]

Although the police were often subjected to assaults by groups of neighbours, friends and family members in poorer streets, the gang attacks of the 1870s were unprecedented. Following the establishment of the Metropolitan Police in 1829, full-time paid police forces were brought in across urban England and from the beginning, the middle class pressured them to enforce discipline on the rapidly expanding industrial working class. This meant not only dealing with crime and disturbances but also with controlling the street by targeting traders, pedlars, gamblers, ballad sellers, singers, entertainers, drunks and those playing games and rough sports. Police intervention into these hitherto mostly overlooked activities provoked a violent reaction in much of northern England, but in Birmingham there was a less hostile response. For a few years from the force's inauguration in 1839, the approach was more cautious, with an emphasis on peacekeeping, thief catching, crime prevention and interfering only when public disorder was threatened. It was difficult balancing what the middle class wanted the police to do and what the working class would allow them to do, but seemingly the Birmingham police succeeded. Though mistrusted and disliked as busybodying outsiders, violence against constables mostly occurred when making arrests for drunkenness, theft and trying to stop fights. That situation was transformed from the late 1860s when, succumbing to the demands of the middle class, the police attempted to put down pitch and toss.[29]

On Sunday 10 May 1868, responding to numerous complaints, George Glossop, the chief of police, ordered a strong force of men in plain clothes to rout the disreputable gangs of pitch and tossers and end their offensive practice. Several gambling sites in some of Birmingham's poorest streets were fixed upon and fifty-one offenders were charged. Aged between thirteen and thirty, most were fined 2s 6d or three days' imprisonment if not paid. Although Glossop used the term gang it was to describe a sizeable band of gamblers and not a group resisting the police. Indeed, only one of the prisoners was charged with assaulting a constable after he was arrested. Pleased with the outcome, the magistrates complimented Glossop and other large-scale actions followed. They failed to stop pitch and toss gatherings and instead were the catalyst for young men coming together in fighting gangs to take on the police. This was made plain on Sunday evening 30 April 1871 when two policemen saw roughs gambling in Weaman Street in the Gun Quarter. Spotting the officers, they ran into an entry leading into Slaney Street, but rather than trying to get away they turned and stood ominously with bricks in their hands. As the officers rushed at the gang, 'they were saluted with a shower of stones and half bricks'.[30]

PC Timothy Falvey managed to catch twenty-year-old Edward Lundy, who fought to break free. In what the officers described as an awful scene, missiles flew above their heads, and one thrown by seventeen-year-old Walter Joyce struck Falvey on the forehead, knocking him out and inflicting a severe wound. As he lay bleeding, several stones were flung at him, and he was kicked by the now released Lundy. A very violent man, it was said he had a dagger and that he shouted he'd settled for one policeman and would do for others if they interfered. Joyce was sentenced to three months and went on to join the Army, but pleading that he was a victim of mistaken identity and supported by witnesses, Lundy was discharged. A year later, he was imprisoned for six weeks for so badly beating a man with a knuckleduster that he was hospitalised for thirteen days. He followed that up with violently robbing a woman and pushing the point of his umbrella into her husband's mouth and through his cheek. Finally, in 1875, Lundy was sent down for four months for assaulting two policemen.[31]

In 1860, Birmingham's magistrates dealt with 227 assaults on constables. That figure jumped dramatically to 467 in 1872 when the slogging gangs were first named. Of course, many of the increased assaults were unrelated to them, yet, as Barbara Weinberger discerned, whilst the police had always been unwelcome in certain working-class streets, the active hostility towards them in the 1870s was a new phenomenon partly due to the behaviour of gangs of youths who came into existence at this time. Philip Gooderson recognised that these noisy and dangerous teenagers were violent rather than criminal, fixated as they were on asserting their masculinity territorially by 'owning' their street against outsiders. Fights arising from one set of lads occasionally raiding another locality were common before the 1870s, but the slogging gangs were distinctive in their durability, firmer identity, indiscriminate violence and hatred of the police. This frighteningly new phenomenon was underlined by concerned residents in Gosta Green complaining of 'the gangs of youths assembling in the streets on Sundays, throwing stones, gambling and so-called "street- fighting" with life-preservers and other dangerous weapons to such an extent that mob law has become predominant, and a reign of terror established'. Prisoners taken into custody were rescued from the police and there'd been other scenes quite as dangerous to the public.[32]

Adjoining Gosta Green, the Gun Quarter was another compact district of a few streets, and it too quickly became notorious for its sloggers. Meeting on Sundays, they were a great source of annoyance to several neighbourhoods and in early April 1872, they caused turmoil with breaking windows and throwing stones. Helping to quell the 'riot', PC Walton was violently assaulted by fourteen-year-old gun worker Edward Head. Sentenced to three months, he served his time in an adult prison. Alleged to be the ringleader of the gang, Joseph Wooley was discharged because of insufficient evidence but was cautioned that 'if he molested or in any way assaulted the witnesses who had given evidence against him and the other prisoners, he would be well punished'.

Unhappily, the molestation of witnesses by sloggers and peaky blinders was to become a dismaying theme throughout Late Victorian and Edwardian Birmingham. Four other teenagers were sent down for six weeks. At thirteen, the youngest was Walter Smith. He could have been sent to a reformatory or industrial school as he was under fourteen.

However, Weinberger noted this option tended to be taken for those deemed morally worthy and capable of profiting from the experience. By contrast, youngsters who lived in 'the roughest areas, who could not produce character witnesses or parents to speak in their favour, or who had previously been in trouble with the police were held to be irredeemable and were sent to prison'. Although reformatories enforced harsh discipline often with beatings, imprisonment with adults would have been horrifying for Walter Smith. Forced into the rigid and punitive regime of hard board, hard fare and hard labour, he would have made mats, cleaned the prison and picked oakum, a particularly dirty and laborious task unravelling and cleaning old rope.[33]

The magistrates believed that Smith and the other prisoners were connected with an organised gang disturbing the public peace and endangering the lives of the inhabitants. It was not the only such gang. Late on Sunday afternoon 23 March 1873, and as they had done so weekly for at least a month, over thirty youths assembled in Bagot Street on the edge of the Gun Quarter. Hailed today as a location soon to rival Birmingham's Jewellery Quarter for city living, it was an overcrowded neighbourhood where the workshops of skilled gunmakers were surrounded by back-to-backs. That day, the sloggers behaved riotously, flourishing sticks, throwing stones and making it dangerous for anybody to pass along the street. A sergeant trying to disperse the mob was assailed by a regular shower of stones. With the help of others, he arrested James Boyle, a gun barrel filer, aged seventeen and one of the ringleaders. Although born in England, his family was from Roscommon in the west of Ireland, as were most of the Irish settling in Birmingham before and during the Famine. He was sent down for two months along with Edward Moore, the other ringleader and a blacksmith's striker like his Dublin father.[34]

Two other youths were each fined 40s, more than twice the weekly wage for unskilled men, or a month if they didn't pay. One of them was seventeen-year-old John Derrick, a shoemaker, living with his father in The Gullet. One of the 'blackspot' streets condemned by the Chamberlainites as a den of vice filled with thieves and prostitutes, it would be cleared in the Corporation Street Improvement Scheme. In reality, its people were amongst the poorest and most vulnerable in the city. Many of them were widows and abandoned wives straining to keep themselves and their children out of the workhouse. Others in the narrow, short gulley-like street were elderly folk waiting to die. One of them was a lodger of the Derricks, their 77-year-old relative, James Derrick. A lifelong criminal, he was my great-great-great-grandfather. As will be related, his grandson, another John, was a leader of the Sparkbrook Slogging Gang and his younger brother, Edward, my great-grandfather, was a wife-abusing peaky blinder.[35]

The Bagot Street disturbance infuriated the *Birmingham Post*, its lead writer raging that it was the town's turn to feel 'the strength of the native savage, and to witness his skill in the manipulation of stones, brick-bats, and other popular projectiles'. Such language charged with racism highlighted how poor young men in the back streets were outcast in forward-looking Birmingham. That's not to exonerate them, as too many were drawn into the untrammelled violence of slogging gangs. One of the worst was the Livery Street Gang, drawing its members from the neighbourhood beside Snow Hill Station. Soon to be cleared of the housing of the poor and renewed as part of Birmingham's architecturally impressive financial district, its 'mischievous youths' gambled in a dilapidated building. Not content with the mild excitements of pitch and toss, 'these precocious young gentlemen' varied their entertainment by pelting passers-by, knocking down walls and hoardings, and smashing windows. Intent on stopping the problem, a group of police went to their hideout. About twenty youths made a short stand, but outnumbered, they beat a retreat to some old cellars in the rear. Reinforced by 'confederates', they kept the officers at bay by throwing brickbats until more constables arrived. Fifteen gamblers were arrested. Taken to Kenyon Street Police Station, they were put in a prison van for the Lock Up at Moor Street Police Station.

By now, though, hundreds of people were swirling about Kenyon Street and when the van pulled into the street, 'a violent concerted attack began, which, if the police arrangements had been less perfect, might have resulted, not only in a rescue, but in serious injuries to the men in charge'. Stones and missiles of every kind were freely used, but supported by a special detachment, the driver and guard contrived to run the gauntlet without serious injury. Eighteen youths aged from thirteen to nineteen were sentenced to between seven and fourteen days, although if they'd been older, the punishment would have been more severe. Over the next year, each week the most savage and unprovoked attacks on constables became more serious. Deplorably, it appeared 'that the rough element of Birmingham spend the greater part of their leisure time on Saturdays and Sundays in creating breaches of the peace and brutally assaulting the police when they interfere to preserve order'. By the summer of 1874, so bad was the situation that upwards of fifty officers were placed on special duty on Sundays 'solely to keep the roughs in check and protect their brother constables from violence whilst in the execution of their duty'.[36]

If the slogging gangs flared up because of police action, then another trigger was the violent approach of some officers trying to control the back streets. Paid only £1 a week, new recruits received negligible training. Although the probationary period was supposed to be a month, after just three days they were sent out on duty with an older hand to show them around and then left to get on with their beat. Working nine-hour shifts in the day and thirteen hours of a night, they received no sick pay and weren't allowed to vote. Mostly from the countryside, constables were looked down upon by the property owners whose rates paid their wages and were disliked as outsiders by the poor. Lacking status, they were exploited by their employers. And there were too few of them. In 1873, the authorised size of the Birmingham Police was 450, but for assorted reasons that full complement was never achieved, and the daily strength was less. With an estimated population of 355,000, this gave a ratio at best of one officer for 788 people. That was noticeably less than in almost all other towns of comparable size in England. Outnumbered as they were and pressured by the middle class to cut down the gatherings of youths and men in the back streets, some officers acted violently.[37]

In 1867, the chief of police asked the Watch Committee 'to entrust some of the most judicious policemen with canes, believing that an occasional stripe administered to a boy was better than taking him to the lock-up'. The rejection of this appeal was praised in the *Birmingham Gazette*, but it remained unhappy that the police could still use belts because, 'We have seen terrible and cruel punishment inflicted on lads by irate and passionate policemen. In fact, the police ought not to be allowed to punish at all. Their business is to preserve the peace, not to inflict sentences on untried people.' The *Gazette* was a Conservative publication, but its concerns were shared by the satirical journal *The Town Crier*, arguing that the example of police violence had increased violence amongst civilians. It urged the Watch Committee to make a collection of policemen's weapons, 'not the authorised staves – but the surely unauthorised gutta-percha bludgeons, lithe canes, twisted hazel sticks, knotted sticks and all the evil weapons with which the police have armed themselves'. The perceptive question was posed: would the children beaten with these weapons remember the police with kindness when, in a few years' time, chance delivered officers into their hands?[38]

Despite such concerns, aggressive policing appeared to have the unspoken support of the Watch Committee and magistrates. They either released defendants complaining of rough handling and gave the officers a mild ticking off, or passed the buck back to the Watch Committee. That's what they did regarding the case of Walter Howkins. A 26-year-old glass blower and hence a skilled worker, he was charged with being drunk and disorderly and assaulting the police in executing their duty in Burbury Street. Because of the gangs of roughs loitering there and annoying the inhabitants on Sundays, constables were put on special duty to disperse the sloggers and stop them gambling. According to the police, Howkins and others were standing by an entry and obstructing the footway. When requested to split up and go quietly home, they refused. Telling the constables that he was at his own door, Howkins became violent and was taken into custody. Resisting, he kicked an officer on the leg and was taken to the police station with difficulty.

The defending lawyer gave a different account. Howkins was 'a very respectable young man, and not a "rough" as described by the constables'. A witness testified that Howkins was talking loudly to a young woman when a constable ordered him to move on. Replying that he was near his own home, he refused to go away. A fellow officer then told the constable to 'bundle prisoner up, use his timber [staff] to him' and 'run him in' for being drunk and disorderly. Another witness, a highly skilled silversmith, said that Howkins did nothing more than bawl to his wife who was deaf, adding that he thought the officers had greatly exceeded their duty. He was ashamed of them, calling them unfit to be policemen.. Howkins was discharged and the magistrates intimated that the Watch Committee would probably further investigate the matter. There is no evidence that they did.[39]

RIOTS AND MURDER: THE NAVIGATION STREET GANG

Whatever the cause of the escalating violence against the police by gangs associated with back-street gambling sites, it was a troubling development. By April 1873, the high number of assaults accompanied by riots was noted as the gravest feature of Birmingham's criminal statistics. Two months later, the *Birmingham Post* deplored the ongoing rowdyism, riotous conduct and gambling in the town on Sundays. Mob law was taking over and although the police brought in the whole of their resources to cope with the growing evil, it had little effect. So bad were things that some residents were talking of furnishing themselves with pistols to shoot the roughs down. Glossop, the head of the police, agreed that disorderly gangs infesting the streets were a major problem. Disturbingly, they deemed it an honour to cowardly stone poor policemen in the discharge of their duty.[40]

One of the unruliest localities was around Navigation Street. Dominated since the 1850s by New Street Station, today it ends at Suffolk Street Queensway but until the late nineteenth century it stretched a few hundred yards further, next to where rises the modern Mailbox shopping centre with its plush shops and restaurants. Within a hop, skip and jump of the Town Hall and Council House and on land owned by the East Anglian aristocratic Gooch family, lower Navigation Street was a neighbourhood of five confined and dismal streets. A focus of the crackdown on pitch and toss meetings, it was packed with back-to-backs, little shops and small workplaces, and was fraught with danger to the police. In March 1873, when the landlord of the 'Greyhound Inn' refused to serve him because he was drunk, an enraged Edward Downes violently assaulted a constable. A 26-year-old bone turner born in Wales and the father of three young children, Downes was backed up by a gang of the biggest roughs in Birmingham and created quite a riot. He was sentenced to just one month.[41]

Within weeks, another disturbance broke out locally. On the last Saturday night of June, a little boy was struck on the head by a gang throwing brick-ends in every direction for a bit of fun. As he was taken to hospital, seven or eight roughs ran down Navigation Street using 'very obscene language' to passers-by. Remonstrating with them after his wife was insulted, the husband was knocked down and kicked. A shopkeeper trying to help was felled by a stunning blow on the side of the head. The gang then insulted a woman standing on her doorstep and upon her brother going to protect her, he was knocked down and kicked black and blue. Attempting to scatter the mob on his own, PC Roby was rushed furiously by James Thornton, swearing he would 'do for him'. Though kicked violently in the stomach, the officer knocked down Thornton with his staff and arrested him. In court, it was stated that he and his companions assaulted people with short sticks loaded with lead. Guilty of violently assaulting an officer, he was given six months.[42]

The disorder in Navigation Street emphasised that the new gangs were not restricted to juveniles but included older men; and as newspaper reports indicated, they weren't always called slogging gangs but gangs of roughs. Gooderson differentiated the two, distinguishing the collective 'roughery' as groups of habitual companionship rather than being organised in any way, although the beerhouse or street corner where they gathered gave them some sense of identity. Their criminal records were for stealing and assault, often rightly dubbed 'murderous'. In effect, this definition applies as much to the slogging gangs and peaky blinders and Gooderson did acknowledge there was an overlap between hardened roughs and the sloggers. Still, he didn't believe that there was a Navigation Street Gang. Contemporaries did.[43]

William Brown served forty years as a warder at Winson Green Prison, Birmingham and was fictionalised as the humane Warder Evans in *It Is Never Too Late to Mend*, Charles Reade's novel attacking abuses in prisons. Having had charge of numerous sloggers, Brown was well informed, remembering that in the 1870s, Birmingham's byways were dangerous to walk along, especially at night, because of gangs of street roughs. Chiefly youths aged fifteen to twenty-five, 'They had no other amusement than pouring out in sets, under certain leaders, in order to molest and injure innocent and defenceless pedestrians.' Lashed horribly about the body and head by buckled belts, their victims were left gashed and bleeding on the pavement after their pockets were rifled. Brown named two gangs in particular whose youths met in 'low' public houses, coming out after closing time to thieve, fight and wage war with each other. The Livery Street Gang pulled its disorderly members, including women, from the abutting streets. So did the Suffolk Street Gang. Made up of 'all the vicious characters who were crowded into that slum quarter', it was synonymous with the Navigation Street Gang, as was the 'Chiving Gang' mentioned in local newspapers and named after the word chiv, meaning to knife someone.[44]

Brown's alertness to Birmingham's gang problem was matched by Will Thorne. Later a great working-class leader, founder of the Gas Workers' Union, and Labour MP for West Ham, he grew up in dire poverty in Hockley and didn't learn to read and write until late in life. Born in 1857, he knew too well that there were 'few rosy patches, if any, in the fight for bread in the lives of the manual labourer with little skill or education. Just long years of drudging work in the past and in the future.' Although living in Farm Street, he had no memories of 'the free air of a farm during those early far-off days; just the ugly houses and cobbly, neglected streets that were my only playground for a few short, very short years'. When still a child, his father was killed in a fight and though his widowed mother did whatever she could to earn money, they were hungry days for her four children who had to work to help. Aged six, Thorne turned a wheel at a rope spinners. It was mighty toil, twelve hours a day Monday to Friday and half a day on Saturday, after which he lathered faces for men wanting a shave at a barber's – as he did again on Sunday morning. Growing older, he went from job to job, working in the brickfields, now Birmingham City's football ground, and as a plumber's mate, lath splitter, cow and pig-hair dresser, brass roller, nut and bolt tapper, builder's labourer and navvy. Aware of much of Birmingham through his varied work, Thorne was streetwise and a fighter able to handle himself during the 'exciting happenings' in Birmingham in the early 1870s when the Navigation Street riots were at their height. A locality of dilapidated houses, it was 'the haunt of a very tough gang of roughs who were always looking for trouble. They found it one Saturday night when they ran afoul of the police. It was a hot battle. One of the policemen was killed with a brick and several others were injured.' Thorne was well informed as he worked with the brother of the rioter sentenced to death for the murder.[45]

The policeman killed was William Lines. Born and raised in rural south Warwickshire, his father was an agricultural labourer and like PC Leach, Lines had been a milkman. Despite the low wages, policing appealed to young men like them. Paying more than unskilled farm work, its regular income offset the strict rules and militaristic discipline. Lines and his wife were both twenty when they married in October 1864 and a month later, he joined the Birmingham Police. It was a baptism of fire. Within a year, he was involved in a desperate affray with five burglars and was frightfully wounded on his head and face by one of the men wielding a jemmy (short crowbar). Undaunted, Lines pluckily held on to his attacker but was under medical treatment for six weeks. During subsequent arrests, he was struck on his head by a poker and kicked on the ground; his skull was fractured when a dangerous escaped convict hit him with a brick; and he was punched and kicked by an abusive husband who'd brutally ill-treated his wife. Soon after that last attack in 1872, Lines left the force. He was not on his own, as it was revealed that whilst the Birmingham Police had an authorised strength of 465, there were only 431 men because of the difficulty in getting recruits. Over a twelve-month period, the force lost ninety-nine officers, almost a quarter of its total. Some died, others retired or were dismissed, but most were young men who left discontented with their pay and regulations and especially with the violence they faced. The local press was sympathetic: 'We cannot profess to wonder at men throwing up a calling which is, perhaps, at once the most thankless, the riskiest, and, in proportion to the duties exacted, the most ill-paid of any under the sun. A policeman in the lower quarters of Birmingham runs almost as much risk of being maimed for life as a collier.' Unlike others who left, however, Lines quickly rejoined. Tragically, it was a bad move for him and his family.[46]

On Monday 8 March 1875, *The Times* reported that the previous evening's disgraceful riot in Navigation Street was expected to have a fatal termination. So bad was the uproar that the *Birmingham Mail* declared it was one of the most serious in the town for some time. As will be discussed in Chapter 2, that was a dramatic statement given Birmingham's bad reputation as a riotous place. In this disorder, the rioters exhibited 'even more brutality than has been the characteristic of recent ruffianly displays, and the police, as usual, have been outrageously maltreated'. The turmoil blew up after two detectives were called to a disturbance at the 'Bull's Head' inn. Amongst the troublemakers was William Downes, who was arrested because he was seen burgling the pub a couple of nights previously. He was the younger brother of Edward Downes who'd caused mayhem locally two years before, and it's apparent that the pair were leading figures in the Navigation Street Gang. As the officers took William Downes along Navigation Street, they were suddenly set upon by a large mob, pelting them with stones, hustling them, and trying in every way to rescue their pal. Though the rioters were 'exceedingly numerous, the officers stuck to their man most pertinaciously' and were joined by Sergeant Joseph Fletcher and PC Lines, who was stabbed. A week later, with his condition deteriorating, his deposition was taken in Queen's Hospital by the clerk of the magistrates' court. He was accompanied by a senior justice of the peace, two detectives and several constables in charge of the rioters who'd been arrested. They were John Cresswell, Aaron Rogers, Thomas Whalen, Jeremiah Corcoran, Richard Smith and Samuel McNally.[47]

Lines said that as the mob and detectives holding Downes came into Navigation Street, Rogers shouted, 'Come along, you will let any poor – get took.' Putting himself between the detectives and the crowd, Lines was confronted by Whalen cursing, 'Now, you – I will give it you.' Rogers then threatened, 'Ah. We want to get you by yourself, you – pig.' He, Whalen, Cresswell and others began to pelt the officers with stones. Still, they strove to move on but reaching a pub, some of the rioters rushed at Lines. Drawing his staff, he met them head-on and ran some of them into Suffolk Street where Sergeant Fletcher was beaten to the ground trying to stop them. Rushing to his assistance, Lines used his staff on the attackers pressing round the helpless sergeant. After hitting Cresswell on the head, he was set upon by Whalen and Rogers. Lines heard Whalen make use of a foul expression and upon that, he was stabbed by the left ear, although he couldn't say who did it. With his deposition finished, the prisoners were taken from the hospital and 'a number of ruffians – no doubt their companions – cheered them, and urged them "to keep their pluck up"'.[48]

Witnesses corroborated much of what Lines said. Beset by roughs clinging to him like rats, they tried to get him down, but he just about beat them back. Then one of them grabbed him by the throat, whilst another ran at him and stabbed him in the neck just below the left ear with a long sharp instrument. It penetrated his head by several inches. Falling to the ground with blood flowing profusely from the wound, Lines was kicked and trodden upon. He'd have been killed immediately if not for Detective Goodman hurrying to him and driving back the mob, who fled when police reinforcements arrived. Brutally kicked and stabbed in three places on his head and once on his face, Sergeant Fletcher was also treated in hospital but was taken home to recover. Lines was not as fortunate. Despite all that medical science and careful nursing could do for him, he died aged thirty on 24 March. A much-respected officer, he was 'a down-right good fellow to work with, and he wasn't the man to fight shy when there was any work to be done'. Lately, he'd arrested a few bad characters in the Navigation Street vicinity and 'a considerable animus was entertained against him'.[49]

CONSTABLE BAITING

The funeral took place on 28 March. Early that morning, policemen were stationed by the door of the Lines's home in the middle of the slogger's haunt of Gosta Green and from 9am, a large, orderly crowd paid their respects. Those closest to the house heard 'the heartbreaking sobs of the deceased's only orphan child – a handsome girl of about 10'. Looking inside, his widow, who'd already suffered the grief of recently losing her eldest daughter, was seen endeavouring to conceal her anguish. People were allowed to enter in twos and threes, and Elizabeth Lines 'gently uncovered the face of her murdered husband. So highly respected was the deceased in life and so deeply lamented in death by his brother officers, that stout hearts gave way, and tears uncontrollable trickled down upon the linen covering in the coffin, and uttering a feeling "poor Lines" they made way for others.' With thousands of people lining the nearby streets, shortly before noon, 210 constables, twenty-one sergeants, seven inspectors and seven superintendents assembled in the courtyard of Duke Street Station round the corner from where Lines lived. The superintendents wore strips of black crepe on their left arms and nearly all the men seemed considerably affected. The force then marched round the square four abreast with the police band playing the 'Dead March in Saul'.

When the gates were thrown open, the street was completely blocked, but the crowd made way for the police procession to move slowly to Lines's home. In a deep and moving mark of respect by the local people, they drew the coverings on their windows whilst shopkeepers closed their shutters. It was estimated that 20,000 people packed into every available corner in Gosta Green. Despite the vast numbers, there was 'a quiet decorum such as is rarely to be seen under so great a pressure, and altogether the behaviour of the multitude was faultless'. The coffin was brought out amidst solemn silence. Placed in the hearse, it was followed by three mourning coaches for the relatives, including Lines's aged parents. An advance guard of sixteen policemen and a superintendent led the long procession to Witton Cemetery five miles outside Birmingham. The whole route was lined with a mass of men, women and children with heads respectfully uncovered. At the boundary with Aston Borough, men from the Warwickshire Police joined their Birmingham comrades. It seemed as if the whole of the district turned out in solidarity as the cortège went on to Aston Parish Church and then the cemetery, where thousands more were assembled. Altogether, it was estimated that about 100,000 people showed their support for Lines, his widow and child, and the police. Amongst the official mourners were councillors from the Watch Committee and Sampson Gamgee, the celebrated physician who'd made every effort to save Lines's life. Noticeable by their absence was the mayor, Joseph Chamberlain, and his leading supporters. There is no record of any of them speaking about the murder of the first officer to succumb 'to the knife of the assassin ever since the formation of the force'. Nor does Chamberlain's name appear on the subscription lists set up for Elizabeth Lines. Over £800 was collected, much of it from workplaces and the 'penny fees of the working classes of the town'.

The 'assassin' charged with murder was nineteen-year-old Jeremiah Corcoran, alias Corkery. His father was a schoolmaster in Birmingham but returned to Ireland when Corcoran was a child, leaving him to be raised by his Irish mother. In the Navigation Street neighbourhood, she was spoken of as a hard-working and tidy woman, always making her 'humble dwelling' as comfortable as was compatible with her means. For all her best efforts in raising her son, when he was nine, he was arrested for wounding, although he was discharged because of his young age. Soon after, he was sentenced to twenty-one days in an adult prison for stealing twelve yards of flannel. This must have been a terrifying experience for a child, and having done the time he was sent to a reformatory for five years. He wasn't reformed. Within weeks of his release, he was imprisoned for six months for theft. That was followed swiftly by two months for assaulting a policeman. Supposedly a metal roller, it's obvious Corcoran didn't follow that occupation as he was back inside again in March 1873, this time for twelve months. He'd thieved a jar of preserves, a bottle of sweetmeats, thirty-six boxes of furniture paste and other items.[50]

Fresh-complexioned with sandy hair and grey eyes, Corcoran was scarred on the right side of his forehead and was merely five feet three inches, compared with the then minimum height of five feet seven inches for Birmingham's police. He was identified as the murderer by several witnesses. One man testified that as the detectives left the inn with Downes the burglar, Corcoran said, 'They are taking Billy, let's go and do 'em.' The next day, the witness met Corcoran, telling him, 'You have got it hot.' He replied, 'I got knocked down with the copper's staff,' and the witness made a movement as if Corcoran was stabbing. A youth living nearby said that as Corcoran came up to Lines with a knife in his hands, the officer hit him above the eye with his staff but was then stabbed near to the ear. Corcoran ran off and with blood pouring from him, Lines staggered against a lamp post. Two men caught him as he murmured, 'Oh dear, oh dear.' Annie Whalen, a young umbrella worker, was the sister of one of the arrested rioters but she also testified against Corcoran, explaining that Lines asked her if she'd tie a pinafore round his head to stem the bleeding. She'd been standing with her friend who lived in the same street and gave similar evidence.[51]

Found guilty of wilful murder at the Warwick Assizes, Corcoran was hanged on 27 July 1875 at Warwick Prison. He was nineteen. Previously, he'd been at Winson Green Prison where he formed a strong bond with the Reverend E. MacCartney, the Roman Catholic chaplain, to whom he wrote several letters. In his last, he thanked the priest, 'Ain't you been and done more for me than my own father.' His mother fainted when the priest came to her house to break the news that her son was dead. Finally recovering, she asked his permission to 'wake poor Jerry', which she did with decorum according to the local press. In the left-hand corner of the one downstairs room was a rude sideboard on which was a pillow in lieu of the deceased's body. This was covered with a piece of white linen and at each corner were lighted wax candles. Maria Corcoran sat alongside. She fainted eleven times, and her many visitors all wept, whilst the entry leading to the back house was besieged by neighbours anxious to pay their respects.[52]

Protesting that he'd been set up, Corcoran pleaded his innocence throughout the trial, although it was claimed he confessed to the killing shortly before his hanging. His fate elicited some sympathy and an elaborate funeral card sold by the hundreds couldn't be printed fast enough according to a street seller in a 'shy' neighbourhood (dangerous area):

CONSTABLE BAITING

In Remembrance of
JEREMIAH CORKERY,
WHO DIED JULY 27, 1876,
AGED TWENTY YEARS.
Be warned by my sudden call,
And straight for death prepare.
For it will come you know not when –
The manner how nor where.
RECQUISICAT IN PACE.

A ballad was also quickly penned and sung on the street. Stylistically poor, 'Corkery's Farewell to his Mother, Brother, and Sister' was like others of its kind – melodramatic, gloomy and moralistic:

We have lost a brave Policeman,
By that awful cruel knife.
And Young Corkery he must suffer,
But do not blame a child of strife.
Cruel Drink, has made unhappy;
Many, many, happy homes,
And the bell will soon be tolling,
To drown the unhappy victim's groans.[53]

Eight years before the Navigation Street Riot, Birmingham was wracked by a frenzied mass attack by an English mob on the Irish of Park Street. As Chapter 2 will relate, this arose from the 'preachings' of a despicable Protestant preacher playing on long-standing anti-Irish and anti-Catholic prejudices in England. In the febrile atmosphere it provoked, that Murphy Riot was unfairly blamed on the Irish, heightening religious and ethnic tensions, and leading to an Irish slogging gang that feuded with nearby English gangs. By contrast, the Navigation Street Gang was made up of men and youths from Irish and English backgrounds and it's noteworthy that the Birmingham newspapers neither blamed the murder of Lines on the Irish nor stirred up sectarian antagonisms, whilst the descriptions of Corkery's mother and priest were positive.

Eleven other men were arrested for their part in the Navigation Street Riot. Aged between seventeen and twenty-three, all were reported as convicted thieves. Several were guilty of assaulting the police, and one was known as the 'Captain' of the 'Chiving Gang', 'whose malpractices were a source of much trouble to the police'. Seven were finally charged with participating in the fatal riot. Aged twenty-three and an iron bedstead worker, Aaron Rogers was discharged along with Samuel McNally, an eighteen-year-old brassfounder. Rogers had previously served time for assault, but contrary to the press reports he wasn't a convicted thief and nor was McNally, who had no criminal record. Of the remaining five, William Kelly, seventeen and a filer, was a reputed thief who'd served three months for assaulting a police officer. Found guilty of the same crime in the riot, he was given five years' penal servitude. The final four were found guilty of wounding with intent to do grievous bodily harm. They were John Cresswell, Thomas Leonard, Thomas Whalen and Charles Mee.

A twenty-three-year-old caster, Cresswell had convictions for assault and theft. So too did Thomas Leonard, eighteen and a tube drawer. His record emphasised how hungry children were thrust into criminality by a class-biased justice system that protected the rights of property owners above all. When he was ten, he served seven days in an adult prison for stealing apples from a garden. Well into the twentieth century, scrumping, as it was called, was carried on by many working-class boys, including my father, uncles and great-uncles. Taking apples from a tree wasn't seen as a crime in working-class neighbourhoods but a vengeful middle class fortunate to have gardens demanded it was punished harshly. The next year, in 1868, Leonard took a cake of bread and was convicted for six weeks. Later sent down for three months for stealing a bowl, in 1871, he served fourteen days for trying to take a shilling. This was followed by four years in a reformatory. He'd only just come out when he was involved in the riot. Denying any part in the row, he said that as Corkery walked away from the stricken PC Lines, he sensationally boasted, 'It's me that chivvied the b–. Feel the blade of this knife. It's wet with blood.'

The last but one of the four was Thomas Whalen, also named as Whalin, whose real name was Whelan. Eighteen and a stamper, he was another child from a poor family criminalised by English law. His Irish father was a labourer, and his English mother took in washing. Both were precarious and badly paid occupations. When their son was eleven, he stole some oranges and was imprisoned for three days and whipped. Unsurprisingly, he became an angry teenager, doing time for wilful damage, two assaults and aggravated assault on a constable. When arrested after the riot, he complained that 'I suppose this has been got up for me. You want to send me away for nothing, same as I have been before. If anything happens in our quarter, it's either me or our kid (meaning his younger brother). I was not there at all.' Sergeant Fletcher, though, told the court that after he was knocked down by several men, Whalen stood over him saying, 'Now for it,' and twice jabbed him with something.

Other witnesses identified Cresswell and Leonard as amongst those who'd kicked Fletcher, but the fourth youth found guilty was a victim of misjustice. Charles Mee was seventeen and a metal roller. Nicknamed 'Barber' Mee because of his father's trade, he was picked out by a witness as having gone down the street with Corcoran before the attack on the police and by another as carrying a policeman's helmet after the row. There was no evidence at all that he took part in the riot, whilst the owner of the factory where Mee worked, and others, gave him a good character. Their pleas failed to influence the judge, who sentenced him and the rest to penal servitude for life. Startled by the severity of the sentence, they burst into tears. Several of their friends in the galleries 'screamed out and sobbed as the prisoners were removed from the dock, bidding them farewells. Two women were carried down out of the gallery swooning, one of whom continued moaning, "Oh! My poor children," and a large number of females in all parts of the Court were in tears.' The scene was described as the most affecting and exciting witnessed in the Warwick Assize Courts for the last fifteen years.[54]

Another street ballad lamented their fate:

Their sentence it has been one of great severity.
Penal servitude for life, oh what an awful fate.
For four young men whose united age is scarcely
seventy-eight.

A petition from his widowed mother and others praying for a mitigation of Mee's sentence was ignored, but in 1886, all four were released on licence. It was too late for poor Mee.

His mental health had suffered and now he was in Broadmoor Criminal Asylum. Cresswell was said to have become a respectable working man, but nothing is known of what became of either Leonard or Whalen, who served his time in Pentonville. So too did William Downes, the burglar whose arrest sparked the riot and who was handed five years' penal servitude. He went on to a life of crime. A notorious thief and pickpocket, he was prominent in the Brummagem Boys, the small gangs of violent former sloggers and peaky blinders plaguing racecourses in the Midlands and the North from the 1890s and from which emerged the Birmingham Gang that fought the Sabinis.[55]

There was no ballad for intimidated witnesses. Soon after they came forward, most were threatened by friends of the prisoners. Others were violently assaulted, and four young women sought the protection of the police after a man and his wife menaced them, accusing them of swearing away the lives of innocent men. The husband then struck and kicked Ann Whalen, sister of one of the accused, and chased her friend, Margaret Morgan, down the street. After his arrest, the husband shouted at her, 'All right, Meg, I will do for you yet.' He was bound over to keep the peace, but Whalen, Morgan and two other female witnesses were so in fear of their lives that it was dangerous for them to go to and from work. A superintendent assured them the police were determined to protect them, 'but if they indiscreetly ventured among the prisoners' friends they might be mobbed'. That advice was of little use, living as they did in the same neighbourhood of the accused. Mind you, Whalen herself was no innocent and was capable of intimidation. Three months after her brother was sentenced, she approached a young woman witness in another stabbing case and threatened to 'do for her', before brandishing a knife and saying, 'This is for you.'[56]

The daughter of Irish parents, Morgan's ordeal wasn't over. A few weeks before the trial, she was accosted by two youths shouting she was one of the 'coppers' (police informants) and stones were thrown at her. Within days, she fled for protection to a police station when threatened by the same pair and three other men. They were arrested with difficulty. One of them, nineteen-year-old nailcaster Thomas Jackson, was previously discharged from involvement in the riot. From an English background and noted in the press as not educated, he'd had several convictions but again he was fortunate to be discharged with the warning to be careful as to his future behaviour. John Cluly was another of the bully boys intimidating Morgan. A seventeen-year-old metal roller, his real name was John Gilhooley. Bound over to keep the peace, he was a most dangerous man whom Morgan rightly feared. As he left the court, he called out that she was 'only squaring herself to tell a lot of lies. If I had my way, I would smash her.'[57]

The next month, Jackson was with Kate Kelly, the sister of another of the accused, and Corcoran's fourteen-year-old sister, Margaret, when they saw the persecuted Morgan. He told Corcoran, 'That is her; give it to her. That's her that went against your Jerry. Give it to the – cow.' After more urging, Corcoran struck at Morgan with a knife. The blow fell short, and Corcoran tried again but again missed as Morgan stepped back. For incitement to feloniously wound, Jackson was sent down for eighteen months, as was Margaret Corcoran for attempting to unlawfully wound. Soon after her release, she was back in court. Working as a news girl, she traipsed the streets six days a week selling thirteen newspapers for half a penny profit, with which she could buy a ha'penny dip from an eating house – a thick slice of bread dipped in the dripping of roasting meat. This time, Corcoran and a news boy were alleged to have led other young newspaper sellers in gambling for a ha'penny a time at pitch and toss. For this seemingly trivial offence, each was given one month.[58]

TO 'CORKERY' A CONSTABLE

Shocked by the riots in the Navigation Street neighbourhood, law-abiding local people petitioned the Watch Committee for a police station. Their plea went unheeded, although an increase of fifty men to the Birmingham Police was authorised. Indicative of the marginalisation of the poor suffering most from the slogging gangs, it was felt this move would have a 'wholesome moral effect' on the rough, and give confidence to the burgesses – men who had the vote because they were property owners. But it was the hanging of Corcoran and the exceptionally severe sentences passed on other rioters that were believed to have 'struck salutary terror to the hearts of some of the worst of the dangerous class'. Hopes were high that the spirit of the local 'residuum' was now fairly subdued, if not positively extinguished, and that with the breaking up of the Navigation Street Gang, organised disturbances were over. Such optimism was squashed by serious disorder in various quarters. They included an attack on the police in February 1876 when the Livery Street Gang fought to release a man arrested for wounding. Thomas Lavell, aged nineteen, was amongst the ringleaders of the riotous proceedings and was sent down for three months. His County Mayo parents settled in the district in the 1840s, but his father died when Lavell was ten and his youngest sibling was a baby. His widowed mother did her best to keep her family on her meagre earnings as a paper-box maker and what the oldest of her seven children pulled in. Other than Thomas, there is no evidence that any of them were criminals.[59]

Fellow ringleader John McDermott was born in Wolverhampton, but by 1861 when he was five, he and his two younger sisters were living with his widowed Irish mother, their paternal aunt and seven others in an overcrowded and decrepit house in London Prentice Street. One of the most deprived places in the town, it too was swept away in the Corporation Street Improvement Scheme. Bridget McDermott was thirty-one and despite the most trying of circumstances, she managed to keep her family together and out of the workhouse. By 1871, through toiling as a washerwoman and helped by her sister-in-law, she was able to rent her own back-to-back. Unhappily, though, her son was pulled into the slogging gangs and in the assault on the police, he cried out, 'Come on, chaps. Belts off, they shan't take him.' When sentenced to four months, he called out that he could do it on his head. After his release, and unlike so many sloggers, he turned his life round and by 1881, he was working as a bricklayer's labourer and married to an Englishwoman. The couple provided a home to their three children, McDermott's mother and two sisters, and a widow and her young daughter.[60]

In the Lionel Street Riot, Lavell and McDermott tried to free 21-year-old John Ellis, who was given nine months for unlawful wounding. A hawker of no fixed address and with convictions for stealing, gambling and assault, he was of English heritage, as were others in the Livery Street Gang. Like the Navigation Street Gang, it coalesced around neighbourhood loyalties not ethnicity, bringing together the sons of Irish migrants with those of English parents. Hating the police, these and other gangs were largely responsible for Birmingham's transformation from a law-abiding town into an exceptionally violent place. As a shocked Recorder pointed out in April 1877, policemen once bore a charmed life locally but 'of late they had been knocked about and ill-treated, stabbed, and in one case, as they knew, murdered'. The next month, in another disturbance by a gang of ruffians in Navigation Street, the John Gilhooley who'd menaced Margaret Morgan threatened to 'Corkery' PC Baldry who'd ordered a crowd of roughs to disperse. The officer was beaten and kicked when trying to arrest Gilhooley but was saved by the appearance of more policemen. Heading to the Lock Up, they were kicked by Gilhooley and stoned and assaulted by the gang following them. As the ringleader, Gilhooley was sent down for six months, whilst Elizabeth Kiblane, an eighteen-year-old button worker, was imprisoned for six weeks for attempting to rescue him and for assaulting PC Baldry. Nothing more is known about her, unlike Gilhooley. A year later, it was 'only by the good providence of God' that his threat to 'Corkery' a constable was not carried out on PC Samuel Copestake.[61]

The Navigation Street Gang drew its members not only from lower Navigation Street but also from the adjoining section of Suffolk Street and Greens Village, where Gilhooley lived. A jumble of narrow streets, close courtyards and confined passages, its drains were blocked, wells polluted, miskins overflowing and privies tumbledown and filthy.

Many of its people were refugees from the Irish Famine, living in decrepit houses overhung with a foetid atmosphere. Like their very poor English neighbours, they were vilified by Birmingham's political elite, with Bunce pronouncing that no family in Greens Village 'could dwell there without destruction to the sense of decency, or peril to health and life'. Unnoticed by him and the rest of the civic elite, its people supported each other through kinship and neighbourly networks, but the presence of such a 'slum' in the developing central business district disconcerted them. Soon, it too was cleared for a new thoroughfare lined with impressive buildings. Ironically, it was named John Bright Street, after the MP who'd coined the offensive term 'residuum'.[62]

Contrary to Bunce's denigration, there were many decent folks in and about Greens Village and they suffered as much from the bullying of the local gang as did the police. The savage beating of PC Copestake made that clear. One Tuesday afternoon in May 1878, a passer-by in the area remonstrated with Gilhooley who was holding a little terrier by the tail and dashing its brains out on the kerbstone. Angered, Gilhooley knocked down the man and threw the dead dog on a handcart. As he wheeled it across some waste ground, another bystander looked at the cruelly treated animal. Just for that, Gilhooley pushed one of the handcart's shafts into his stomach and hit him. Retaliating, the man knocked down both Gilhooley and his pal, Stephen Fay, before he was tripped up by another gang member and kicked on the ground. With great difficulty, the victim got up and ran off for the police. Returning with PCs Copestake and Walker, they found Gilhooley amidst a large crowd by a pub in Howards Place, a short street off Suffolk Street and the street where the Corcorans lived. Copestake took hold of Gilhooley, who kicked out, declaring 'with an oath that he would not be taken to the lock-up'. In scenes chillingly reminiscent of the Navigation Street Riot, Fay yelled, 'Don't let the bleeding coppers take him.' Immediately stones, brick-ends, coals and other missiles were flying about in all directions. Copestake was struck on the cheek with a large piece of coal and on the ribs by a brick-end thrown by Frederick Farmer. Felled to the ground, the officer loosed Gilhooley who then floored PC Walker and tried to strangle him. Struggling up through the hail of missiles, Copestake throttled off the attacker and pulled him away a few yards before he was struck on the head by a brick-end. As Walker tried to keep the mob back, Gilhooley hit Copestake three times so violently with his own staff that he fell almost insensible. Still trying to hold on to his prisoner, he had to let go when his hand was bitten and Gilhooley ran off.

More dead than alive, Copestake was saved from the mob by brave local people and put in a cab to hospital. He'd suffered a partial fracture of the jaw, ruptured muscles and a one-inch wound in the back of his head, and he also had pains in the loins. It was thought his injuries would be fatal, but he recovered slowly, though he was unable to take any solid food for months. As for Walker, his helmet was broken in three places by the stones and bricks thrown and his uniform was torn, but fortunately he got away with cuts and bruises to his face. A witness who challenged one of the gang throwing bricks was as lucky. Shoved against a wall, he was seized by the throat before he was rescued. Later that evening, two constables went to another pub in Howards Place and apprehended Gilhooley for assaulting Copestake and Walker. He resisted violently, kicking and striking the officers. As earlier, a large and angry crowd quickly appeared, hooting and throwing stones until the constables succeeded in reaching the Moor Street Lock Up. One of them had only just returned to duties after an extended period off sick, and with his hand now lacerated by the teeth of one of the prisoners, he had to go to hospital. During the remainder of the night, 'the neighbourhood was in a state of excitement, a report having been circulated that a member of the force had been killed.'[63]

For intent to do grievous bodily harm to Copestake, Gilhooley, Fay and Farmer were each sentenced to seven years' penal servitude. An eighteen-year-old bricklayer apparently from an English background, Farmer was a convicted thief, having stolen the paltry sum of 2s 9d. As for Gilhooley, he was the Birmingham-born son of Irish parents. With his father a tailor and skilled man, he had a different background to many other gang members and there is no evidence of a criminal record for his older brother. By contrast, at twenty years old, the younger Gilhooley already had a long record, having served time for throwing stones and assaults, including on the police. Purportedly a metal roller, he lived by criminality. He never changed. Within months of his release on licence for the attack on Copestake, he was convicted of robbery with violence, despite the scared victim changing his story when the case went to court. Pronounced as insensible to the suffering of others, he was sentenced to five years' penal servitude, with the judge decreeing that he was to receive thirty strokes of the cat so he might feel the pain he'd caused.

This was a fearsome punishment. Bare-backed, the prisoner was fastened to a wooden framework with his hands strapped to the upper part and feet to the lower, and a strong belt around his waist and the frame. Two stout warders administered the flogging with a 'cat': a thick, straight, wooden handle about one and a half feet long, to which was attached about a dozen thongs or lashes of strong whipcord, two feet or more in length. Each thong was considerably thick, well knotted and twisted to make a most formidable weapon. Standing about two feet away, the warder deliberately and firmly lashed the back in a slant from the shoulder to the waist, so that no part escaped the blows. After the whipping, the back was left with livid flesh. It was reported that Gilhooley undertook it with tolerable firmness. Despite such a terrible punishment, he went on to be labelled a habitual criminal in 1889, by which time he bore several scars and had various tattoos.[64]

Gilhooley adopted aliases, as did his eighteen-year-old friend Fay. His real name was Stephen Gannon, but mostly he was recorded as Fay, the birth name of his County Cork mother. As with Gilhooley, Fay's family circumstances differed from most sloggers. His older brother was in the Army and his Roscommon father was a blacksmith's striker, whilst it's apparent that his parents were a supportive couple. In 1881, in their tumbledown house in Greens Village, they gave a home to their four sons, oldest daughter, son-in-law and three young grandchildren, and an English lodger. Unlike them, their second son was in trouble throughout his teenage years, having convictions for assault, using obscene language, theft and drunken and riotous behaviour. Fay was incorrigible, and although he said he was a machinist, he became a travelling pickpocket and violent thief. Just under five foot four inches and with several scars, in 1899 in

Manchester, he was sentenced to death for murder, although this was commuted to life imprisonment.[65]

SAVAGE ATTACKS: THE HIGHGATE STREET AND SPARKBROOK GANGS

Copestake never recovered from his brutal beating and had to retire in 1880 with a pension of 28s a week. That year, a constable was knocked out when he and a fellow officer were stoned by a gang in the Gun Quarter, but over the ensuing decade, assaults on policemen dropped to 366 in 1889. That fall didn't arise from a decrease in slogging gang activity as they carried on fighting each other, disrupting political meetings, abusing women and beating innocent people. Rather, it seems that lone constables were more wary of putting themselves in danger by interfering with gatherings of youths playing pitch and toss, obstructing the footpath or rowing. Some evidence for this is indicated by letters to the local press. In 1880, a shopkeeper called the attention of the police to the considerable number of men congregating Sunday after Sunday to gamble in Lancaster Street, complaining that the nuisance was growing worse by the week. His concerns were echoed five years later by an Aston resident angered at the lack of police action against the intolerable evil of the mob of youths assembled each Sunday for pitch and toss on waste ground near his home.[66]

Further support for the belief that the police were avoiding potentially riotous crowds of youths and men appeared in *The Times* in a condemnation of a 'Disgraceful Scene'. One March Sunday afternoon in 1891, two young men fought in Hurst Street, on the edge of the town centre and near to where the Birmingham Hippodrome would soon be opened. One of them was armed with a buckled belt and the other with a loaded stick (cosh) and they were urged on by the choicest young ruffians to be found in Birmingham. People flocked to see the brawl and though at least 200 were milling around, not an officer was to be found. The fight went on uninterrupted and the 'sickening crack which could occasionally be heard over the din as one or other of the combatants was struck on the head by the buckle or stick was sufficient to make one shudder'. It was too dangerous for anybody to try and interfere, although a woman dashed into the throng endeavouring to drag one of the fighters away. The protagonist with the cosh now had blood pouring down the side of his face from a very severe cut on his temple, but the woman was roughly pushed aside, and the fight went on as fiercely as ever. After about a quarter of an hour, two policemen finally appeared and after blowing their whistles, more arrived. Seeing them, the crowd dispersed, and the fighters bolted away with their pals. Having watched the goings-on, the reporter asked if anybody was arrested. The answer was none, at which the question was posed, 'You were a long time coming, one would think you were asleep round the corner.' The constable's reply was telling, 'We always are.' Sardonically, the journalist commented, 'Judging by the marked absence of the police for so long a period it might be thought the officer told the truth.'[67]

The caution of the police was understandable as the force was badly undermanned. Though it increased by fifty officers in 1890, there were thirty less for patrol duty because of assignments to the tramways, traffic duty, the Art Gallery and the detective section. The next year, Birmingham extended its boundaries, bringing in an extra seventy men from county forces, making a total of 670. Yet with the city's population having grown substantially, this was still much too few. With one officer to 715 citizens, this ratio compared unfavourably with 1:432 in Manchester with its scuttler gangs and 1:482 in Liverpool with its corner boys. Birmingham's enlargement brought another problem: each constable now covered nineteen acres compared with fourteen previously. For that and for facing danger, they received a starting rate of 24s a week, up a shilling, rising to a maximum of 30s.[68]

They were at risk not only on duty, as PC Daniels found to his cost on a Monday afternoon in August 1887. Off duty and in civilian clothes, he went for a drink but was followed into the pub by several men. One of them remarked, 'That's the – who had me.' A few minutes later, Thomas Welch, twenty-two and a bricklayer, darted at Daniels and hit him in the right eye before landing another blow on his nose. Thomas Finn, a twenty-four-year-old labourer, joined in, blackening the left eye of the officer before he was again punched on the nose by Welch. Staggering through the doorway into the street, Daniels was pummelled by Welch and Finn and hit from behind by James Cain, a labourer aged twenty-five. Exhausted and semi-conscious, the battered constable fell to the ground where he was kicked severely about the body before the attackers ran off, allowing passers-by to help him. With twenty-one previous convictions mostly for violent offences, Welch was handed two months by the stipendiary magistrate, a full-time judge who heard more serious cases than those of justices of the peace. Though it was the heaviest punishment he could inflict, he emphasised that it was too lenient. Finn received the same sentence, whilst Cain and another man were each fined £1 or a month in prison if they didn't pay. It was apparent that they were in a gang as three of them in this savage attack lived in the same street in Ladywood, which had several bands of sloggers.[69]

Yet if there were fewer attacks like this on Birmingham's policemen, their fellows in the adjacent towns of Aston and Balsall Heath were subjected to more slogging-gang violence. Today, Balsall Heath is an inner-city area, but until 1891 it was an independent local authority in Worcestershire just across a main road from Birmingham. As early as 1866, disorderly gatherings of Sunday gamblers on wasteland were causing concern and by the start of the 1880s, Balsall Heath was plagued by 'gangs of low, foul-mouthed blackguards' pulled not only to pitch and toss but also to a local concert hall. Prominent amongst them was Henry Butterworth, whose background contrasted sharply with other fighting men. Both his parents were from rural Warwickshire, with his mother a dressmaker and his father an advertising agent. Having a large family, however, they lived in Highgate Street, a poor neighbourhood with its own slogging gang. Butterworth joined it, soon gaining a bad name and doing time for five charges of drunkenness and three of assault. Then on a Saturday night in January 1888, he and others were seen behaving disgracefully in Balsall Heath, 'challenging everybody they met to fight, and pushing and striking those they met'. An officer remonstrating with them was attacked most brutally. Tussling with Butterworth and one of his pals, he was kicked violently on the left leg. A constable arriving to help took hold of the other slogger, but Butterworth violently threw the first policeman on the ground, kicking him in the side. He did the same to a third officer until at last, he was overpowered and handcuffed. As he was frogmarched along the street with his arms pinned behind him, a 'confederate' came up from behind and stabbed a constable on the right hand. Named as the captain of the Highgate Street Slogging Gang and branded a very dangerous character with a bad record, the police asked for Butterworth to be dealt with severely as several belts were used in the affray. He was given four months for assaulting the police and another fourteen days for being drunk.

Early on an autumnal Sunday that year, two other ring-leaders of the gang met up in a Balsall Heath street, stripped to the waist and ready to fight each other. Though brothers, they'd obviously fallen out and until the 1950s, it was common for men who'd rowed drunkenly on the Saturday night to settle it man to man the next morning. Two officers told them to go away, which they did. But with all animosity between them forgotten in their mutual loathing of the police, they came back armed with pokers and a knife and attacked the constables. Running off, they were chased and caught. On the way to the station, they constantly threatened the police, with one of the brothers doing so again when sent down for two months. Both were warned that if either of them interfered with the police when out of prison, their sentence would be doubled.[70]

It seems they heeded the warning, but others in the Highgate Street Gang remained intent upon attacking the police in Balsall Heath. On a Saturday night in early December 1889, Thomas Cox was arrested for kicking a woman on the ground in Longmore Street. The same location of previous assaults and merely a few hundred yards away from Highgate Street, it was the main entry point into Balsall

Heath. As two constables tried to handcuff Cox, he called on his pals to rescue him. They'd just been thrown out of the Sherbourne Concert Hall, a nearby music hall bedevilled by ruffianism. Numberless stones were hurled at the officers and seeing they were in a perilous position, a bystander ran to the district's only station for help. A sergeant and a handful of constables rushed to the scene but were almost powerless among so many roughs. Trying to reach the safety of the station, a policeman was knocked out by a large stone hitting his head. In the melee, Cox escaped whilst two bystanders assisting the police were assaulted, one of them having his cheek severely cut. With the handcuffs on his wrist, Cox was soon spotted and taken into custody. He appeared in court along with five others of the gang. A witness horrified by the violence said it was 'outrageous, and an utter contempt for law and the sacredness of human life'. Throughout the attack, 'the police stuck bravely to their prisoners, notwithstanding that they were assailed with stones from all directions'. As for the injured policeman, he appeared with bandages around his head after treatment in hospital. Two men sentenced to six months were told they'd had a very narrow escape from being committed for murder. They were eighteen-year-old nailcaster Henry North, known as 'North Pole', and Frederick Thompson, twenty-two and a polisher.

Cox, eighteen and a brass caster, got four months. A contemptible man, he was embroiled in criminality. The next year, 1890, he was again named as in the Highgate Street Gang when he and another member pounced on a Worcestershire constable like two dogs. As the officer blew his whistle for help, one of them said, 'Now we'll give it him.' They did until assistance arrived. Cox was handed six months. When

71

appearing in court, his partner in crime was wearing a pair of bell-bottoms. Seeing this, the magistrate said, 'Ah, I see you have got the regulation cut.' He then added, 'We know you gentlemen; we all know the regulation-cut trousers, and the sooner you alter the fashion and get to work the better. They have found it out at Birmingham at last, and we shall know how to deal with each of you. If ever I have anything to do with fellows with those trousers, I shall never give them the option of a fine.' Five years later, in December 1895, Cox was reviled as a 'Midland Savage' for beating his partner in a drunken rage. Pulling her by the hair, he kicked her savagely. Breaking free, she fled upstairs. Terrified as he was right behind her, she had no escape except to jump out of the window, suffering severe injuries. This time he got only three months. By 1907, Cox had five convictions for theft, one for burglary, eleven for assault, six for drunkenness, and one each for fighting, begging, illegal pawning, sleeping out and using obscene language.[71]

Imprisonment didn't deter him nor Butterworth, who went on baiting constables. In April 1890, he was arrested as amongst the most turbulent of his gang fighting and swinging a piece of catgut in Longmore Street. Arrested by PC Lysons, he resisted violently, and his companions assaulted the officer unmercifully. Kicked and struck on the head, his left hand was bitten badly by Butterworth. A young man endeavouring to help was 'so promptly assailed that he ran away. Meanwhile the crowd had grown considerably, and not another person dared to lift a hand to rescue the policeman for fear of attack from one or more of the many roughs.' Hemmed in, Lysons struggled to ward off the blows raining down on him. Furiously trying to release his brother,

Arthur Butterworth struck the officer with a piece of catgut loaded with a lump of lead at the end. Somehow and despite the battering he was taking, Lysons dragged his prisoner into a butcher's just inside the Birmingham boundary, but was pulled out again. Battling bravely, he scrambled back and the butcher in 'a spirit in striking contrast to that of the crowd, which had passively looked on, stood in the doorway with his cleaver and kept the roughs back'. After twenty harrowing minutes, Lysons was saved by a couple of Birmingham constables, but his ordeal wasn't yet over as on the way to the Lock Up, another attempt was made to free Henry Butterworth. He was handed six months after the court was told his gang infested Longmore Street. Their conduct was so disgraceful that the police were scarcely able to perform their duty, whilst the public were afraid to assist as they'd be immediately set upon. Having one previous conviction, Arthur Butterworth was handed six weeks. He'd obviously hoped for less as he said he'd taken the pledge not to drink alcohol by joining the Gospel Temperance Mission and was striving to reform his character. Another brother, Alfred, was fined 20s for throwing a lump of coal at Lysons.

The Butterworths carried on causing trouble. Not long after his release and for all his protestations that he was going to change, Arthur was back inside for a month for a drunken assault on a constable. Then in June 1891, Henry Butterworth was brought before the courts for robbery with violence after he and two others beat up a young man and stole his tobacco. Condemning it as an outrageous assault and a perfectly barbarous treatment of the victim, to everybody's great surprise the judge sentenced Butterworth to five years' penal servitude. Up to that point, he'd treated the proceedings in the most light-hearted fashion but was crying when removed to the cells. That term didn't change him. Released on licence after doing four years, it was revoked when he was convicted of another assault. A habitual criminal, he did another fifteen months in 1903 for theft. He was thirty-two. At just under five feet five inches, he carried the scars of slogging on the top of his head, the nape of his neck, each elbow, the back of his right hand, and the thumb and a finger of his left hand.

Younger by five years and a smidgeon taller, Alfred also bore the scars of fighting and like his brother was a bully. On Christmas night 1893, he and another rogue showed no goodwill when they dragged a boy along the pavement in Highgate Street. Catching hold of Butterworth's arm, the concerned Peter Nyland asked them to stop. At that, the slogger called to his accomplice, 'Let's cut him.' The response was chilling, 'Let's chivey him, and put his – light out.' Deciding discretion was the better part of valour, Nyland went towards his house, followed by a crowd. Suddenly, his young son shouted, 'Look out, Daddy! He's got a knife!' Swiftly turning round, Nyland saw Butterworth running at him with a knife. Stepping out of the way into the street, he was belted on the head twice by the other ruffian and then Butterworth struck at his head with the knife. Putting up his right hand to ward off the blow, the blade passed clean through the hand and into his lip. A neighbour saved Nyland by felling Butterworth with a jar. Getting up, he and his mate scarpered but were soon captured. In court, Nyland explained that he was a tailor and that so severely cut was the first finger on his right hand that he could no longer sew. He'd lost his living. For that, Butterworth was given three years' penal servitude. He was twenty-one.[72]

CONSTABLE BAITING

The viciousness of the Butterworths was matched by the Harper brothers. Living on the edge of Balsall Heath in Sparkbrook, they were the driving force of the local slogging gang. So much did they terrorise the neighbourhood and waylay foot passengers, especially women and children, that the local police had to be increased. John Harper was the oldest. Convicted of scrumping when he was fourteen and sentenced to fourteen days, he went on to do time for stealing ducks, fowl, a pair of boots, tools and a coat – for which he was handed eighteen months. Originally a boatman working on the canals, he later said he was a tube drawer. Pigeon-breasted, slender of build, scarred on the right neck, left cheek, eyebrow and back, he was merely four feet eleven inches, but though small, he was an alarming man. In 1889, he and his brother, Henry, were seen drunk, stripped to the waist, and looking for a fight in Alfred Street. It's a street I know well. My father, Alfred 'Buck' Chinn, grew up there at number 19 and opened his illegal betting shop across the road in the late 1950s, whilst for many years I drank at the Royal Oak at the top of the street. Dad and his three brothers were boxers and could handle themselves, but they never assaulted the police, although our family had convictions for illegal bookmaking. By contrast, the Harper brothers were police baiters and when approached by a constable, they behaved like madmen kicking out at him. Helped by another officer, they were finally arrested. In court they were also charged with assaulting a blacksmith. He'd been in Alfred Street when they knocked him down and kicked and hit him until he was insensible. John Harper was sent down for a total of six months and Henry for three months.

The next year, John and two other brothers, William and Thomas, were named as notorious characters and members of a dangerous gang of roughs, the Sparkbrook Slogging Gang. Alerted to an assault by them late on a Saturday evening in April 1890, three constables went to arrest them 'but this was a task that they were able to effect only with the greatest difficulty, and not until, it is alleged, they had sustained severe personal injuries from the resistance of the prisoners'. On the way to the station, the officers were attacked by other members of the gang. One received a blow on the back of the head with a large piece of blue brick, harder than the normal red bricks. Another was kicked on the knee and the left side of his face and had nasty abrasions from a missile flung at him. Thomas and John were exceptionally violent, and only after a Birmingham constable came to help were all three brothers locked up. Witnesses of the affray were too afraid to give evidence against them, whilst one of the policemen explained that he'd apprehended a member of the gang a few months previously and since then, the Harpers and their companions had watched for an opportunity to pay off old scores. Thomas was handed six months and William six weeks. Having been convicted for similar offences numerous times, John was sentenced to eighteen months, with the warning that 'the Court intended letting the "Sparkbrook slogging gang" know what they would get when they came there. The law did not allow the Court to flog him, or he would certainly have been flogged.'[73]

John Harper last came to notice in September 1894 when he was discharged for stealing fowl. He was fortunate as he'd just done six months for the same offence and was out on licence. Moving from address to address, neither he nor his brothers appear on censuses, but by 1892, court records indicate they'd shifted from Sparkbrook about a mile down the road to Charles Henry Street, Highgate. Born the next year, my great uncle Bill Chinn recalled it as a place with a hard reputation where young men used to walk about in a gang. They did and joining it, the Harpers were soon causing trouble. Along with Arthur Croton, Thomas and William were charged with assaulting a customer in a pub after the landlady refused to serve them. With some doubt as to the extent of his involvement, Thomas was discharged but William was given a month and Croton six weeks. Like their brother, both Harpers disappeared thereafter. As for Croton, he was a cowardly ruffian. One of the Charles Henry Street bell-bottom crew, in late 1891 he set about an old lady running a little shop when quarrelling over his change for something he'd bought. Grabbing a bread knife from the counter, he tried to stab her. Dropping the weapon, he picked up an advertisement board and struck the poor woman with a blow on the back of the head. Even though the magistrates thought it was a very bad case, they only imposed a fine of 40s, or in default, a month.

Croton was as obnoxious as the Harpers and in 1894, aged twenty-four and working as a scale maker, he abused Sarah Jones. In the patriarchal and misogynistic language of the time, the attack was blamed on the female victim for arousing his jealousy. After a week living together, she went to another man's house, leaving Croton in the lurch. Meeting Jones in the street, he assaulted her. Breaking away, she ran into her house, but he was right behind her. Pulling out a penknife and threatening to 'stick it to her heart', he struck at her. Twisting round to escape, she felt two blows to her shoulder. One wound was only slight, but the other was two inches deep. For that vile act of violence Croton got two months.

He'd learned his despicable ways from his father, another abuser of women. In August 1881, after rowing with his wife, Croton senior left the house only to come back with a carving knife. After making several attempts to strangle her, he stabbed her through the thigh and arm and tried to strike her in the bowels, failing because of the thickness of her skirts. Leaving the house, he told some friends he'd done for her. Again the woman was blamed, as he defended himself by claiming his wife was living with another man. Though in a dangerous condition, thankfully she recovered and left her husband.[74]

The Harpers may have gone from Sparkbrook, but the local police had no respite from its slogging gang, which had new leaders. One of them was John Derrick, a labourer and my great-grandfather's oldest brother. Aged eighteen in the summer of 1889, he was one of two youths bound over to keep the peace for six months with a surety of £5 for his part in an affray. As a labourer, he'd have found it very difficult to raise that amount unless his pals had a whip-round and intimidated local shopkeepers to pay into a 'fund'. Two years later, he was described as well known to the police and belonging to a gang of roughs who created a disturbance in Thomas Street. Now part of Highgate Road, it's dominated by the Paradise Banqueting Deluxe Asian Wedding Hall, boasting a lavish interior and five-star reviews. Back in the late nineteenth century though, the street was filled with old cottages, small shops, four pubs and the retailing symbols of a poor quarter: a pawnbroker; wardrobe dealer selling second-hand clothes; marine store dealer buying and selling old metal, timber, rags and any waste a bit of money could be made from; and a tripe dresser providing a cheap takeaway food by cooking the inside of a cow's stomach with onions in a clear sauce and serving it up into the jugs of customers.

With half of Thomas Street in Birmingham and the other in Balsall Heath until late 1891, it was a popular meeting place for the Sparkbrook Slogging Gang as they could hop between two different police forces when causing trouble. On Saturday night 31 January that year, a lone constable trying to quell disorder in the street arrested one of them. His mates had other ideas and attempting to rescue him, Derrick threw a brick which missed its target and instead hit the arrested slogger. In court, the local superintendent said that Derrick was a constant source of annoyance as a leader of the district's rowdies. He was given six weeks. Like many other peaky blinders, he then joined the 6th Warwickshire Militia, the forerunner of the Territorial Army. Part-time service appealed to unskilled men, especially those in casual employment, as the pay topped up their irregular income whilst they could pick up work again after time away at camps. Derrick died of pneumonia on one such camp in Essex in January 1900. He was buried with military honours at a service conducted by a Roman Catholic priest, the faith passed on from his Irish grandparents.

Both were criminals. James Derrick was a thief and ne'er-do-well sentenced in 1850 to transportation to Australia for stealing brasses from a mine. Instead, he did almost five years' penal servitude in Dartmoor. A labourer by occupation, he could neither read nor write and whilst inside, his common-law wife, Eliza née Hennessy, was sent down for six months for theft. That was the end of both their relationship and her bond with her three children. They were put in the Wolverhampton Workhouse, a horrible institution where children were beaten and if Catholic, 'encouraged' to become Protestant. My great-great-grandfather, John the elder, was six. Nine years later, he was living on his own and working as an ironstone miner in Walsall, but soon after, he moved to Birmingham where he married a widow. He had a fierce temper and was fined for assaulting a police officer after striking the wall with a tremendous blow with a poker during a row with his wife. Like his parents, John Derrick the elder ended up in the workhouse and was buried in a paupers' grave. And like him, his sons John and my great-grandfather Edward were violent, whilst Edward and another brother followed their grandfather into a life of thieving.[75]

MAIMING MEN IN BLUE: THE WHITEHOUSE STREET GANG

Frightful as the upsurge in violence against the police in Balsall Heath was, it was exceeded in Aston. A more populous authority, it was policed by the Warwickshire County Force until becoming part of Birmingham in 1911. Taking responsibility for the district in 1882, Superintendent Henry Walker quickly realised that slogging gangs were usually under the control of a recognised chief and were formed to retaliate against someone committing an imaginary offence against the ethics of 'Sloggingdom'. Recruited from the class from which the peaky blinder evolved, generally they took their names from streets where most of their members lived and, in some cases, they comprised forty to fifty of the very worst local characters. Causing endless trouble to the police, they created such a reign of terror in Aston that after 10pm it was unsafe for any respectable householder to pass along the streets for the three miles from the Birmingham boundary to the bottom of Gravelly Hill on the edge of semi-rural Erdington. Officers were not only badly maltreated but some of them were so seriously injured as to be practically incapacitated from service. Having an antipathy against 'coppers' which no amount of punishment seemed to destroy, they immediately rose in the estimation of their fellows if one of them succeeded in maiming 'a man in blue' (the colour of police uniforms).

The Whitehouse Street Gang in particular was feared for its reckless violence. Although there were other slogging bands in the district, its infamy meant that it was also known simply as the Aston Slogging Gang. Short at less than 200 yards, Whitehouse Street today has a few industrial premises on one side and an empty space on the other, but until the mid-1960s it was a busy back street filled with factories, a scrapyard, coffee house, infant school, dance hall and back-to-back houses. Amongst its people was my mother, Sylvia Chinn née Perry, who lived at seven back of six until she married at eighteen in 1954. Her grandparents moved to the street in 1915, staying until their deaths fifty years later. My half Irish great-grandmother, Lily Wood, was the street's layer-out of the dead, unofficial midwife, wise woman and matriarch to thirty-five children and grandchildren living within yards of her. Her oldest daughter, my nan, Lil Perry née Wood, didn't leave the street until 1961 when she was allocated a new maisonette nearby, but she and Mom often took me down there visiting my great-grandparents and family members working in the scrapyard and factories. I still go there, drinking in the Albion pub on the corner after going down the match at Villa Park, home of Aston Villa

Football Club. Now called Christopher's Lounge, it's well known for its 'colourful Jamaican British carvery attire'.

My great-grandfather, William Wood, was a fighting man and so were his three oldest sons. As a teenager in the early 1950s, my mom wouldn't let a chap walk her back to her street on a Saturday night as too often her uncles were scrapping outside the pub. Georgie Wood, a sergeant in the 2nd Battalion SAS during the Second World War, was especially hard. In one straightener (man-to-man fight), he beat the 'cock of Aston', the bloke with the reputation as the toughest in a very tough district. In another, he sorted out what my nan called a 'whoer (whore) monger', a husband who slept around and whose wife gassed herself through the shame. Yet Uncle George always emphasised that when he was a teenager in the late 1920s, fighting was fair:

> We used to fight as kids with other streets. Avenue Road, Chester Street, Holland Road, Rocky Lane. Oh, we was cock o' the fuckin' north, Whitehouse Street. There was me, Dougie Ayres, Jackie Hunt, Herbert Mortiboy, Bobby Steel and another lot. People used to watch us fight. Fists. Knew you worn't hurting each other. Once you was on your arse you was out the fight. Never seen any kicking. If you was fighting then, you fought with a ring round you, copper'd only muck in if there was somebody getting hurt.

That recent change towards a code of fair fighting was explored in *Peaky Blinders: The Real Story* and *Peaky Blinders: The Aftermath*. None of my family knew of the Whitehouse Street Gang, which disappeared shortly before they arrived and contrastingly, its members were dirty fighters using weapons rather than fists, as James Brown's injuries proved.[76]

Becoming a constable in 1884, he looked back on Birmingham then as a cesspool of crime and vice where slogging gangs roamed. One of them injured him severely at the Old Pleck. Then at the northernmost edge of Birmingham close to the border with Aston, this large plot of wasteland was 'the melancholy resting place of old boots, dead cats and multitudinous assortments of malodorous rubbish'. Covered with stones ranging from small pebbles to granite setts, it was the battleground for rival gangs of peaky blinders and 'the locale of many a stirring struggle' where the police were ever worried with stabbing affrays, serious assaults and violent robberies. Though just in Birmingham, it was the domain of the Whitehouse Street Gang, who attacked anybody whether or not they were enemies. Called to such a disturbance there in 1888, Constable Brown was violently assaulted by 'the bell-bottom trouser ruffians'. They didn't fight fair and with thick buckled leather belts they beat the young policeman to the ground, leaving him unconscious. Off sick for some time, he went on to become a detective sergeant, figuring in some exciting adventures, especially of a nighttime when he had to battle for his life. Unhappily, though, the pasting he took at the Old Pleck was so severe that it was mostly responsible for him having to retire early from the force with ill health.[77]

Like the other most violent gangs, the Whitehouse Street sloggers included notorious brothers: the Simpsons. A wire worker from Hull, their father was twenty years older than his partner from Shropshire, and after moving around, they settled in Whitehouse Street where they raised their seven sons. Five of them became some of the worst police baiters of all. The oldest, John, was fined 2s 6d or seven days in March 1886 for punching a constable in the face outside a music hall. Within four months, his younger brother, seventeen-year-old Alfred, was arrested for throwing stones in a Sunday afternoon disturbance so serious that police from Birmingham had to be called in. A well-known character, he was fined just 10s and obviously regarded it as a paltry punishment. Three weeks later, when a mate was arrested, he led the gang in hurling such a storm of stones at the two constables that they were forced to shelter in a shop. Going up to one of them, Simpson warned 'that he would put it in for him, and immediately afterwards one of the stones which were flying about in all directions struck him on the back of the head'. An unfortunate passer-by was knocked out by another stone. With every one of his family having appeared before the local magistrates, Simpson was handed twenty-one days.[78]

One of his mates was as nasty. Ostensibly an edge tool maker, at eighteen William Newman was named as the leader of the Whitehouse Street Gang and the terror of Aston after he and four others laid into a man in his garden. Beating him with broken palings (wooden fencing), they broke an arm in two places. With previous convictions and having just done a fourteen-day stretch for assault, Newman was handed two months along with a companion, Ernest Mack. As detailed in *Peaky Blinders: The Legacy*, Mack provided another link between the sloggers, peaky blinders and the Birmingham Gang that fought the Racecourse War of 1921. Newman was also a very bad character, joining the Simpsons and their pals on street corners around Whitehouse Street and forcing pedestrians to move off the footpath. Fines for obstruction didn't deter them from intimidation nor from bullying. Having a melancholy catalogue of misdeeds by 1886, Newman joined in a cowardly mob-handed assault caused by another Simpson brother, George, hitting a boy so hard he made him cry and caused his nose to bleed. Seeing this, a householder asked Simpson why he'd done it but was threatened that his brains would be knocked out if he didn't go away. He didn't get a chance to. Struck on the head with a severe blow by another youth, he was stoned by Simpson, cutting his skull to the bone. Trying to help, the father of the boy was knocked to the ground and kicked savagely. Newman was one of two men arrested. Like Simpson, he got away with it and the Whitehouse Street Gang carried on terrorising the neighbourhood and beating the police.

Gathering on the Aston Road North on a summer afternoon in 1887, they intimidated everybody going past. Moving into Whitehouse Street, John Simpson and another man used bad language towards a woman. Overhearing this, two constables tried to arrest them but were resisted violently. Joining in, George Simpson lashed both officers about their heads and faces with his buckled belt, forcing one of them to draw his staff. In court, John Simpson accused the police of beating him without the slightest provocation, whilst a witness asserted that George only got involved because his brother was ill-treated. Preferring the evidence of the abused woman and the constables, they handed John Simpson three months. Having been released from prison just a few hours before the assault and with many previous convictions, George Simpson went down for six months.[79]

Soon after, it was the turn of another brother when James Simpson and George Betts, a neighbour from Whitehouse Street, were convicted of assaulting Louise Smith. Crossing the Old Pleck with a friend, she was suddenly surrounded by a gang of about twenty. She must have been terrified. Shouting, 'We have you now, you – !' the leader punched her in the mouth and then stabbed her on the shoulder, the knife going in one and a quarter inches. Falling to the ground, she was savagely attacked by the furious mob with Simpson and Betts striking her, kicking her and finally belting her. In their defence, the prisoners slandered Smith and her friend as women of ill fame who'd got a gang to beat them up with sticks the night before. Their lies weren't believed and each of them was sent down for two months. Both Simpson and Betts were aged nineteen, five feet four inches and filers. The 'chiver' was William Butler, an eighteen-year-old labourer from Whitehouse Street. He was handed fifteen months for unlawful wounding. Like Simpson and Betts, Butler had plenty of previous convictions. The same height, he was scarred on his forehead, the back of his head and on his bottom lip, and amongst his tattoos was a shamrock on his right forearm.[80]

Reporting on this case, the *Birmingham Mail* asked, 'Where are the Police?' The answer was simple. There weren't enough of them. With only fifty-two officers for a population of 68,000, a ratio of 1:1,307, the Aston police were even more badly undermanned than Birmingham's force. Responding to the slogging gang problem, the force was increased by twelve men. This still left the ratio of officers to people too high at 1:1,062, meaning that there were too few to contain serious outbreaks of violence. And with the Birmingham border just a two-minute walk away from Whitehouse Street along the Aston Road North, the town's police were also at risk. On a Saturday evening in January 1888, one of them heard a disorderly gang of roughs hustling everyone they passed.

After arresting one of them for being drunk and disorderly, the officer was challenged by Alfred Simpson roaring, 'Are you going to let the b – go!' As he did so, he punched the constable under the ear. Straight away, the rest of the gang closed round him, but determinedly he held on to his prisoner until two more policemen came to help. Though arrested, Simpson struck one of them so violently that two of his teeth were broken. As the pair of sloggers were dragged along the road by the police, a barrage of stones and brick-ends was hurled from a mob of about fifty. George Heeley was seen with a brick in his hand and ignoring warnings not to do so, he flung it at the policeman holding Simpson, smashing his helmet and 'inflicting such injuries as to incapacitate him from duty'. Although nearly blinded with blood, the constable struggled on and finally landed his man at the Lock Up. In court, one of the five men arrested proudly boasted that, 'It took three to take me.' In response, the magistrate's clerk remarked, 'I am afraid that that is not much in your favour.' Explaining that all the prisoners belonged to the slogging gang which had occasioned the police both of Aston and Birmingham a great deal of trouble, Superintendent Walker read out a lengthy list of previous convictions against Simpson. He was sent down for three months. Heeley and two others were each given two months and the last prisoner, six weeks.

James Simpson was as much a leading figure in the notorious organisation of the Whitehouse Street Gang as was his older brother. A hawker with several convictions for petty theft, in April 1888 he was one of the band stoning a solitary policeman. Undaunted, he chased off his attackers, capturing nineteen-year-old brassfounder George Willoughby who was too drunk to get away. His pals circled the officer, who was hit on the back by Simpson wielding a brick. Another policeman was at hand and with his stave, he hit Simpson to the floor. Both men had been repeatedly convicted for assault, but just as sentence was about to be passed, Willoughby said he would at once join the Army if discharged. Thinking 'this would be the best way in which his bellicose spirit could be kept within bounds', the magistrates sent him under escort to the recruiting office with instructions he be brought back for punishment if he wasn't accepted. Willoughby didn't seem to make any further court appearances. Despite his bad record, Simpson was merely fined 40s and costs or in default, a month.

Within weeks, and prompted by a rowdy May Bank Holiday Monday, a local newspaper despaired of the 'Aston Road loungers', 'Phillips Street bucklers' and the average slogger of 'the Simpson type'. Having graduated with 'knavish credit through all the degrees of local ruffianism and roguery, the "slogging" of a member of our constabulary is a source of unadulterated felicity and glory'. An 'amusement' requiring much physical strength and endurance, it also evoked 'a certain amount of excitement, calling for a display of all those demerits so indelibly associated with "roughs"'. The most brutal, cowardly and sanguinary 'slog' ever witnessed on the Old Pleck or elsewhere 'never afforded to the most susceptible of the "sloggers" the one-hundredth part of the delight – or to his more active, more aggressive and more murderous comrade the one-fiftieth part of the glory and renown – which accompanies the knocking of a policeman's head in, or the pulverising of his face; for in the "slogging" of a "slop", or the "buckling" of a "copper", the consummation of a "rough's" enjoyment is indubitably attained.'[81]

CONSTABLE BAITING

As the main road into Birmingham, Aston Road North had several streets running off it, meaning there were corners aplenty for the Simpsons and the Whitehouse Street Gang to gather on. According to Walker, 'If anyone passed they were insulted, and if they dared to remonstrate they were immediately buckled and maltreated. Only a brief time ago, two persons had their heads cut open by being so rash as to resent the insults of such a gang, and one of them was still in the hospital.' In response, he was obliged to place plain clothes men on duty in the neighbourhood. Incensed at what it perceived as the powerlessness of the police, a local newspaper announced that it seemed 'no less preposterous, disquieting, and astounding to be officially informed in this civilised, humanised, and be-policed period that one of the principal and busiest thoroughfares of Aston is virtually monopolised by a horde of blackguards, who take initial delight in insulting people, and then supplement their felicity by severely maltreating them'. With Alfred Simpson and other ringleaders now imprisoned, it was hoped that the Whitehouse Street Gang was no longer as fearsome. It was a false hope. Those sloggers still at large carried on with the terror-inspiring banner of 'sloggism'.

Worried that it would be years before they would disappear, the local press despaired of the ongoing brutal proclivities of Aston's sloggers or larrikins. Week after week, newspaper columns reported 'unprovoked and savage attacks either on policemen or members of the public. Police constables have been placed *hors de combat*, and quiet unoffending pedestrians maltreated with such persistent frequency that it is not at all surprising that the name of Aston is becoming associated with a band of ruffians the bare mention of whose appellation – Aston Slogging Gang – arouses feelings of dread and alarm.' Unfortunately, the increase of twelve men to the local police didn't help, as most of the constables knowing the district were removed to other stations. They were superseded by 'a lot of bucolic fellows whose entire knowledge of constabulary duties is of that inefficient and elementary kind which a police officership in the smallest of small, and quietest of quiet villages is best calculated to impart'. The force was now composed largely of 'the youngest of men and the oldest of boys, who until they came to the Manor had no idea of a real Aston slogger or a Brummagem rough, save that which he had formed from the reading of a newspaper report of a "slog"'.

Unafraid of the police, the Whitehouse Street Gang had little to fear from the courts. Highly organised, it was reported in the summer of 1888 that they had a system of compulsory assurance by means of contributions to a common fund, out of which fines were paid. However, recently, that insurance scheme received a rude check because Aston's magistrates decided to send all convicted members of the gang to prison without the option of a fine. To keep up their courage and maintain their discipline under these trying circumstances, the gang came up with the plan of organising a 'subscription' for the benefit of any member newly released from prison. To this end, in August 1888, Alfred Simpson and several of his associates went about demanding money for a fund for Betts, who'd just finished three months for assaulting a policeman. When approached in his garden, one resident said he couldn't afford to 'donate' because he'd a wife and large family. Furious at his refusal, they kicked and beat him before pulling off their belts and laying into him with their buckles until he escaped into a neighbour's house. Betts himself was in the gang and after an exciting chase, he was caught by a constable and was soon back inside. Simpson was also fetched before the magistrates. Appealing for another chance, he promised that he'd leave the country if leniency were extended to him. His pleas were ignored. Told that it was a very bad case, in fact one of the most infamous cases ever brought before the court, he was given two months.[82]

Later that year, the Whitehouse Street Gang grabbed attention nationally. According to London's *Daily News*, they'd enjoyed a great field day:

A member of their fraternity had that morning been released from the gaol in which he had been confined for stabbing a woman, and the occasion appeared to his comrades to be a fitting one for marking their sense of this interference with their liberties by a public demonstration taking the form of a procession through the streets. Thoroughly consistent and practical in their mode of assorting their claims, the sloggers seem to have begun operations by violently assaulting a young unmarried woman, who as she was on her way to her work was struck violently in the face, knocked down, and brutally kicked about the head and body.

The woman was Laura Solloway, a seventeen-year-old press worker from Lichfield who was lodging locally. She had the misfortune to be going to work when the drunken sloggers were parading. As she went by, Betts spoke to her in a blackguardly manner. When she asked if he was addressing her, he hit her in the eye with such force that she went reeling into the gutter where she was brutally kicked by Betts and others. At considerable personal risk, a Good Samaritan pulled her into his chemist shop just within Birmingham. Straight away the gang began smashing its windows and bawling that they'd fetch her out to murder her. With no police to be found for almost an hour, they besieged the chemist's, terrorised the inhabitants and had the locality at their mercy. Eventually, a detective and inspector arrived and chased the rowdy mob along Chester Street. The detective grabbed eighteen-year-old James Casey, but having 'conquered and handcuffed his man', he was felled to the ground by two severe blows from a brick. It was brandished by another usual suspect, James Simpson, revelling in his violence as 'he was not in Aston, where the Bench gave it to them so hot' [where the magistrates imposed severe sentences].

Releasing the man he held, the inspector ran to help his fellow officer and as he came round, they sought refuge in a pub. Seeing what was happening, a local man drove his horse and trap to the nearest station in Duke Street, Gosta Green. Fortunately, as the shift was changing there was a large number of men there and led by a superintendent, about fifteen officers raced over half a mile to Chester Street. Facing them were about thirty roughs who'd chosen as their stronghold a piece of wasteland well stocked with bricks and stones. They barraged the police as they advanced, but 'the strife was but a short one, for the gang were ousted with five arrested'. Still, several officers were injured with the detective seriously so. Two of the gang were fined 20s or in default, a month. One was from Gosta Green and the other from the Summer Lane neighbourhood, indicating the pull of the Whitehouse Street Gang for sloggers from further afield. Betts and Simpson were each charged with malicious wounding. As the magistrates could hand them no more than six months, they sent them to a higher court hoping that a heavy punishment would be meted out. Betts's grievance was that 'Solloway dared answer him, and he wasn't going to stand any woman talking to him.' It was he who'd come out of prison only the day before, and within the past year, he'd spent ten months inside for numerous assaults. Simpson's total reached twenty. Each of them was given fifteen months not only to punish them but to deter others of similar inclination from following their example.[83]

Casey was lucky as he was discharged from unlawful wounding. He lived just in Birmingham, in Pritchett Street, merely a ten-minute walk from Whitehouse Street. Unlike the English Simpsons, Betts, and the rest of the band, his parents, were Irish, hailing from Roscommon. Casey's father was a bricklayers' labourer and his mother a press worker, and he started out in the way of most lads from poor, unskilled backgrounds as an errand boy on pitiful wages. His older brother, John, was named as an old offender when sent down for three months for stealing six bottles of beer worth 2s in 1887. Later that year, he and his mother, Sarah, were charged with assaulting a man without any provocation. Quarrelling in the dock, she spat in her son's face. She was let off, but John Casey was given a month. When out of prison, he was said to be always with the Whitehouse Street sloggers and would go on to do six months for assaulting a constable by smashing a wooden plank on his head.[84]

By the late 1880s, several of the Simpson brothers were also living in Pritchett Street. Though still calling themselves the Whitehouse Street Gang, this shift led to them also becoming known both as the Aston Slogging Gang and simply the Slogging Gang, so frightful was its reputation. Any thoughts that severe sentencing would deter them were quickly dispelled. In early 1889, Alfred Simpson was imprisoned for three months for assaulting a policeman. Within three weeks, the rest of the band went on the rampage led by that other incorrigible young rough, Casey. Having got away with it for the Chester Street affray, he'd gone on to be discharged for assaulting several officers on the Old Pleck. He must have thought he was untouchable and on a drunken Saturday night in February 1889, he brutally kicked an officer striving to arrest him. Alerted by the blowing of the police whistle, two more constables came to help, but Casey was so violent that it took the three of them to frogmarch him to the station. Sentenced to two months for each assault, he threatened several of the constables and was given an additional month. Assuming an air of bravado, he said he didn't care and would still make it hot for the 'coppers' when he came out. Unhappily, he kept his word and after disappearing for three years, he was sent down for three years' penal servitude for knifing two men in what looked like a gang fight. That stretch was followed by another spell inside for assaulting a policeman and by 1902, he'd amassed fifty-five convictions. As Chapter 3 will reveal, one more was to come, following the last attack of the Whitehouse Street Gang.[85]

The baiting of Aston's police went on into the summer of 1889. One evening in June, a pair of sloggers were arrested for kicking two brothers and beating them with the 'dreadful buckle'. On their way to the station, the constables were stoned. Amongst the crowd slinging missiles and using obscene language was fourteen-year-old Lizzie Hands. The only one taken into custody, she was said to have violently assaulted a policeman. Slammed as a 'juvenile virago', she was imprisoned for twenty-one days followed by five years in a reformatory. This was noticeably a harsher sentence compared with those on young teenage lads charged with first offences. Hands had it rough and in 1901, she and her illegitimate eleven-week-old son were lodging with another family in a back house in Pritchett Street. He was named Albert after her older brother. It was an unfortunate choice. A ruffianly fellow, he was a well-known character in the Whitehouse Street Gang and joined the Simpsons when they assaulted a married woman. Hitting her several times with his hat, he then kicked her, insulted her with filthy language and threatened to kill her. Later, he was acquitted of indecently assaulting a sixteen-year-old woman. Despite the support of witnesses for her account, he was found not guilty because she was deemed as consenting because she'd received sixpence from him.[86]

Albert Hands seems to have steered clear of the police after that. James Simpson didn't. He went on making it hot for the police. In 1891, he slashed a constable on the head with his belt whilst another officer was belted so hard by someone else that the buckle broke. Knocked down, he was then hit by Simpson. In court, he and another man said they were assaulted by the police without any provocation and struck severely on the head. Though both wore blood-stained bandages, the sergeant in charge of the Lock Up said neither had any injuries. At that, the magistrates had the bandages removed and it was clear both were play-acting. Simpson was given six months. His older brother, John, was fined 10s and costs, or in default fourteen days for assaulting an officer at the police station. Two years later, George Simpson was sent

down for two months after he attacked a pair of policemen.
Though James Simpson joined in he got away with a fine, but
it didn't take him long to be back inside. Damned as a pest
to society and a disgrace to humanity, he did another three
months for assaulting two constables in December 1893.
Resisting violently, they needed two more to frogmarch him
to the station. By then he had twenty-eight convictions, some
of which were for assaults on women. In court he presented
a dishevelled appearance, his face being scarred and bruised
in several places. Less than eighteen months later, he was had
up for the thirty-eighth time. He was twenty-five. After that,
there's no mention of him breaking the law and in 1901 as a
single man, he was lodging with his younger brother, Robert,
his wife, and two of her relatives. Robert Simpson had no
convictions, although in 1886, when he was fourteen, he was
discharged from assaulting a married woman in Whitehouse
Street when, unsurprisingly, she didn't turn up at the hearing.[87]

AN EPIDEMIC OF RUFFIANISM

It was hot for many policemen in the 1890s, the decade when
the peaky blinders thrust themselves into both Birmingham's
history and its urban myths. A few weeks before their name
first appeared in the press, policemen were savagely assaulted
in the Deritend Riot of Saturday night, 25 January 1890.
Today a creative hub that's part of 'cool' Digbeth, Deritend
boasts trendy cafes, bars and pubs as well as independent
shops, arts and dance venues; then it was crammed with
back-to-backs and workplaces overshadowed by high railway
viaducts crossing the valley of the River Rea. The ringleaders
of the Deritend Riot were 28-year-old Joseph Bostock and

his brother, John, nineteen. Both were brass casters living with their Irish father and English mother and both were members of the Milk Street Gang. That night they caused mayhem and as the older Bostock fought PC Dowell trying to arrest him, a general riot broke out in which the roughs joined with seeming delight. In a melee reminiscent of those in Navigation Street fifteen years before, PC Hemming strove to keep back the gang as Sergeant Betts now took hold of Bostock and started for Moseley Street Police Station. Showered by stones, the officer was felled by John Bostock creeping up behind him and striking him with a loaded stick. With his jaw broken, somehow Betts was fetched to hospital.

Taking over from him, Dowell just about got Joseph Bostock a few hundred yards closer to the station before he was forced to stop by the furious mob. With brick-ends and stones falling thickly about him, he sheltered in an entry, dragging Bostock with him. One of the gang came up to the beleaguered officer, saying menacingly, 'Dowell, I have got a boxing glove here for you, and a – hard one, too.' Told to mind his own business or he would get into trouble, instead the slogger pointed to a huge stone in his hand, threatening, that 'I will knock your – brains out with this before you get to the station.' A little later he did throw the missile at Dowell. Seeing it coming, he drew back and pushed Bostock forward so that it struck him on the head, causing it to bleed profusely.

Fortunately, Hemming and four others came to the rescue of their fellow constable, but they had a warm time with the rioters kicking them about their legs whenever they could get near. Unable to reach Dowell, the rowdies vented their rage in smashing a confectioner's window. Reinforcements arriving, Dowell moved on, but he'd hardly done so when

John Bostock rushed at him, dealing him a terrific blow on the back of the head, and nearly stunning him. Helped by a colleague, Dowell pluckily kept hold of his prisoner who was still trying to grapple his way free. The younger Bostock then made a dash at both policemen, but was caught hold of by Dowell who sprang back sharply. As if reporting a wartime battle, the *Birmingham Post* wrote that 'all this time the police were being injured with stones and kicked. They fought the roughs gallantly to the very last. Had they once shown the white feather some of them would in all likelihood have been maimed, probably for life. They made use of their staves, but in the height of the affray three or four of the constables were disarmed.'

Joseph Bostock had a bad record. In 1881, he'd been sent down for two months for assaulting the landlord of the Two Swans' in Deritend and three policemen who came to arrest him. A frequent offender and key figure in the Milk Street Gang, he'd other convictions for assault and in 1886 he, his brother John and a companion cowardly attacked a mother. Seeing them chasing after her son with buckled belts, Mary Kemp ran over to them, begging them not to touch her boy. Instead, they set upon her, with Joseph Bostock kicking her and fracturing her ribs. It was a vengeful assault as a few months before the Bostocks and their pal were each imprisoned for three months for breaking into Kemp's house. Now for the Deritend Riot, Joseph was sent down for four months. As for his brother, John, for stealing some bread when he was twelve, he'd been imprisoned with adults for fourteen days and then passed to a reformatory for five years. At just under five foot five and with numerous scars from fighting, he was found guilty of unlawfully and maliciously wounding Sergeant Betts and PC Dowell and given five years' penal servitude. In passing sentence, the Recorder said that had the loaded stick he'd wielded struck Betts a little higher on the head, probably he'd have been hanged for murder. It was absolutely essential that the police should be protected in exercising their perilous duties, and not be subjected to such attacks. Unfortunately, more of them were to be baited, whilst an extraordinary feature of the affair was also to be repeated many times: the riot was witnessed by about 500 people, none of whom showed a disposition to aid the police.[88]

A few weeks after the Deritend Riot, Chief Constable Farndale insisted that the slogging gangs were declining in numbers and power. He was taken to task by the *Birmingham Mail* drawing attention to an 'epidemic of ruffianism' that had exploded recently. In Digbeth, a hotbed of sloggers, the local tradesmen had lost what faith they had in the police, who appeared wholly unable to cope with the roughs infesting the district. Together with stories of wanton ruffianism and brutality from other parts of the city, the public's confidence in the police force was shaken, although not so far as the individual bravery of the men was concerned as 'almost every day bore testimony to the courage which policemen were prepared to exercise in the discharge of their duty'. There was also a strong feeling of class discrimination. With its markets, shops, workplaces and masses of back-to-backs, Digbeth, along with the Bull Ring and Deritend, was the working-class heartland of Birmingham, yet it was thought that too few policemen were stationed there. By contrast, an unwarrantable number were on duty in the middle-class shopping thoroughfares of New Street and Corporation Street. Away from these entitled enclaves, mob law held sway, with shopkeepers living in terror of the gangs prowling about at night levying blackmail and committing unprovoked assaults.

Hardly a day passed, railed the *Mail*, without slogging cases in court and each week brought with it its crop of attacks with brick-ends and buckled belts upon the police. At present, several were incapacitated from duty by injuries inflicted in the street riots they'd tried to quell. It was all very well saying that the respectable public should be keener to join the police in subduing this rowdyism, but recent experience had shown that 'the interference of a civilian on behalf of the police is likely to be attended with serious results, and it is not at all surprising that there should be wholesome dread of "sloggers" amongst the public.' The 'Birmingham rough' was feared as having no equal for ferocity, evidenced by assaults on the police. In Manchester, a policeman was assaulted for every twenty arrests for drunkenness, in Liverpool the ratio was 1:13, and in Leeds 1:12½. By contrast, in Birmingham it was 1:7½, and these figures took 'no cognisance of assaults committed by ruffians who are not in a drunken state'. Importantly, in nearly every recent case of serious assault in the streets, the rowdies had worked in gangs.[89]

The intensification of gang violence was frightening and if constables tried to avoid gatherings of roughs, some of them had no qualms in beating youngsters. In March 1891, a group of teenagers were playing a game like tig in Greens Village. Branded as a nuisance for running back and forth and having supposedly stoned passers-by earlier, three policemen were sent to clear them off. Approaching from three different directions to 'middle' the lads, the officers made an onslaught. As the youngsters fled, several of them were hit with buckled belts, including sixteen-year-old William John Whittaker, who was heard to cry, 'Oh, my poor head.' Badly injured with a depressed fracture of the skull and another head wound, he was taken to hospital where he died. At the inquest, the coroner was scathing of the officers' conduct, making it clear that it was absolutely necessary that they should do their unpleasant duty legally and properly. Belts were part of policemen's costume, but they had no right to take off a belt even in self-defence. It was apparent, though, that the officers wanted to catch the lads and give them a blow and they didn't care whether they did it with a buckle-end or anything if it had the effect of breaking the lad's skull. The police had no right whatsoever to strike in that way and still less any right to strike boys when they were running away. It might be that the constables 'got their blood hot, and being greedy, they liked to run their prey down; but they should remember that they were only executing a duty for the general public, not for themselves, and they must not go beyond that'. They should have identified the boys, got their addresses and brought them before the magistrates for obstruction in the street. That offence was not to be punished by knocking a boy down. Arriving in support of the three officers chasing the lads, PC Watson was named as having struck young Whittaker with his belt. Found to have done so unlawfully by the jury, he was charged with manslaughter but because of contradictory evidence, the case was not proceeded with.[90]

The inability of the police to deal effectively with the gangs of roughs terrorising the poor contrasted starkly with such an attack on boys larking about, reinforcing the negative opinions held of officers in poorer districts and feeding the ranks of the peaky blinders with angry, aggrieved youths. Though receiving less attention in the newspapers, attacks on constables reached a high of 494 in 1894. The next year, on a Saturday night in late October, two policemen turned out a gang of between twenty and thirty peaky blinders causing trouble in a pub close to the Bull Ring markets. Once on the street, they reared up on the officers. Though arrested, Charles Warner viciously resisted, whilst the constable was whipped by the belts of others and made to let go of his prisoner when kicked by James Cuson. Scarpering off, Warner was chased by Constable Telfer and caught in an entry in Inge Street, right by the National Trust Back-to-Back Museum in modern Birmingham's Gay Quarter. There was another desperate encounter and Telfer was in peril until PC Bennett came up. Both officers were then beaten about their heads by the buckled belt of Thomas Groves. A seventeen-year-old brass caster appearing very frequently in the police books, he was given three months. Having a very bad character, Warner was sent down for six months. Aged twenty and purportedly a goldbeater, if he were a skilled man he was a rarity amongst the peaky blinders. As for Cuson, a 28-year-old labourer with eighteen previous convictions, he was sentenced to six weeks. All the men lived near to the offence and their wide age range emphasised how peaky blinder/slogging gangs included men as well as youths.[91]

The Bromsgrove Street Disturbance was quickly followed by the Watery Lane Affray. When chatting with a civilian, PC Farley was approached by three men, one of whom asked what they'd been talking about. Suddenly and with no warning, Thomas Plumb hit the officer on the cheekbone whilst the other pair took up a fighting attitude on either side of him. Plumb charged at the constable who struck him on the back with his staff. It broke in two, allowing Plumb to grab hold of Farley.

CONSTABLE BAITING

Defenceless, he was hit on the head and kicked on the legs by Arthur 'Nugget' Morris and an associate. Picking up part of the staff, Plumb belaboured the officer on his head. Knocked down, he was kicked so badly that one of his ribs was broken and with his whistle snatched, he couldn't sound the alarm. Having lost several teeth and with one eye closed, somehow the battered constable pulled himself up, reeling against a wall. With the beating happening so quickly, the shocked civilian who'd been chatting with Farley was rooted to the spot but now the gang turned on him. Hit with the broken staff so hard that his head was covered with blood, he fell unconscious, remembering nothing else until awakening in hospital. Hearing shouts of murder, a witness begged the attackers to stop. Instead, they ran across the street to beat him with part of the staff. Another bystander was too scared to intervene.

Plumb was sent down for six months, but having a bad record, Morris was given five years' penal servitude. A 22-year-old galvaniser, he was taken aback at the severity of the sentence. As he shouted with an oath and many filthy expressions that he'd hang for Farley, his friends at the back of the court caused a commotion. Though still young, Morris did have a bad record. At thirteen, when convicted as an associate of thieves, he was sent to industrial school for five years. After his release, he was found guilty of assault and stealing coal, rope, fowl and mutton amongst other things. A hardened criminal, a stretch of five years didn't change him. After doing more time for theft and assault in 1909, he was involved in the notorious Garrison Lane Vendetta and given twelve months for his part in a riotous attack.

Outraged by the brutality of the Watery Lane Affray, a local newspaper complained bitterly that the peaky blinder was having things too much to his own liking. Imperatively, he had to be taught 'to respect the policeman sufficiently to refrain from battering, assaulting, and half-murdering the guardian of the peace'. A peaky blinder rarely acted alone because he was an arrant coward singly, but he performed astonishing deeds of bravery when in 'the company of blackguards, and the common enemy is a solitary policeman'. Though he'd shown commendable courage, PC Farley paid a severe penalty in wounds and bruises and deplorably it was apparent from this and other assaults that the Reign of the Rough was again imposed upon Birmingham. It was. By the mid-1890s, Birmingham was notorious across the land for the violence of its slogging gangs and undesirable class of youths generally known as peaky blinders. An exasperated journalist in a best-selling national Sunday newspaper was baffled that they hadn't been exterminated by the police long ago. Constituting a danger to all classes of citizens, they seemed to stop at no deed of violence when on one of their brutal excursions. Yet the average sentence inflicted on them by Birmingham magistrates was merely two months. Little wonder that they were undeterred from their wild career of smashing up policemen, knocking down inoffensive old people and hitting and striking everywhere.[92]

THE CITY OF DREADFUL NIGHT

Birmingham's ill repute for violence condemned it as 'The City of Dreadful Night' whilst its dialect name became a slang term for attacks on policemen. When some Coventry youths set about two police officers to free one of their pals, 'their war cry was, "Let's give 'em Brummagem."'

Hauled before the court, three of them were sternly informed that 'if Birmingham permitted rowdyism Coventry did not!' Within Birmingham itself, there was a pronounced feeling that the violence of the peaky blinders was accepted, a sentiment encapsulated by a correspondent to the *Birmingham Mail* in February 1896. Denouncing an attack on a volunteer (part-time soldier) by a gang of peaky blinders, 'Civis' asked if it were not time to check the rife rowdyism. Hardly a day passed without brutal and unprovoked assaults on citizens, yet it was only when anything exceptional happened that they found their way into the papers and then the public was aroused. From personal observation and scrutiny of the press, the dismayed letter writer believed that 'We are rapidly coming to a similar state of things which years ago culminated in the murder of Police-constable Lines.' They were prescient words.[93]

In 1897, there were 589 assaults on constables, considerably up from 346 a decade before. There was also one murder, that of 29-year-old PC George Snipe. The second oldest of eight children and the son of a farm labourer, he grew up in the rural districts of north Worcestershire, soon to be subsumed into Birmingham. Constable Snipe followed his father into unskilled agricultural work before becoming a groom and then joining the Coldstream Guards for three years. At just under five feet ten inches, he was accepted for the Birmingham Police in February 1890. Within three months, his left elbow was fractured when grappling with a drunkard causing trouble in a pub. The next year, he was kicked badly on three occasions, hit in the back by a brick, attacked by a thief, and kicked like a madman by a dangerous ruffian with numerous convictions for assaulting the police. Snipes's woes continued into 1892 when he was attacked three times, and then in August 1893, he was the victim of a dastardly assault. One evening when walking along a main thoroughfare, he was struck from behind with a heavy blow from an unknown man. Snipe was hospitalised with his right jawbone fractured and a severe injury to his head. Two further assaults followed in 1894, in one of which he and other officers were mobbed by a crowd trying to free prisoners. A year later, he was kicked and bitten by a drunken woman and suffered a savage assault from an abusive husband. Entering the house to help the wife, the constable was attacked with a poker and a knife, his helmet was smashed on his head, and he was hit with glass and crockery. His attacker swore that the officer should not leave the house alive and 'he had the utmost difficulty in escaping without serious injury'. The abuser was fined merely £1 or in default, a month.[94]

Such numerous acts of violence perpetrated on just one constable received only brief notices in the local press, emphasising that police baiting was now regarded as intrinsic to Birmingham. The killing of Snipe, however, drew countrywide attention to the perils of the city's police in combating the epidemic of brutality of the peaky blinders. About 10pm on Sunday 18 July 1897, as the pubs were turning out, Snipe and PC Mead arrested William Colerain for disorderly behaviour. A labourer aged twenty-three, his last name was also given as Kilrane and he had two previous convictions for assaulting the police. Heading towards Bridge Street West Police Station, the officers had to pass through what the prosecution called an undesirable neighbourhood. This was the Summer Lane district, rooted in Birmingham folklore as one of the toughest parts of the city where policemen only ventured in pairs well into the twentieth century. According to the *Liverpool Weekly Mercury*, as was usual with 'the denizens of such a district as this, popular sympathy was all in favour of the man under arrest'.

A determined attempt was made to rescue Colerain, but keeping hold of him the officers also managed to arrest Charles Edward Elvis. Aged thirty-two and a plasterer, he had a long record for drunkenness, theft and assault. The inflamed crowd started throwing stones in a ferocious attack on the policemen. Blowing their whistles for help, they were joined by another constable in a stubborn battle against serious odds. Volleys of stones rained on them and 'those of their opponents who could get opportunity used foot and fists in savage fashion' to release the prisoners. As they reached the corner of Well Street and Bridge Street West, just opposite the Star beerhouse, Snipe was tripped up by Colerain. As the officer pulled himself up, someone darted from the crowd and from within a yard or so flung a brick at him. It struck him with fearsome force on the temple. Knocked senseless, he fell almost into the arms of Polly Mullins and lying unconscious on the ground, he was kicked by Colerain before several 'respectable' people bravely tended to the policeman. Seeing that, PC Mead went on to the station, grappling with the very violent Colerain who repeatedly threw himself down. As for poor Snipe, he was rushed to the General Hospital. Briefly regaining partial consciousness, he demonstrated his devotion to duty by saying he would go back to the row. Falling back unconscious, he died a few hours later of a haemorrhage. His head was fractured in two places and on one side the skull was driven in.[95]

Colerain was sent down for eighteen months, whilst Elvis was imprisoned for nine months along with two others also found guilty of unlawful assault on peace officers. They were Thomas Hodges, thirty-one and a labourer, who'd done time for housebreaking, drunkenness and assaulting a constable, and 24-year-old Thomas Moran, with one conviction for drunkenness. As for who'd hurled the brick that killed Snipe, PC Mead couldn't say. Mary 'Polly' Mullins could. Aged twenty-six and a tin solderer, she clearly identified James Franklin, a nineteen-year-old filer and peaky blinder who was charged with wilful murder. As Mullins was the most important prosecution witness, there was a little flutter of excitement when she was called for in court. Testifying calmly and intelligently, she explained she knew Franklin by sight and saw him in the crowd following the police and then throwing a brick from about a yard and a half away. After picking up the felled officer, she put his helmet in her apron, exclaiming at Franklin, 'You – scamp. You've killed him.' Running off to the police station with the helmet, Mullins was chased by Franklin. Catching her, he demanded the helmet and hit her when she refused. Freeing herself, she ran off again but once more Franklin caught her, threatening that if she didn't give him the helmet, he'd kill her. Snatching it from her, he jumped on it, telling her that Colerain was a friend of his. Despite Mullins's persuasive evidence, other witnesses strongly denied that Franklin threw the brick, and he was discharged to loud applause from the public gallery. Soon after, he threatened Mullins.

During the trial, the brick thrower was named by several people as nineteen-year-old George 'Cloggy' Williams, so called because he wore clogs like the men of Lancashire. One of those witnesses was James Jones, supposedly a friend of Williams, who stated that, along with others, they were with Colerain when Snipe ordered them off for obstruction. When the hurling of missiles began, Jones testified that Williams picked up a brick, saying that he was going to knock out the policeman's brains with it because Snipe had once sent him down for two months. According to Jones, after hurling the brick, Williams said, 'He ain't hurt much.' Eventually arrested after absconding from Birmingham, Williams was tried in March 1898. A glass beveller working a machine, he was praised by his employer as very industrious but the same witnesses who'd supported Franklin affirmed that Williams had thrown the missile to have his own back. Found guilty of manslaughter, he admitted he'd been in the crowd but asserted his innocence. When sentenced to penal servitude for life, his mother swooned and fell forward.

At five feet two inches, Williams was discharged from breaking into a house in 1895. The photograph then taken of him by the Birmingham Police shows he was a peaky blinder, with prison-cropped hair and a quiff plastered across his forehead from the left. This look was commented on during his trial: 'His hair, which is of a light colour, was dressed in the approved "peaky-blinder" style, short at the back, and pulled down in a fringe over his forehead.' Unusually though for a peaky, he was a skilled worker in regular employment and a member of a trade union, whilst his father and older brother were highly skilled whitesmiths, and his mother ran a small shop. Younger than the others convicted, it seems he was drawn into the local gang but perhaps because he didn't quite fit in; it looks like he was 'fitted up'. Several of the witnesses against him were friends of the discharged Franklin and were dismissed contemptuously by the defending counsel as testifying from the gutter. In particular, Jones's crucial damning testimony was repudiated as tainted by his attempts to cover up his own involvement in the assault on Snipe. Nicknamed 'Chicken', presumably because he was derided as a coward, Jones was challenged that he'd boasted to Williams's older brother that he'd hit PC Snipe with a bottle. The sibling's reply was instructive: 'Chicken, where did you get the pluck from?' Jones answered, 'Pluck or no pluck, I "knacked" him [hit Snipe] with a bottle and would have "knacked" him with a knife if I hadn't had it knocked out of my hand.' Reinforcing the belief that Jones had something to hide, immediately after the attack he went to his sister's in Bolton taking with him Williams, who then went off elsewhere.[96]

Whatever the justifiable doubts about Jones's evidence and that of other witnesses, Cloggy Williams was the one who did the time, although his sentence was reduced to eighteen years in 1907 when the Home Secretary's attention was drawn to his case. He was a model prisoner. After the first six months, he was at Dartmoor where his servitude necessitated digging to reclaim land never cultivated. He accepted his lot stoically stating, 'It was a hard job. Still, the life of a prisoner is very much what he makes it. It is no use his running his head against a brick wall, because if he does he will get hurt.' After five years, Williams was put on basket making then work in the library, where he did quite a lot of reading and took the opportunity of improving his education. Four and a half years of his sentence were then remitted for good conduct, and upon his release in 1911, the Home Secretary, Winston Churchill, directed that Williams need not report himself to the police as was required of other convicts on licence. Still asserting his innocence, it was widely reported that he looked bronzed and well and was going to take up his old job as a glass beveller and marry his old sweetheart who'd stayed true. Writing to the *Birmingham Gazette*, Williams denied he'd a sweetheart and that it was his brother who'd been nicknamed Cloggy and not him.[97]

ACCURSED PEAKY BLINDERS

Eight months pregnant and with a two-year-old toddler, Snipe's widow, Dorothy, was grief-stricken at her husband's funeral in Warstone Lane Cemetery. Taking a last look at his coffin in the grave, she fell insensible into the arms of relatives, whilst her brother-in-law fainted. An enormous and respectful crowd gathered in sympathy, but for all that support, constables remained at risk. Two nights after the manslaughter of Snipe and in the same district, an officer was badly mauled by a buckled belt when roughs tried to free an arrested man. Another policeman who'd served throughout the Indian Mutiny was disabled for months after he was struck from behind by a gang, whose leader only got two months. The hardened young 'Peaky Perisher', it was said, liked nothing more than pummelling a policeman on his beat, although a single-handed bout was naturally not to his liking. As a retired officer spelled out:

They drop upon you in a band, and you've not one, not two, but twenty-two to tackle. Off come their belts, out come the brick-ends and the loaded sticks, and in a twinkling the fun begins. Before you can stir you get a buckle into the middle of your back, a brick-end lands on your head, and you feel the weight of that loaded stick. They're at you on all sides like tigers, and if you're a particularly precise and obedient fellow anxious to follow the Stipendiary's direction . . . you'll be very careful not to hit the blackguards in a way that will hurt 'em; rap 'em over the head and you might fracture their skulls. But your own skull doesn't count; you're paid for the work and have to take the risks.[98]

With the frightening ruffianism of the peaky blinders seemingly unstoppable, a public meeting was called in the locality where Snipe was killed. Speakers defended the police but firmly placed the root of the evil with the local magistrates for their apparently fixed determination not to inflict severe punishments for assaults on constables. The usual sentence was a few shillings fine and only occasionally were perpetrators imprisoned, and then for just three months at the most. That prompted the *Manchester Evening Chronicle* to sneer that there were people in the world who looked upon Birmingham as 'if it were an earthly paradise, saying with more or less obvious pride that it was the best governed city in the Kingdom'. If that were the case, it was strange that street rowdyism was allowed to exist and street ruffians to flourish. Flourish they did, and it was less than a year after the manslaughter of PC Snipe that PC Leach was so badly beaten by peaky blinders. Violent men with long-held grudges, they bided their time for vengeance, something that John Hession knew only too well. Formerly an officer in the Warwickshire Police Force covering Aston, he'd become a munitions worker. In February 1900, he was outside a pub when he was knocked down and kicked by a man wielding a file. The powerfully built and odious Edward Hayes joined in. Filled with spite against Hession for once arresting him for assault, he kicked the ex-policeman and stabbed him three or four times in the head with a knife saying, 'Kill the – this time.' Picked up after the assault by concerned bystanders, Hession was covered in blood. Two pocketknives, one with a broken blade, were found on the ground. Hayes was sent down for six months for malicious wounding. Aged twenty-five, he'd previous convictions for assaulting constables and would go on to serve time for grievous bodily harm and manslaughter.[99]

Four months after Hession's beating, a serious affray erupted in June 1900 in Barford Street, below the Bull Ring markets. Deprecated in the press as 'the local Alsatia', a sanctuary for criminals, it had a long-standing and notorious slogging gang. Brothers Thomas and Albert Harris, twenty and eighteen respectively and both in the metal industries, were arrested by two officers for disorderly behaviour and using obscene language. They didn't go peacefully. One of them belted a constable and suddenly, an angry crowd milled around. Another policeman came to help, but as the three officers strained to reach Moor Street Police Station, two were stabbed in their left shoulders. Although the blades penetrated to the bones, neither suffered serious injuries and they were able to arrest the offenders: twenty-year-old labourer Henry Attwood and Percy Langridge, a polisher aged sixteen. The disorder raged on even after the arrival of two more constables and Frederick Long, sixteen and a filer, 'was so anxious to secure the release of his friends that he interfered, swore at the officers, and threatened them'. Eventually, the constables reached the safety of their station with their prisoners. Thomas Harris was fined 10s 6d whilst his brother was handed three months and Long a month. Described as of the peaky blinder class, Langridge complained to the magistrates that he'd been hit in the face by one of the constables. When asked if that was so, the officer replied he'd struck with his fist when kicked. Langridge was admonished: 'You must not expect to have it all your own way when you begin to assault the police.' He and Attwood were each sent down for five years' penal servitude.[100]

During their appearance in court, the dangers faced by the police were made clear. In 1899, there were 557 convictions for assaults on them and over the previous decade, the total was 4,462. Nine officers were presently disabled because of injuries. Responding to these serious and alarming figures, an editorial in the *Birmingham Post* pronounced that just as epidemics of disease required special measures for their extinction, so too did the city's epidemic of ruffianism. The exuberant vitality of the hobbledehoy and hooligan necessitated severe repression for just as slogging gangs made certain districts intolerable, 'the baiting of policemen is indulged in until repeated sharp punishment brings about at least a temporary cessation.' Unhappily, there was no cessation and the policeman's lot remained an unhappy one.[101]

Birmingham's rampant ruffianism was deplored locally as a disgrace to any civilised city. Woefully, there were some parts 'where police patrols literally carry their lives in their hands, and where the Hooligan looks upon it as his privilege and amusement to assault anyone who wears a policeman's uniform'. One of those taking his life in his hands was PC Charles Phillip Gunter. Tragically, he lost it. A Welshman and copper smelter whose older brother and family lived in Birmingham, he joined the city's police in March 1900 and was assigned to Duke Street Station in Gosta Green. A hotbed of the peaky blinders, it was regarded by the police as a rough neighbourhood where they had considerable trouble. As a bachelor and under the supervision of a superintendent, Gunter lived with twenty-eight other constables on the premises. Only one was from Birmingham, although two others were from the immediate locality. Fifteen were English, with eleven of them from rural areas. Three came from industrial districts and one from London. There were two others from Wales and eight from Ireland. The racism of peaky blinders will be addressed elsewhere, but it's probable that their animosity for the police was fuelled by a loathing for the preponderance of officers drawn from agricultural England and from Ireland and Wales.[102]

In a short notice in its late edition of 23 July 1901, the *Birmingham Mail* related that earlier that day, PC Gunter was found stunned and bleeding on the ground by a passer-by who blew his whistle for assistance. He'd been set upon by a gang of roughs who'd thrown bricks, with one hitting him in the face and causing a nasty wound above the left eye. Taken to the General Hospital, he was soon sent home although he was expected to be incapacitated for several days. Unfortunately, the injury to his head developed 'unfavourable symptoms' and quickly he was back in hospital in a critical condition. The follow-up on his condition was even briefer, although slightly fuller reports on the murderous attack ensued. With his skull fractured, PC Gunter's condition was precarious, necessitating trepanning, and towards the end of August it was announced that his strength was gradually diminishing and there was no hope of his recovery. Operated on three more times, a month later his doctor stated he remained in a very unsettled condition. His brain was altogether out of working order, and it was doubtful whether he would ever be of right mind again. Unable to speak and partly paralysed on one side, and despite the almost 'superhuman efforts' to save his life, PC Gunter died on 26 October. Five days later, his body was taken from the General Hospital to Snow Hill Station, hence by railway to his parents' home in Carmarthenshire.[103]

The local Welsh newspaper praised the scene in Birmingham before the coffin was placed on the train. Thousands congregated to show their respects, and the procession was headed by the police band playing the 'Dead March in Saul'. Behind them came a hundred comrades walking with slow and measured steps ahead of the hearse. The coffin itself was all but hidden in masses of white flowers. Alongside it walked six constables chosen to act as bearers. Three or four mourning coaches brought up the rear, carrying amongst others, PC Gunter's brother and father, who'd kept vigil at his dying son's bedside. Under the headline, 'Burry Port Policeman Killed by Hooligans of Birmingham', the *Llanelly Mercury* reported that the funeral itself was one of the largest and most impressive ever witnessed locally. Back in Birmingham, a memorial service led by the Reverend Bass was held at St Laurence's Church, Gosta Green.[104]

Four men were charged with wilful murder: Joseph Adey, twenty-three, George Callaghan, thirty-three, and John Davis, thirty-one, were all polishers whilst George Fowles was a nineteen-year-old brass filer. On the dreadful night, they and others left a pub at about 11pm and with a barrel of beer went to Callaghan's back-to-back yard. With their singing and drinking disturbing the neighbours, just before midnight Gunter told them to be quiet and move on. As they did so, one of them was heard urging the others: 'Let's go down and do him in.' The officer was then called to a nearby house where there was a family upset. Mary Ann Bruce lived there, and she stated that the constable was followed by seven men, including Adey and Fowles. Her cousin added that as the officer left the house, 'They all got round him. Bricks went.' More men joined in, and Gunter was surrounded and felled by a brick. A nightwatchman from a nearby factory saw a man in a trilby hat pick up a brick and break it on the kerbstone. It was obvious he was about to throw it when a girl standing at the bottom of an entry called to him, 'If you do, I'll blow you [report him to the police]'. At that, the man hit her, and he was joined by someone else. One of them threw something and the policeman collapsed. Running from the factory to help, the nightwatchman found the constable lying on the ground bleeding from a wound to the forehead. The next morning, a sergeant reported that the place was strewn with brick-ends.

Another onlooker heard Adey telling his wife he'd been in a row and broken a brick in two and that Fowles knocked out a policeman with a brick. The witness added that Adey was wearing a trilby hat when leaving home in the morning, but a cap when returning that evening. When he was arrested, a trilby was found in a drawer in his house. The potman of the pub where they'd been drinking also gave evidence against the defendants. As a 'copper', he was threatened by one of their friends who later cut his head open. As the postman fled home scared, a brick was hurled at his back. Reaching his doorstep, he fainted and was taken to hospital. The next night, his attacker ran at him threatening to 'do him in'. For that threat, he was merely bound over to keep the peace for six months. Charles Bailey was another intimidated witness. One of the crowd who gathered around Gunter, he ran off when he saw Adey, Fowles and Davis with bricks in their hands. Testifying 'with some misgivings that his own personal safety would be jeopardised as a consequence', he was right to be worried. Fowles went looking for him to 'roust' him and 'sherrick' him [have a go at him] for making off when the bricking began.[105]

At the beginning of the trial, Callaghan's charge was withdrawn as it was clear he'd also run away from the trouble. He then turned against the other three, saying that Fowles admitted he threw the brick at Gunter, hitting him 'chock on the nut' [full on the head].

In his summing up, the judge explained that although there was an absence of motive for the killing, this didn't matter. That was because it was quite possible that certain sets of men had a lasting spite against the police doing their duty in grave danger in neighbourhoods like Gosta Green. Consequently, the jury had to consider what was actually done, with the judge suggesting strongly that if a set was made against Gunter with the intent of causing him serious injury, then the verdict should be murder. The jury, however, could conceivably bring a verdict of manslaughter if it were thought the men were so inflamed by anger and passion that they scarcely knew what they were doing. To the surprise of the judge, manslaughter was the decision. Fowles, Adey and Davis were each sentenced to fifteen years' penal servitude. Locally, the press was incensed, all the more so because 'Cloggy' Williams had been given life for the same offence. The *Birmingham Gazette* raged that the case reflected a 'namby-pamby spirit'. PC Gunter's brains were dashed out by a brick and he lingered in agony for weeks before succumbing, whilst every impediment was placed against collecting evidence in

Gosta Green, 'the haunt of the accursed "peaky blinder", a savage beast in human form', who'd imposed a reign of terror. And just as the name of Corkery was once used to terrorise constables, now to 'Gunter' an unpopular officer was already in the peakies' vocabulary.[106]

Adey had four convictions for assault, fourteen for gambling, wilful damage and other offences, and had also served eight months for shopbreaking. Although only nineteen, since he was twelve, Fowles had spent almost five years in prison for stealing and burglary and had other convictions for vagrancy and obstruction. In court, Adey and Fowles turned against Davis, accusing him of throwing the fatal brick. What is certain is that he was a much more violent man. Since he was thirteen and amongst other thefts, he'd served time for burglary and stealing a dead rabbit and a cake as well as for numerous assaults, including on the police. Not long before the bricking of Gunter, Davis was sent down for six months after so violently resisting his arrest when drunk and disorderly that the officer had to strike him with his staff. On the way to the station, Davis bit the constable's thumb so viciously it broke the bone. Refusing to let go, he was struck over the head by another policeman who tried to choke him off before his jaws were finally prised open with a penknife.[107]

Like his older brother, George, Frederick Fowles was a criminal. In 1904, the Birmingham Police took his photo when he was sent down for five months for housebreaking. It shows him with the close-cropped hair and donkey fringe of the later peaky blinders. Interestingly, though, George Fowles, Adey and Davis weren't referred to as peaky blinders but as the hooligan type. 'Hooligan' was a new word describing a young street rough in a street gang, having suddenly appeared in London newspapers in July 1898. It swiftly gained wide currency and within a month, one commentator was recognising that 'Birmingham like certain districts of London has its Hooligans, though in the Midlands the ruffians are known by the euphonious name of peaky-blinders.' The term hooligan quickly took hold within Birmingham and elsewhere, so much so that in 1901, reports of the conviction of Thomas Walters for stabbing a policeman referred to him variously as a peaky blinder and hooligan.[108]

A nineteen-year-old brass polisher, his father was a highly respected chimney sweep in Nechells, a district noted for its slogging gang. It's apparent that Walters was in it as he'd already done time for throwing a brick at an officer and knocking a piece off his elbow. Now, he was fetched before the courts for what the judge pronounced was one of the worst cases of unprovoked assaults he'd ever known. The trouble arose after a group of youths was ejected from the Carlton Theatre on the Saltley Road for disorderly conduct. Carrying on causing trouble outside, they were warned by PC Bennett. Riled, they went for him. Badly mauled, he was stabbed in the back with a long pocketknife by Walters. The wound was a very deep one and if it had been an inch lower, it would have gone into his heart and killed him. Surprised that Walters was not charged with attempted murder, the judge gave him five years' penal servitude, regretting that he couldn't be more severe.

Walters's nephew, George Thomas Nicholls, knew that his great uncle was a peaky blinder who served a long stretch for wounding a constable and was told that he 'used to fight in the Bull Ring for his beer money and was a hard man.' He was, even though like so many peakies he was small at five feet two inches. No one was safe from him and out on licence for knifing Bennett, the drunken Walters quarrelled with his sister and brother, waving a cut-throat razor at them. Petrified, they barricaded themselves in a bedroom. In another example of wartime metaphors when describing peaky blinder violence, the *Evening Despatch* thundered that 'with the aid of some furniture the fort was held for some time against the infuriated assailant, and subsequently the brother and sister took advantage of a temporary cessation of hostilities to escape into the street'. Discovering this strategic movement, Walters chased his brother, vowing to cut his throat, until the razor was knocked out of his hand by a smart blow from a constable's staff. Walters was sent down for fourteen days.[109]

BARBAROUS BIRMINGHAM

'Barbarous Birmingham', thundered the *Evening Despatch*, might well be the heading of the Chief Constable's report for 1901 with its returns on assault and battery, malicious wounding, manslaughter and murder. In many parts of the city, peace-loving inhabitants were dominated by small bands of ruffians with no fear of the law, whilst the police were the victims of the most wanton and violent outrages. Constable baiting was unchecked, with the *Birmingham Mail* lamenting that 'still the peaky is with us, and the notion that the policeman exists only as a target for brick-ends had not yet been expelled from his mind'. Its rival publication, the *Birmingham Gazette*, was as dismayed. Worryingly the enmity between the peaky-blinder element and the officers of the law was now regarded as normal and had risen to such a pitch that the dangers of the policeman's lot were immeasurably increased. They were. Just weeks after Fowles, Adey and Davis were sentenced, peaky blinders almost killed PC Ernest Blinko when his head was split open with a cleaver in a murderous attack. Hailing from rural Oxfordshire, like so many constables he was the son of a farm labourer. Moving to Birmingham as a young man, he delivered goods on a horse and cart for the Great Western Railway before joining the police at the end of 1895 aged twenty-one.[110]

On the fateful afternoon of Tuesday 28 January 1902, he was on duty walking along Longmore Street, the scene of many previous assaults on the police. A tram route, it was now one of the busiest thoroughfares in the city, making the attack even more extraordinary. Three men were seen slinking about and peeping from behind a street corner as if watching out for someone. One of them went off and another was heard saying, 'Hey up, here he is.' A peaky type, he stealthily approached the constable from behind and horrifically dealt him a murderous blow on the back of the head with a cleaver taken from his coat. The officer collapsed to the ground and more blows were landed on him. His callous assailant was about to strike again when his companion approached him saying, 'We have done him in. We had better get off.' The attacker replied, 'We may as well stop. We have killed him.' They didn't stop. Concealing the cleaver dripping with blood in his clothing, the cowardly attacker and his partner ran off. Nobody tried to pursue them, 'the horrible character of the crime and the desperate demeanour of the assailants seemingly paralysing the few onlookers into a state of dazed inaction'.

Two women were the first to rush to aid the fallen officer. Screaming when they saw the blood pouring from several ugly wounds, they fainted. A man coming to help blew the police whistle, whilst another bystander got hold of a cab to take the terribly injured and partially conscious constable to the Queen's Hospital as speedily as possible. Arriving in a critical condition, he had three wounds close together at the back of the head. Each was more than three inches long and beneath them, the bone was driven in. All three were dangerous. There was another wound lower down, close to the junction of the neck, a superficial cut on the left side of the forehead and a bruise over the left cheek. An operation enlarged the wounds and took out the driven bone to the extent of six inches. A tear one and a half inches long through the membrane of the brain was then found. As the brain substance was escaping through this rent, it was sewn up to stop the bleeding. The fragments of bone were then cleaned and put back in place and the skin drawn over and stitched together, but with a draining tube left in. Next, the wound near the neck was searched and the damaged bone scraped. In a critical condition for almost two weeks and hovering between life and death, the unfortunate Blinko was left helpless and incapable of moving. At first, it wasn't known whether he'd entirely recover, but remarkably, he did thanks to the skills of the surgeon, Dr Jordan Lloyd and his assistant, Dr Quirke, and to the care of Sister Wills and Nurses Heap, Shaw and Hooper. All were honoured for their dedication, with Dr Lloyd noting that the patient's recovery would have been impossible without recent advances in the science of surgery and anaesthetics. Remarkably, PC Blinko returned to duty three years later in May 1905, retiring seventeen years later.[111]

The man striking the blow was short and wore peaky blinder clothing with a neckerchief (daff), a soft cap pulled down over one eye, a cutaway coat and bell-bottomed trousers. His companion was dressed similarly. From the evidence of witnesses, the police realised they were the notorious brothers David and Frank Cherry. Aged twenty-eight and purportedly a painter, David Cherry was described in court as short, with a receding forehead, prematurely bald, and having a closely cropped beard and moustache. His younger brother, nineteen and a labourer, was similar except he was clean-shaven and had forelocks well plastered down over the forehead in orthodox peaky fashion. Both were said to be as unsettled in their place of living as nomads. They were apprehended by two constables a mile away in the George inn on the Ladypool Road, Sparkbrook. Now a South Asian boutique in Birmingham's famed Balti Triangle, I drank in the pub in the 1970s and '80s when it looked the same as at the turn of the twentieth century. Its main feature was a long bar with only one entrance on the corner with Alfred Street, so that the brothers would have readily seen the officers coming in. Frank Cherry was taken without bother, telling his brother, 'Go quiet, David, we are beat to the wide [have no chance]'. David Cherry didn't go quietly and started to take the cleaver out of his coat pocket to strike the other officer. In a severe struggle, the weapon was wrested from him and he was thrown on the floor and handcuffed. The constable must have been charged with fear and adrenaline, fighting with all his might knowing what had happened to Blinko. When the struggle was over, David Cherry said, 'I done it. He [meaning his brother] never done anything.'[112]

Like numerous other peaky blinders, the Cherry brothers were taken to the Steelhouse Lane Lock Up, next to the now Grade I listed Victoria Law Courts. Both were opened in 1891, with the Lock Up operational as a police cell block until 2016, after which it was transformed into the unique West Midlands Police Museum. Because Blinko was unable to attend the magistrates' court hearing for several weeks, the Cherrys were held at the Lock Up for longer than usual before transferral to Winson Green Prison. Whilst they were still there, Frank Cherry unlawfully wounded eighteen-year-old William Owen. He'd waited with the brothers for Blinko to appear, but when he was spotted, Owen was heard saying, 'Come on, I'm going out of this.' Turning on his erstwhile pals, he became a prosecution witness and when fetched to the Lock Up to identify the brothers, Frank Cherry struck him a slinging blow in the eye necessitating hospital treatment.[113]

Both brothers were sentenced to penal servitude for life for wounding with intent to murder. Having a very bad record and like all peaky blinders, Frank Cherry was a bully, even though like his older brother he was short at five feet two inches. In September 1900, after he and other rowdy youths took over the children's play area at Calthorpe Park, Cherry turned off a little boy from a swing, boxing his ears and making him cry. An attendant intervening was punched and then hit with a shovel. Cherry was fined 20s. The next year he was sent down for fourteen days for assaulting a constable and within weeks of his release, he served three months for a dastardly attack on another officer. His older brother had an even worse record. Born in Taunton, Massachusetts, USA, his father was from Lancashire and his mother from Birmingham. Returning to England in the late 1870s when Cherry was a toddler, the parents settled in Balsall Heath, best known today as the birthplace of UB40. His mother and father must have regretted the move for not only were David and Frank Cherry violent but so too was their brother, John. As will be revealed, he served five years' penal servitude for stabbing a man to death.[114]

David Cherry's life of criminality began in 1887. Aged thirteen, he was fined 10s for stealing from a local shop. Given a good character, he was said to have been led astray by another youth but was cautioned to be careful for his future. The warning went unheeded. A fourteen-day stretch for scrumping was followed by others for burglary and stealing beer. Though just under five feet three inches, thereafter he became a most dangerous man. One of a gang causing a row in December 1891, he was sent down for a month for kicking a constable and hitting him with his buckled belt. Just weeks after his release, he and other peaky blinders cruelly beat a Jewish man in a racist attack. After serving two months, it was only days before he was back inside for assaulting another constable. Four months later, in October 1892, he was again before the magistrates for the same offence. Given three months, he laughed. Almost despairingly, the magistrate told Cherry he'd begun a very bad life. Only nineteen, he'd been before the court nine times and 'there was only one form of punishment that would do such a fellow any good, and that was a good whipping, which the magistrates were sorry they could not order. Prisoner would not laugh again if he had a taste of the cat.' As it was, they 'really did not know what to do with such a fellow'.

It's unlikely that either the cat or any other punishment would have had a positive effect on Cherry. After doing more time for assaulting yet another constable in July 1893, he was sentenced to three years' penal servitude for robbery with violence. Once released, he went back to live with his parents in Balsall Heath where he demonstrated he had no qualms about whom he beat up. One Saturday night in 1896, he refused to fetch a bag of tools from the workplace of his elderly and unwell father. Upset and angry, the old man told his son he wouldn't have such a lazy good-for-nothing about the house. Cherry then 'savagely turned upon his father, and, after knocking him about severely, attempted to put him on the fire'. Two police officers called to help were kicked and beaten. Hopelessly, a local newspaper asked, 'What can be done with a ruffian like David Cherry?' Nothing it seemed could change such an 'incorrigible savage', who quite clearly was on the road to the gallows. Handed two months, he again served it locally in Winson Green Prison. It's obvious he was undeterred and certainly unreformed by a regime of having to walk the treadmill to power the grinding of wheat, and by occasional stone breaking, pumping water, mat making, tailoring, shoemaking and oakum picking.

Cherry was clearly a leading figure in a peaky blinder gang with a very bad reputation for outbreaks of ruffianism in the lower part of Balsall Heath. In 1897, he was with them when they badly mauled a policeman and bit off part of his ear. Of no fixed abode and a heavy drinker, after an eighteen-month stretch for attacking yet another constable, in July 1899, Cherry tried to strangle a young woman in the Bull Ring. Arriving to help, an officer was tripped up by Cherry's associate and kicked unmercifully. Three more policemen were viciously beaten, one so badly that it was thought he'd be unable to carry on with his duties. Feared as a desperate fellow, Cherry was imprisoned for six months, followed in June 1900 for twenty-one months for housebreaking. Unfazed by prison, he attacked a sergeant whilst inside. Embittered by a ruthless loathing of the police, he needed little or no reason for tearing into them. Although PC Blinko knew Cherry, he'd never arrested him, but his head was cleaved merely because the day before he'd been with another officer who'd served Cherry a summons for loitering. Over the first decade of his life imprisonment for this brutality, he attacked other prisoners and staff. Then, in 1911, he was transferred from Parkhurst Prison to Broadmoor Asylum for the criminally insane where he died in 1945. His younger brother, Frank, was sent to Portland Prison and released in 1917 to fight in the First World War with the Dorset Regiment. Injured badly in battle, he died of his wounds and was posthumously awarded the Military Medal for bravery in October 1918. Was it redemption? He is buried in Gézaincourt Communal Cemetery Extension by the Somme.[115]

HUNTERS OF PEAKY BLINDERS

In sentencing the Cherry brothers, the judge emphasised that there seemed to be a disposition on the part of such men to hunt policemen to death, but he'd do his best to put a stop to it. Previously, he'd punished 'Cloggy' Williams for causing the death of a policeman, but this attack was far worse. The brothers deliberately planned their crime and that they weren't sent to be hanged was only by providence and medical skill. Applause greeted the sentence of penal servitude for life, whilst the *Birmingham Gazette* hoped that exemplary as it was, it would check the unruly hooliganism existing among the peaky type. Still, knowing the peaky blinders as well as they did, it yet remained that whenever they attacked a policeman, 'black murder and nothing else is in their hearts, whether they seek to accomplish it an "in an affray in the street" or by prowling about with a chopper in wait for their victim'. In the eyes of the blackguards who infested the city's streets, to 'Snipe', to 'Gunter' or to 'Blinko' a policeman was considered an act of the highest heroism. Despite this gloomy assessment, prosecutions for assaults on constables began to drop, from 507 in 1901 to 416 a year later. Though welcomed as a gratifying decrease, it was felt that the peaky blinder hadn't been tamed. Soon he would be.[116]

In a striking and sharp turnaround, gang attacks declined quickly and noticeably. In 1905, only two serious slogging gang battles were reported and just a handful of peaky blinder assaults against the police. One was an 'exciting' struggle in Hockley. Arrested for drunkenness, 22-year-old polisher James Brough struck out, knocking down the constable and kicking him about the body and face. Two other policemen arrived but were set upon by a pair of Brough's mates trying to free him. They would have succeeded 'but for the prompt assistance rendered by several bystanders, who clung tenaciously to the prisoners and rolled over on the ground with them'. After what was said to be an hour's struggle, all three were arrested. One of the constables was unconscious and taken to hospital. So too was Brough, whose clothes were almost torn off him. With a lengthy list of convictions, he was given one month along with one of his pals, whilst the other was fined 20s.[117]

Thereafter, peaky blinders all but vanished from newspapers, so much so that in 1907, a visiting journalist observed that a few years ago, Birmingham was even more notorious for its peaky blinders than South London for its hooligans. Two years later, assaults on the police fell dramatically to 360. With satisfaction, the authorities affirmed that in all respects,

Birmingham was quieter and more orderly than a few years previously and now it compared more favourably with some other great towns. Most of the slogging gangs were broken up, once frequent night attacks upon pedestrians were few and far between, and street outrages of all kinds had decreased appreciably. The main reason for this extraordinary change was the disappearance of the peaky blinders, a phenomenon emphasised by a judge when praising the remarkable absence of serious crime in Birmingham in 1909. By comparison, when he'd first visited in 1887, the peaky blinder was an aggressive force, a standing menace to all respectable citizens, and a continual danger to the police. Happily, this class of hooligan had ceased to be an element in local criminal life.[118]

It had. As the First World War approached, peaky blinders were looked upon as a disgraceful feature of the city's past. They'd carried out dark deeds in the side streets where they'd waged warfare, but no more was 'a midnight walk from Birmingham through Slumland to any of the suburbs an adventure fraught with danger'. During the war itself, it was noticeable that many former peaky blinders were making good soldiers, whilst others had found respectable, regular jobs as unskilled workers. With the coming of peace, there was no revival of peaky blindism nor were there any modern-day successors. As one informed commentator asserted, they were extinct. That reality was highlighted by officers who'd clashed with the peaky blinders. Retiring in 1919 after thirty-three years in a police division embracing many criminal areas, Detective Inspector Herbert Davies was thoroughly familiar with evildoers. Entitled 'one of the hunters of the peaky blinders', he recalled that a couple of decades previously, the peaky blinder was a notorious and vicious character, spreading terror through his dirty work. Dressed in bell-bottom trousers and generally armed with a knuckleduster, 'this individual was equal to anything in the way of crime, and robbery with violence was one of his favourite evil works'. It wasn't safe for the police to take him on, but they'd done so and succeeded in stamping him out. Detective Superintendent Burnett agreed. In 1920, when reflecting on his twenty-five years' service, he was proud that Birmingham's streets were no longer infested by prowling gangs ready to commit any violence to carry out their depredations and that nowhere was now unsafe to go through after dark. Peaky blinders were evil-doers and a menace to the city in the far-off days of the 1890s, but Burnett declared they'd been suppressed because of the relentless vigilance of the police.[119]

As related in *Peaky Blinders: The Real Story*, social developments also contributed to their disappearance. Youths were pulled away from the street and the gangs by the popularity of football and boxing as participatory and spectator sports, by youth club facilities provided by socially aware clergymen and women, and by the attraction of the pictures (cinema). For all their importance, though, the crucial factor was undoubtedly the robust police action launched by Birmingham's chief constable, Charles Haughton Rafter. Appointed in 1899, it was understood locally that his most pressing task was to stamp out the dangerous element of 'Peaky Blindism for the bell-bottomed fraternity has reigned far too long'. Rafter succeeded where his predecessors failed. In 1910, the knowledgeable J. Courtney Lord, chairman of the Birmingham Juvenile Court, stressed that when Rafter arrived, the city was infested by a large number of rowdy peaky blinders, but within a few years they'd practically ceased to exist. His achievement was driven by a rapid recruitment campaign increasing the Birmingham Police from 700 to 920 men by 1907 and to 1,413 in 1914. This significant strengthening ensured that within a few years, no constable would walk a beat on his own. In office until his death in 1935, Rafter's powerful personality loomed large over the Birmingham Police for decades. It was said that he demanded three things from his recruits: 'Can they read? Can they write? Can they fight?' Young, well built, fit and at least five feet ten inches tall, Rafter sent his men out in pairs to take the fight to the peaky blinders. Fight they had to.[120]

R. W. Hawkins remembered that when a gang tried to rescue a peaky blinder from the police, they had the worst of it because the constables 'were mostly big and stalwart, and the tykes were usually short and tough'. 'Tykes' was a term used briefly in the mid to late 1890s instead of sloggers and peaky blinders. Retiring as a detective chief inspector in 1930, James McArdell recollected that when he joined in 1896, he was quickly mixed up with the notorious peaky blinder gangs terrorising the city. Month after month, he and his fellows were engaged in the suppression of this hooliganism and 'often we had to fight for our lives with these gangs'. Under the headline, 'Prisoners Severely Mauled', a rare contemporary report from just before Rafter's appointment made it clear just how bloody this fight was. In early February 1899, there was 'a lively scene' in Allison Street. Late one evening, three men were causing a commotion and refusing to go home, one of them, Edward Welch, was arrested. Resisting violently, he waved a knife at another constable and knocked off his helmet. John Casey of the Whitehouse Street Gang and a John Moran joined in, and the arresting officer was beaten down and kicked. Finally, after a third policeman turned up, the three offenders were taken into custody.

Appearing in court the next morning, Casey's shirt was considerably blood-stained and his head was bandaged. Having four cuts, so too was Welch's. The stipendiary observed that he'd been badly knocked about the head, whilst Casey looked awfully punished. A witness said the staff of one of the policemen was broken against Welch's head, and he showed a piece he'd picked up. Emphasising that where possible, it was advisable to disable a man by striking the legs rather than the head with the staff, the stipendiary sentenced Welch and Casey to twenty-one days each. He commented that it would have been nearer six months had they not been so severely punished by the police. Moran received fourteen days. A violent man of no fixed abode, he'd served time for several assaults over the previous decade.

Welch was of the same thuggish ilk. Unaffected by his previous time in reformatory school and by this lenient sentence, merely days after he was released in March, he so fiercely fought against his arrest for drunkenness that it took five constables and two bystanders to hold him down. Fuming at the sentence of three months, he yelled at the police, '– if I don't swing for one of them.' Welch seemed intent upon carrying out his threat as quickly as he could after this stretch. In July 1899, he severely mauled a constable but escaped. Weeks later, he was found in a Park Street pub by an officer, whom he asked to show the warrant for his arrest. As the unsuspecting policeman put his hand in his pocket to take it out, Welch set about him right and left, punching and kicking him so much that he had to pull out his staff in self-defence. A six-month term was handed out for these offences. Blasted as an incorrigible rough, Welch lived up to his bad reputation. In 1902, under the headline 'More Peaky Blinders', he was described as a ferocious-looking man who'd badly knocked about a constable in Park Street. In this, his fortieth appearance in court, he was sent down for three months. Later that year, he was convicted of highway robbery with violence and was sentenced to four years' penal servitude.[121]

Rafter's resolve for young, fit and tough recruits was embodied by Bromsgrove-born Arthur David Penrice. A giant of a man at six feet one inch, he was twenty-three when he joined in April 1903 after eight years' distinguished service in the Grenadier Guards. A keen athlete and swimmer, he rose quickly through the ranks and as a superintendent in the 1920s was a familiar figure astride his white horse in the Aston division. Before that, though, he was entangled in several fights breaking up gangs of peaky blinders. The most savage was in July 1905 when some women called him to a yard in Weaman Street in the Gun Quarter where the drunken Henry Cotterell was smashing windows. Though resisting violently, he was arrested and dragged to the entry by Penrice, who was challenged by an unidentified man and Joseph Fox, menacingly saying, 'Loose him, or we'll do you in.' Fox tried to do so, kicking and hitting the constable and forcing him to let go of his prisoner. Regaining hold of his man, Penrice was accosted by Joseph Jennings asking, 'Do you want assistance?' He replied, 'Yes, take hold of his other arm.' It was a ruse. Getting behind the policeman, Jennings knocked him down with a powerful blow to the jaw, shouting, 'That's the sort of assistance I'll give you.' John Murphy joined in the attack, jumping on Penrice's chest and kicking him viciously in the abdomen. Though battered, the officer still held on to Cotterell but, getting weaker and weaker, he had to let go. Fortunately, a civilian picked up Penrice's whistle and blew it to fetch other constables to the scene. Penrice was hospitalised although the offenders were arrested.[122]

They all lived in Weaman Street and were clearly members of its slogging gang. Cotterell and Fox were each sent down for three months whilst Murphy and Jennings were each imprisoned for two months. Soon after his release, Murphy was fined 20s for throwing a jug at a landlady of a local pub, the Green Man, and cutting her eye. Three years previously, Fox was given two months for hurling a glass at its landlord and causing him severe injuries. He was an unsavoury character and a few months before the beating of Penrice was imprisoned for three months for theft. Fox was heavily involved in his street's slogging gang and in 1901, he was beaten up and stabbed in a revenge attack after a row between two bands.[123]

Penrice's harsh experience emphasised that Rafter's recruits were enmeshed in a bloody, punishing battle against the peaky blinders. But as more tough, fit and well-built officers came on to the streets and through working in pairs, they gained the upper hand. Seeing the strength of the police, working-class people gained confidence that they'd be protected when witnessing against peaky blinders. Importantly, the chief constable was also supported by magistrates and judges imposing stiffer sentences for 'police baiters'. The importance of these factors was appreciated by ex-detective superintendent W. J. May. Starting his career in 1894 during the 'reign of the ruffians', he quickly became aware that it was quite a proposition for the police dealing with the peaky blinders and slogging gangs because those they injured wouldn't give evidence for fear of revenge. Yet the continual vigilance and war against organised gangs went steadily on and the police were well backed by the Recorder, the part-time circuit judge, John Stratford Dugdale KC. Rarely did his courts open without cases of unlawfully wounding, and if a knife or other dangerous weapon were used, almost invariably the offenders were sentenced to penal servitude unless there were extenuating circumstances.[124]

Many of Rafter's new recruits were Irish, leading to suggestions that the city's police were becoming 'Hibernianised'. It wasn't but the Irish were a significant minority. With eighty-seven men out of 860 in 1904, they made up just over 10 per cent of the force compared with only 1 per cent of the city's population. The fighting prowess of the Irish constables passed into Birmingham folklore. Born in 1898, my Great Uncle Wal Chinn grew up in Studley Street, regarded as the toughest in Sparkbrook, remembering that:

The coppers used to come down in pairs . . . There was two of 'em had to come to keep things ship-shape and I've seen 'em stand outside the Gate and they were nearly all Irish coppers at the time. Charles Haughton Rafter was Chief Constable in Brum at the time and his recruits come from Ireland, and they were all big, broad Irish blokes. They didn't know A from a bull's foot. But it didn't matter to him. They could carry out a job that he wanted them to do. A bit of order, never mind about being educated.

They used to come round, a couple of 'em and perhaps if they found a bit of a disturbance at the Gate or any of the other pubs. They'd come down two-handed and they used to wear a cape rolled up, you know, on their belt. They'd go and sort them out, find out who the culprits was and give 'em a warning, get 'em out the road and say, 'Off Home!' If they didn't comply with the coppers' orders, they used to set about them and if they wanted to tek it out on 'em, they hadn't used to use their truncheons, they used to use their cape and set about them that way. And after it all cleared up, nice and tidy and they'd got 'em on the way home, the gaffer [of the pub] used to come out, 'Thank you ever so much,' to the coppers, you know. 'All right, guv'nor. How you fixed?' 'Yes, hang on a minute,' and the old gaffer used to pull 'em a couple of pints out.[125]

One of the Irish recruits playing a crucial role was Sergeant William Henry Doughty, a former cavalryman responsible for the fitness of the police in his role as gymnastic instructor. In 1984, I interviewed one of his sons, Stan, in the George, the Sparkbrook pub in which David Cherry resisted arrest. Born in 1907, Stan Doughty called to mind his father's early career in the police:

I can tell you something about this. As a constable his wage was 25s per week . . . For that 25s he was a gymnastic instructor, a bandsman and also he used to have a special class of inspectors and superintendents which he used to teach jiu-jitsu. All for 25s per week. When he was made sergeant, I can remember quite plainly, because he come into the house so excited, and he'd still got his helmet on with the spike on the top, and he knocked his helmet off and I heard him say to Mom, 'Maud. I'm a sergeant.' And he upped our ha'penny a week pocket money to a penny a week and that's as true as I'm a looking at you.

William Henry Doughty was born in 1875 in Bangalore, India. His Irish father was a soldier but died when Doughty was a toddler and so he and his widowed mother were shipped back to Dublin. As a military orphan, he was sent to the Royal Hibernian Military Schools where he had 'twelve months sewing, twelve months boot making, twelve months in various things that were supposed to or would equip you to face life. And he finished up in the English Army as a bugler boy for thre'pence a day. That was before he attained to his physical culture expert.' Joining the 4th Hussars for twelve years when he was fourteen, Doughty served his last six in India and after returning to Aldershot and marrying, he drove a horse and cart for R. White's, the soda and mineral water business:

But always being on the lookout for summat better and knowing his own qualifications, by this time he's a musician plus the fact he's a gymnastics instructor and he got all this in the Army, he's looking around for a job and the next thing he sees an advert or hears about an advert for Bradford City Police. And he took Mom up to Bradford. He used to tell us how he used to mek a bit of extra money by doing people's night work, policemen who would transfer their night work to him if he was plucky enough to do it because there used to be a lot of bell metal in those days around the graves, see, and the thieves were pinching the bell metal of a night time and the coppers were getting knocked about.

And so he used to tek anybody's night work on . . .
And then he seen the advert for gymnastic instructor
required by Birmingham City Police and he applied for
it and he gorrit.[126]

Fit, fearless and well able to defend himself, Doughty joined
the Birmingham Police in June 1904. Within five months
and unusually for someone new to the service, he received
an award for vigilance in three cases. Promoted to sergeant
in 1912, with the coming of war two years later, he served as
an instructor to Army recruits. After returning to duty, in
October 1918, he was one of the three sergeants instrumental
in forming the Birmingham Branch of the new National
Union of Police and Prison Officers. The Government
responded by increasing pay but in refusing to recognise the
Union, it triggered a strike on 1 August 1919. Like Doughty,
those withdrawing their labour were dismissed. With an
unblemished and exemplary record, he sacrificed much
for his principles, not only losing his income but also his
pension. As with other strikers he was blacklisted, his son
remembering bitterly, 'Wherever he went he was barred.
This man is dangerous.' After nearly five years out of work
and relying on his wife's paltry earnings taking in washing,
Doughty was called in by Rafter who gave him the two
instruments he'd played in the police band – the tenor and
bass trombone. With these he got a job in a little orchestra of
eight playing for the silent movies at a picture house.[127]

Other than Rafter himself, the most notable Irish
policeman in Birmingham was his deputy chief constable,
Superintendent Michael McManus. Beginning in 1873 when
he was twenty, his remarkable career of forty-five years

encompassed almost the whole of the seemingly interminable and perilous period when Birmingham was plagued by gang violence. Battling the sloggers and peaky blinders in the back streets, McManus took a leading role in their downfall, retiring in 1918 soon after they'd ceased to exist. A Roman Catholic from Newfield, County Mayo and formerly a labourer, he started out in the first year of Chamberlain's mayoralty. According to McManus's obituary in 1928, it was a time when 'There was a good deal more lawlessness than there is to-day – when it was unsafe for policemen to venture singly into some of the streets in the slum quarters of Birmingham.' McManus knew that all too well, remarking that the city was a big rough village when he arrived and that he carried permanent marks of its roughness on his body. Proudly, though, he wanted it known that when attacked he'd always found it best to protect himself with the weapons nature provided him, rarely drawing his staff.

McManus's fighting prowess with his fists was tested soon after his arrival. One summer evening in June 1874, he went to a disturbance in Lichfield Street, soon to be cleared for the Corporation Street Improvement Scheme. Two men were beginning to fight but on seeing McManus, they moved from one spot to another until reaching the Old Pleck. Hundreds gathered around them, 'but despite the manifest signs of hostility to any interference on the part of the police, McManus forced his way into the crowd and arrested one of the belligerents. He was quite alone at the time, and no sooner had he seized his man than he was struck on the head by a half brick thrown from the crowd.' Floored and partly unconscious, McManus managed to get up, chase and catch the missile thrower. Badly injured, the young officer was in the General Hospital for several weeks. Not long after his release, he suffered another brutal assault.

Less than a year after that second attack, in June 1875, 32-year-old married man William Langford went to a pub in Bagot Street shouting he'd fight anyone for the large sum of £5. Unlike most back-street Brummies, he was 'a big fellow, standing over 6ft in height and scaling upwards of 16 stone in weight'. Refusing to leave when the landlord wouldn't serve him, McManus was called to fetch him out.

Recognising the substantial character of the man, the constable addressed him in courteous and persuasive tones and advised him to go away. The man turned round, and, seeing that his adviser was a comparative youngster, threatened to carry him away and 'chuck' him into the canal. He followed up this threat by pouncing on McManus, and a terrific struggle ensued which lasted upwards of half an hour, during which the young and vigorous constable was bereft of the greater part of his garments. Although the man was assisted by several of his friends, the fortunes of war fluctuated between him and his captor until the pair reached Legge Street, where they both seized a lamp post.

Of the hundreds watching the fight, some strove to help Langford, but only one came to support McManus. Together, they battled to take the prisoner to Duke Street Station. Having received shocking and terrible injuries in this savage, gross and brutal assault, McManus was again hospitalised. Langford was given three months, and several others were fined 10s and costs, with fourteen days if they didn't pay.[128]

Worse was to follow. Having only just returned to duty, in September 1875, McManus was stabbed. Six months previously, PC Lines was killed, and this new attack attracted national attention for its close similarities with that terrible event and for the fear that Corkery's execution for the murder hadn't 'the remotest effect on the class it was hoped it would impress'. One local editor even despaired that if capital punishment couldn't put down the rampant reckless rowdyism in Birmingham's back streets, then the police would have to be armed in their own defence so dangerous was it for them. The stabbing itself happened when McManus was on duty in plain clothes in Lichfield Street. Seeing a notorious ruffian called Bernard McCarthy and others kicking a man on the ground, McManus rushed over, hauling McCarthy off by his collar. As he did so, Thomas Byron called out, 'Loose him; what are you taking him for?!' McManus retorted, 'Stand back; I know you, and I shall have you if you do anything.' In return, Byron bawled, 'I don't care. I shan't see my pal taken.' Helped by the victim, McManus grappled his prisoner down the street until knocked down by McCarthy's punches. Though kicked by Byron as he lay on the ground, McManus wrestled his way back up in the midst of an infuriated throng. Trying to pull McCarthy free, Ann O'Hara urged the rest to join her, with seventeen-year-old Annie Shaw shouting, 'You are a nice lot of men to see your pal taken by one – copper.'

Another woman yelled, 'Chivey the –,' but gripping McCarthy with his left hand, McManus hit out with his right fist, single-handedly holding the mob at bay. Desperate to stop him, Byron rushed in from behind, striking the constable hard and painfully with something below the right shoulder. It was a knife. Pelted with missiles, McManus was wounded on the face by a brickbat thrown by Shaw, who then smashed a brick against the head of the victim helping the belaboured officer. Someone else struck McManus in the mouth with a buckled belt, knocking one of his teeth out and cutting his lip. Though he fell, somehow he still grasped his prisoner even when hit on the head with a stone by Shaw bellowing, 'The – swine gave me fourteen days, and I will either settle him or do fourteen years for him tonight.' As others kicked McManus, Margaret McHale flung herself over him to protect him and take the kicking. It was her father who'd been beaten by McCarthy and McManus was certain that without her bravery the mob would've killed him. Thankfully, two officers arrived, saving him and McHale and dispersing the mob. Alongside McCarthy, Shaw was also taken into custody. Kicking and biting McManus all the way to the station, chillingly she cursed him, 'I am sorry I did not knock your brains out; you did not get half enough.' Once there, she launched herself at McHale.

It was only after the tumult that McManus realised he'd been stabbed. Besides that and the injury to his mouth, he'd sustained bruising and abrasions across his body and wounds in his right leg and right eye, impairing his vision for a while. In hospital for three weeks, he was allowed only milk to drink. Found guilty of assault and occasioning actual bodily harm, McCarthy was given eighteen months. A hinge filer aged twenty-six, when he was ten, he'd served three months for stealing forty-eight yards of flannel. He went on to do time for gambling, assaults on the police, and drunkenness and riotous behaviour. Shaw had been working as a general servant since she was at least eleven when she lodged with a widow. Recently released from twenty-one days for assault, she was found guilty of unlawfully and maliciously wounding and was handed fifteen months. The same term was given to O'Hara for assaulting a peace officer in the execution of his duty. Aged thirty-two and a gun barrel polisher, she was a thief. Under her own name and aliases, she'd served several years for stealing but also had a conviction for assault. As for Byron, the chiver, he'd been free only weeks after doing six months for larceny. Now found guilty of unlawfully and maliciously wounding, he was imprisoned for five years' penal servitude. Aged twenty and a hinge filer, he'd a long record of theft, assault, and drunken and riotous behaviour and though just under five feet two inches, the scars of fighting were on his forehead, neck, arms and legs. After his release, he was sent down for six months for hitting a woman with a chair and then stabbing her in the hand with a knife.[129]

Promoted to sergeant in 1879, a decade later, McManus was a superintendent. Though no longer in the front line of the fight against the sloggers and peaky blinders, still he made his mark, as recollected by the famed 'king of the showmen', Pat Collins. From the mid-1870s and with a little set of steam horses, he attended the Birmingham Onion Fair held each September on the Old Pleck. It was a dangerous place where the gangs were the lords of misrule and did much as they liked. Cliques of these tykes went round blackmailing the owners of the shows with the dodge that one of their pals had lost a child or wife. Producing a book, they'd ask for a donation to the funeral expenses. As another showman stressed, refusing to give half a crown (12½p) 'meant more than any of us could risk. If you withheld the money you were marked and might as well shut up shop and clear out, for if you stopped, your show would be 'queered' (targeted) and a row created by the roughs.'

Collins explained that the fun started in 1892 when he took control of the fair by leasing the whole of the Old Pleck:

I resolved from the very first week of my tenancy agreement to stop these ruffians, so I, with bold front, approached the No. 1. Division Police Station in that district and I recall as if it is today, I met Inspector McManus, a fine big Irishman. 'Well,' he said. 'What is your pleasure?' I then told him I had taken the Old Pleck Ground over for fifteen years, and he said, 'God help you.' I said, 'Yes, and with your help too.' I informed him I wanted the Police for protection against the Black Mask Gang and the Peaky Blinders. I said I wanted at least 10 to 15 Policemen, and believe me he nearly jumped out of his skin. He said he would have to consider the matter with the Chief, but eventually I was granted protection by way of ten Policemen. Well, then the game started. Inspector McManus walked the policemen down to the Old Pleck Ground and of course concealed them and awaited the Black Mask Ruffians. Down they came and up to me comes one big fellow with two big scars on his face and cauliflower ears, then the police came into action; the old inspector used the real old Irish kick on this ruffian and no sooner he was put down away they went for their life and he told all the others what had happened. An hour later down comes the Peaky Blinders, the police of course were waiting for them also, and they got the same dose . . . This broke the Black Mask Gang and the Peaky Blinders, and it was entirely due to my action in obtaining the Police that they were wiped out.[130]

The Old Pleck was off Newtown Row, in the 1890s a district viewed by the police as infested by ruffians of the worst type.

Bedevilled as it was by several gangs of peaky blinders, it is likely that one of them was the Black Mask Gang noted by Collins. There is no mention of such a gang in any source other than his reminiscences which appeared in various publications in the 1930s. However, during the interwar period, newspapers carried reports of several juvenile gangs of thieves calling themselves the Black Mask Gang. This was in imitation of either American gangster films or, more likely, the stories in the *Boys' Magazine* by the 'famous cowboy of the films Buck Jones, in which he dealt with "the Black Mask Gang" – the terrors of the Wild West'. Whatever the case, the name was in popular currency. Steeped with dread and gangsterism, it suited Collins's purpose to claim he alone was responsible for wiping out the peaky blinders. Of course, he wasn't. The peaky blinders remained a fearsome force for another fifteen years and it was McManus and his fellow officers who stamped them out.[131]

Chapter 2

RIOTOUS GANGS

THE LLOYD GEORGE RIOT, 1901

Throughout 'the reign of the ruffians', Joseph Chamberlain bestrode Birmingham's political stage like a colossus. Authoritarian, charismatic, dynamic and driven, he kept his grip on the council even after 1876 when he was elected as a Liberal MP for the town. Bolstered by a dedicated clique of influential followers, he quickly became a powerful parliamentary presence disparaged by his Conservative opponents as 'Radical Joe' for his republicanism and contempt for the landed elite. Yet abandoning his allegiances over the issue of Home Rule for Ireland, he joined the new Liberal Unionist Party to forge an alliance with the Conservatives. Transmuted into a 'True Blue' imperialist, he was appointed Colonial Secretary in 1895 and four years later, was the key figure in the Second Boer War. 'Joe's War', as it was condemned by other politicians, was ardently opposed by the new star of the Radical Liberals, David Lloyd George. A gifted and magnetic speaker, he also accused Chamberlain's family of profiteering from munitions contracts to their various manufacturing companies. Audaciously, the 'Welsh firebrand' agreed to speak out against the war at a meeting in Birmingham's Town Hall on 18 December 1901. It was a rash decision. Through all his twists and turns, Chamberlain held on to the fervent support of most of Birmingham's working class. Infuriated at Lloyd George's nerve, they gathered in their thousands to protest – a protest that blew up into a riot.

Stirred up by local newspapers, hundreds of Chamberlainites gained entry to the meeting with forged tickets. A medley of patriotic songs belted out with gusto was followed by a variation on a popular song, 'We'll throw Lloyd-George in the fountain, and he won't come to Brum anymore.' Those words held a real threat as behind the building was the Chamberlain Memorial Fountain erected in honour of 'Our Joe'. As the singing ended, 'hundreds of men stood on benches and sang, shouted, stamped their feet, imitated the barking of dogs, the blowing of steam whistles and cat calls, whistled, clapped their hands, and rapped sticks on the seats'. The clamour was incessant, growing even louder when Lloyd George entered the stage. His attempts to speak were drowned out and then a stone was thrown through one of the windows. At that, a reporter went to the doors guarded by some of the 400 police on duty – half of the force's complement. Looking out, he saw a crowd of many thousands and heard a man shout, 'Come and let's break the doors. We are not afraid because there happens to be a traitor there.' In a rush for the doors, some were smashed in and had to be barricaded. A few roughs then tried to storm the stage but were stopped by the police. Lloyd George was escorted away and at that 'moment of triumph for the rowdies inside the hall, those outside – where it was snowing heavily – increased the vigour of their attack'.

Stone after stone was hurled at the Town Hall windows, some by hand, others by catapult, brick-ends came crashing through and pistols were fired. Inside, 'a group of rough-looking fellows, who continuously menaced Mr. Lloyd-George and his supporters with angry outcries' was held at bay by a large body of police, staving off possible disaster to life or limb. Outside, 'The more respectable part of the crowd began to move away, but there were still some thousands left, and the more rowdy part had a better field for their efforts, and were able more effectively to concentrate their energies.' A furious section tried to storm the doors, yelling they wanted to get at that traitor Lloyd George. Heaving a thirty-to-forty-foot scaffolding pole like a battering ram, they crashed it into a massive double door pinned with heavy iron bolts, splintering it into matchwood. Fearful of the mob flooding in, the police drew batons and charged to clear the area. More charges followed outside. Over 100 policemen were injured, one of them paralysed by a brick hitting his head. Many of the crowd were hurt and one man died after he was struck by an unknown constable.

After the riot, a leading Conservative councillor sent a gloating telegram to Chamberlain: 'Lloyd George, the traitor, was not allowed to say a word. Two hundred thousand citizens and others passed a unanimous vote of confidence in the Government and admiration for your unique and fearless services for king and country.' Although condemning the violence, Chamberlain blamed it on Lloyd George for trying to exercise his right to free speech. The next day, the Liberal politician explained that he'd escaped from the chaos dressed as a constable, telling a London newspaper that he'd been warned that the police had information that gangs were organised for physical violence towards him. Supposedly, there was a deliberately planned conspiracy to kidnap him before or after the meeting, and one of its ringleaders was 'described as a man who had been in every disturbance in Birmingham during the last thirty years'. Other newspapers emphasised that the Town Hall was the scene of the most violent 'peaky-blinderism' and that the police were involved in a series of fierce scrimmages with the roughest element of the crowd, locally called peaky blinders. Sardonically, the *Morning Leader* noted that whilst these were sturdy stalwarts of Church and State, some of these patriots combined 'the enthusiastic defence of these venerable institutions with pocket-picking and dog stealing'.

Mr G. T. G. Gardiner was an eyewitness of the riot. A Welshman then living in Birmingham, he felt that whilst the howling, passionate mob of 40–50,000 people was made up of all classes of society, there was a preponderance of the peaky blinder element, whose passions and habits were of a worse order than those of brute beasts. The blasphemous and murderous expressions of their intentions towards Lloyd George when they got hold of him were 'blood-curdling, and no power on earth could have saved him from their clutches – had they caught sight of him'. It's most probable that peaky blinders, whether in gangs or individually, took part in the riot but the majority were enraged supporters of Chamberlain. Of the ten charged with offences, only Richard Westney could be regarded as a peaky blinder. A twenty-year-old painter, he'd kicked two constables and bit the hand of one of them. Handed a month, it was his second stretch for assaulting a policeman, whilst he'd also done time for gambling and theft. No evidence was ever produced that gangs had been organised to physically harm Lloyd George or kidnap him. Still, Chamberlain's loyalists had form for using gangs to disrupt the meetings of political opponents; whilst the unrestrained turbulence of what was inaptly termed the Lloyd George Riot was matched only by the Murphy Riots of 1867.[132]

THE MURPHY RIOTS, 1867

Birmingham was a riotous place. Ranging from gang brawls in the back streets to widespread uproar provoked by fierce political rivalries, rioting blemished the reputation of 'the best governed city in the world'. From the 1870s to the dawn of the twentieth century and the disappearance of the peaky blinders, riots ensnared the police and gangs in desperate conflict. Ironically, two other upheavals were instrumental in the appearance of both peacekeepers and peacebreakers: the 1839 Bull Ring Riots precipitated the formation of the local constabulary, and the 1867 Murphy Riots spurred the emergence of street gangs along with the coincidental 'crusade' against pitch and toss. The first of these was an explosion of anger arising from the exclusion of working-class men from the extension of the vote in 1832. Defiantly, they went on to organise the Chartist movement to agitate for inclusion in the political nation and seven years later, Birmingham was at its epicentre. That summer, raucous large-scale meetings were held in and about the Bull Ring, alarming the newly enfranchised middle class now in control of the town council and magistracy. But having no proper police force locally and no means to stop the gatherings, they called in a body of London's Metropolitan Police to bring order. It was a disastrous move. Arriving on the evening of 4 July, the police charged into a crowd, indiscriminately cracking heads. Outraged, the working men tore down shop shutters to make bludgeons (clubs) and picked up missiles of every kind. Split up into smaller groups, the police were stoned, kicked, stabbed and saved only by a detachment of dragoons from the nearby barracks. The next day and again on 15 July, Birmingham was wracked by more disorder set off by too forceful policing. Calm was restored only by a noticeable military presence.

Responding to these Bull Ring Riots, the Government swiftly passed legislation for the establishment of the Birmingham Police. Thereafter, the town seemingly became more peaceful until the mayhem of the 1867 Murphy Riots instigated by the inflammatory 'preachings' of William Murphy. An Irishman baptised and brought up a Catholic until his father converted the family to Protestantism, Murphy absorbed bigotry. Moving to England, he became a virulent anti-Catholic speaker, travelling the country for the Protestant Electoral Union. In February 1867, he turned up in Wolverhampton, insulting 'Papal slaves' in a 'talk' loaded with unsubstantiated sexual allegations against priests. Infuriated Irish Catholics disrupting the meeting were blamed for the commotion rather than the offensive Murphy. Intent on more troublemaking, he announced that he'd 'lecture' in Birmingham throughout June. The town was fertile ground for his sectarianism despite its reputation as a liberal place tolerant of all religious beliefs. Although anti-Catholic prejudice was rife nationally, locally it was intensified by two factors. The first was the surge in Irish migrants from the late 1820s, peaking in 1861 at 11,322, almost 4 per cent of the population; and the second was the 1850 consecration of St Chad's Church as England's first Roman Catholic Cathedral since the Reformation, heightening fears of a Catholic revival.[133]

Fearful of a repeat of the disorder in Wolverhampton, Birmingham's mayor refused Murphy permission to hire the Town Hall for his events. Angered, he instructed his supporters to put up a temporary wooden 'tabernacle' on waste ground in Carrs Lane, deliberately sited to outrage the Irish living just a few hundred yards away in Park Street, the town's main Irish Quarter. On Sunday afternoon 16 June, three thousand people attended his first 'sermon', dismissed by *The Times* as in singular bad taste. It was, with the Pope ridiculed as a rag-and-bone gatherer. As Murphy hoped, hostile Irishmen and women milled about outside, groaning and hissing, and some throwing stones. Only six policemen were on duty so as not to create more excitement than was possible. That ploy failed and they struggled to control the swelling crowd until the arrival of reinforcements armed with cutlasses. Bombarded with bricks and stones, the police charged at the angry protesters several times, hitting out with the sides of their sabres.

At the evening 'service', a strong presence of 300 officers protected the 'tabernacle' and patrolled nearby streets where numerous angry Irish demonstrators gathered. Priests went about them, exhorting them to remain peaceful. In stark contrast, Murphy grasped the chance to whip up more strife. Revealing that the home of one of his leading local supporters was vandalised in a dastardly outrage by 'the Papists', he urged Protestants and Englishmen to band together and tell

Catholic immigrants 'that if you interfere with the rights of an Englishman, then John Bull will . . .' The sentence was finished not with words but a violent stamp of his foot. To the ringing cheers of his supporters, he inveighed that every 'popish priest was a murderer, a cannibal, a liar, and a pickpocket'. Murphy's vengeful rant achieved what he wanted. He roused the rabble.

The next day, anticipating repercussions for rousting Murphy, hundreds of Irishmen massed at the top of Park Street, just across the road from the Bull Ring. Now overshadowed by the eye-catching, futuristic Selfridges luxury department store, the street was one of the most deprived in Birmingham and in the racist attitudes of the time was said to be 'infested' with the 'low Irish'. In reality, most of the Irish were hard-working and badly paid labourers vital to the building trade in a fast-expanding Birmingham and they were right to gather defensively. That afternoon, a huge, seething English horde armed with bludgeons of every kind poured towards them. Made up principally of 'pugilists, pick-pockets, garroters, and that grade in social life termed the "dangerous classes"', they hurled stones at the Irish who retaliated in kind along with brick-ends, tiles and other missiles from the windows and roofs of their houses. The fighting went on for several hours until the police 'coalesced' with the English mob, misnamed as the 'party of order'. Shamefully, the force's head officer admitted that the 'respectable' portion of the mob 'formed up in front of the police and returned the stones thrown by the Irish with such force that the police became entire masters of the street'. Their culpability in the onslaught was made plain by Lawrence Tipper. Then eleven years old, he witnessed the fracas outside Murphy's tabernacle but stayed away from watching the attack on the Irish Quarter for fear of ugly scenes. Importantly, though, he heard the story going about afterwards that 'a police superintendent on horseback was among the crowd and that he called to the mob, "Why don't you go after those fellows in Park-street?"' Although the officer later denied this, the police did take an active part in the sacking of the street.[134]

The overwhelmed Irishmen were forced away or arrested. With no protection, Irish women and children huddled in corners 'all in a silence only interrupted by some half frantic wail of lamentation or the bursts of crying from the children'. A disgusted eyewitness saw some of the police joining the rioters in breaking into Irish houses, where they 'beat women, children, old men, and old women, stole their goods, their clothes, their food, and everything they had in the world, broke everything they could not take, and drove the people into the streets almost naked'. Other than a few English properties, almost every house was wrecked, 'every window broken, the frames generally torn out, the contents of the shop thrown out amongst the mob, and the furniture taken and destroyed'. Having looted the houses and shops of hams, flour and money, the 'party of order' paraded up and down the street 'armed with fragments of window shutters, wainscoting, chairs and tables, bedsteads, and singing the 'Glory Hallelujah' and 'John Brown's Chorus''. Later that evening, St Michael's Catholic Church in Moor Street was attacked as was the home of Father Sherlock, a priest who'd tried to pacify the Irish. By now the Riot Act had been read, and to prevent further outrages, police armed with cutlasses and troops were stationed in the Irish parts of Birmingham.[135]

Of the ninety men and women first charged with offences connected to the rioting, most were described as Irish Roman Catholics. Their disproportionate arrests and the police involvement in the gutting of Park Street inflamed their hatred of the police. A few weeks after the Murphy Riots, more fuel was added to the fire with the killing of 24-year-old Michael McNally on 16 July. Arrested as one of the ringleaders of the ruction outside Murphy's meeting and out on bail, he and two other young Irishmen confronted Morris Roberts in his pub in Dale End. A former bare-fisted boxer and 'captain' of a band of fellow pugilists, Roberts was a staunch Murphyite and was seen as the chief leader of the English mob. In a furious row, witnesses said Roberts was attacked, and pulling out a revolver, he shot McNally in the chest, killing him. Roberts claimed self-defence and a coroner's inquest found he'd committed justifiable homicide. Subsequently, neither a charge of murder nor of manslaughter was proceeded with, yet the Irish companions of McNally were convicted of assault and imprisoned for short terms.[136]

Amidst continued tension, sectarian clashes broke out again in November. There was fierce fighting after a young Irishman led a charge to defend St Chad's Cathedral from an attack by an English mob, which split up with the arrival of the police. Seeking out other Catholic buildings to vandalise, one section marching around the town centre was 'evidently under recognised leaders, whose orders were not merely obeyed, but were obeyed with a precision and promptness almost worthy of a volunteer corp. The cry of "hold on", or "halt", or "come on", was instantly followed by compliance on the part of a few score men, who walked at the head of the crowd, and who acted together, while the number following were composed of roughs.' Blowing up in the same year as the 'crusade' against pitch and toss was already antagonising poorer youths, the Murphy Riots and their aftermath showed that the police could be resisted violently, further encouraging the rise of gangs. These were a new and worrying phenomenon as highlighted in 1869 by a resident in a 'rowdy district'. In a dozen such neighbourhoods, 'roughs from 16 to 20 years of age, in gangs of ten or more, may be seen for hours at the corners of certain streets, in the evening, who are ready for any mischief, and are the terror of their neighbourhood'. Responding to angry complaints about these gangs, the Chief Superintendent admitted that as presently organised and managed, the police force was not strong enough to cope with the danger. He was right. It wasn't and it could do nothing to stop gangs springing up across back-to-back Birmingham.

IRISH AND ENGLISH GANGS: THE PARK STREET, MILK STREET AND BARR STREET GANGS

The Murphy Riots whipped up a specifically Irish band. This didn't happen elsewhere in the town. Both the Navigation Street and Lionel Street neighbourhoods had large Irish populations, but neither was attacked in the Murphy Riots and their nascent gangs were mixed Irish and English. But traumatised by the destruction of Park Street, its young first- and second-generation Irishmen joined forces with their fellows in the adjoining Allison Street to form an Irish Catholic gang. Having their own pitch and toss site at the out of commission burial ground halfway along the street, they shared the general loathing of the police aroused by attempts to put down gambling and control street life. That hatred was now inflamed by the blatant police prejudice against the Irish in the Murphy Riots and the need to defend their community against English crews.[137]

Below Allison Street, the rest of Digbeth and all Deritend were overwhelmingly English. Here, the Murphy Riots stirred up anti-Irish Catholic gangs like the (Great) Barr Street Slogging Gang. It originated with 'a number of idle and disorderly persons' meeting at John Bond's pub, The Edge Toolmaker's Arms. Well organised and instructed in drill by a discharged soldier, they and Park Street Gang were quickly entangled in a cycle of attacks on each other's territory. On Saturday 26 December 1868, William Bonner was leaving Bond's pub when he was surrounded by about seventeen of the Irish gang. Though beaten with a bludgeon, he pushed his way through the melee. Running off, he was pelted with sticks and stones and then the gang smashed the windows of the pub. The only one arrested was 21-year-old Thomas Manion, sent down for two months for assault followed by the same stretch for wilful damage. A slater born in Ireland, he lived at various addresses in Park Street and Allison Street. The previous August, he'd badly beaten up an old Irishman and in the same scrimmage, struck a woman with a crutch and assaulted two policemen. For these offences, he was handed a total of six months. Nicknamed 'Smasher', Manion already had twenty convictions. He went on in the same vein. By 1884, he'd made twenty-two assaults on police officers and served a term of penal servitude for attacking a warder in Winson Green Prison. That year his arm was broken when arrested for yet another fight with a constable.

The Barr Street Gang quickly sought revenge for the

attack on their headquarters. Aware of this, the next day, Sunday 27 December, the police were prepared when a large band of youths armed with formidable-looking bludgeons showed up on the edge of Park Street. A mob of more than 100 'roughs and thieves of the worst description from the neighbourhood of Great Barr Street' were primed to attack the Irish. With more and more English arriving to join in, the police were under pressure but finally pushed the gang away. On their way back, they smashed the windows of a pub in Milk Street because of 'ill feeling towards some persons inside'. Later that afternoon, a large body of police led by their chief went to Bond's pub, where they found about sixty men drilling in preparation for a revenge attack from Park Street. The pub was then cleared of thirty of the neighbourhood's most disreputable characters. Two brothers, Thomas and William Swasbrooke, were each sent down for two months for damaging the pub in Milk Street. Aged thirty-eight and thirty-four respectively, both were older than their enemy Manion and were gamblers, although their youngest brother, Joseph, had a conviction for assaulting the police and theft.[138]

John Morris was another leader of the Irish Gang. A labourer born in Galway, his parents migrated to Birmingham when he was a toddler a few years before An Gorta Mór, the Irish Famine. Aged thirty, he was at the forefront of the attack on Murphy's afternoon meeting, shouting, 'Come on, lads; we will have the boards away; we will force it in, and we will kill Murphy.' Joining in an assault on a constable and having several previous convictions, he was sent down for six weeks. The next year, in January 1868, he was arrested for fighting in Cheapside. Across Digbeth from the Irish Quarter and leading from the Bull Ring Markets, Cheapside was crossed by Barford Street, where another gang with a pitch and toss site sprang up. It was also an English grouping and one of the others arrested for the fight in Cheapside was Peter Harris, a nineteen-year-old plasterer from Barford Street. Clearly one of the instigators of its gang, in March 1872, he was fined 40s or two months if in default for beating a man and causing a riot with a great many others. The next month, Morris was seen heading and inciting an Irish Gang battling with English opponents. Supposedly 400 roughs were throwing stones at each other, and as the ringleader of a dangerous and disorderly band, Morris was also ordered merely to pay 40s.[139]

He was patently a fearless fighting man as he was living amongst his English opponents in Barford Street. Still, the stronghold of the Irish Gang was Park Street and Allison Street and amongst its enemies was another English band from Milk Street. Just four streets away, it was looked down upon as a neighbourhood so infested with roughs of both 'sexes' that it was dangerous for a policeman to work a beat alone, the mob actually hunting and stoning him off the streets. In common with the Navigation Street and Lionel Street gangs, those of Park Street, Barr Street and Milk Street included older men as well as young teenagers like fifteen-year-old factory worker, John Thomas Kirkham. Tragically, he paid with his life for his involvement after he was stabbed by another youth in 1874. The son of a bricklayer and shopkeeper, when lying critically wounded in hospital, Kirkham deposed what happened to him:

I was walking along Cheapside about seven o'clock opposite the dial. There were about thirty lads there and some of them called me to them. I stopped and they came to me. The prisoner 'Jacky' Joyce got behind me and stabbed me in the neck by the ear, and I pulled the knife out of my neck. I cried, and some men came to me and put me in a cab. Two of the men came in the cab with me. One of them took possession of the knife and I was taken to the Queen's Hospital. The lads ran away when I was stabbed. I know the prisoner and knew his brother. There are two sets of boys in the habit of fighting each other. Joyce belonged to the Park Street set and I belong to the Milk Street set. All the others [of the Milk Street set] had gone away while I was looking through a window. There had only been a few of the Milk Street party and no fighting. Some of the boys on both sides carry knives and use them. Some carry buckles and there is stone throwing. I never use a knife but I am obliged to carry a belt with a buckle to it. I never had a quarrel with the prisoner myself. The lads in different streets are in the habit of what they call slugging [slogging] one another . . . I saw him get behind me and stick the knife in me. I saw his arm moving.

The knife pierced Kirkham's right vertebral artery causing his death by haemorrhage and exhaustion on 28 February. He was the first person killed in a gang fight in Birmingham. Unfortunately, he wouldn't be the last. A witness told the Coroner's Inquest that on hearing cries of 'Murder!' he looked round and saw the youngster staggering about in the road like a drunken man. Blood was gushing from a wound on the right side of his neck, where a large, very much worn pocketknife was sheathed to the hilt. The verdict was wilful murder.

Shocked by the evidence given, the *Birmingham Gazette* felt that 'some of the boys among our lower classes are likely to give the local police trouble for some time to come'. Despite the class-biased language, this prediction was fulfilled: the genie of gang violence was well out of the bottle.

The youngest son of Irish parents with his father a builder's labourer, Joyce was a tin plate worker. Described in the press as a boy murderer and as a child by his defence, there was some confusion as to his age. Although the policeman in charge of the case believed he was over fourteen, at his trial he was noted as thirteen based on what he'd said when imprisoned. This mattered as the judge made clear in his summing up. Under seven, a child was legally incapable of committing murder; over that age and up to fourteen, he was responsible for this crime if the jury decided the accused acted with personal malice and intention to take away life; over fourteen years, there need not be evidence of malice to constitute wilful murder. If he were over fourteen and found guilty, Joyce would have been hanged. However, given that he was not, if the jury believed he didn't act with personal malice, then they might find him guilty of manslaughter. This was the verdict, with the recommendation of mercy on the grounds of his youth. He was sentenced to a month in prison and five years in a reformatory. After his release, he stayed out of trouble. Returning to the Park Street neighbourhood, he took up his work in the tin trade and married Katie Flanagan.[140]

The killing of young Kirkham heightened the hostility between the English and Irish gangs. At the lower end of Bordesley Street there was a small Irish 'colony' in the Milk Street Gang's territory and on Sunday 21 June 1874, a quarrel ignited a 'donnybrook [fight]' between the two sides. Stones flew thickly overhead and when the supply of this ammunition ran short, 'the women tore bricks from the wall, smashed them into pieces, and gave them to the men to throw'. So frequent was rioting in and around Park Street and Milk Street that this melee attracted little notice in the press. Less than a month later, though, local newspapers were outraged when a regular combination, or gang of roughs, fomented the Bordesley Street Riot on the evening of Monday 14 July. Houses were stormed, lives and limbs were endangered, business was suspended, and the violence didn't end until 'the army of blackguards was met by a considerable force of police'. Their fury was stoked by their hatred of the police and 'coppers'. Having given evidence supporting a constable leading to the imprisonment of a gang member, a local man was 'hunted down through a labyrinth of streets, and at last run to earth in a house in which he sought refuge from the violence of the mob'. All its windows were smashed along with those of the adjoining houses. Missiles flew in all directions and the neighbourhood was completely terrorised until a large number of police restored order with great difficulty. Several rioters were arrested and as they were marched to the lock-up, an immense crowd followed, hooting and groaning at the police, and turning the streets on their route into a state of turmoil.

Seven people were brought before the court for riotous conduct. Named as a ringleader, William Moran was a twenty-five-year-old labourer born in Birmingham and living with his Irish parents in Allison Street. He was sent down for four months. Irishman Henry Manning, another labourer from Allison Street, was given a month along with sixteen-year-old brass caster James Keegan. From Park Street and the son of Irish parents, he would do more time, unlike Moran and Manning. In early 1876, Keegan had a stretch of two months for assault; later that year it was six months for assaulting a constable; in 1877 he did fourteen days for stone throwing; and in 1881 he served six months for another assault. It's apparent that Keegan was in the Park Street Gang, and it was they who'd targeted the unfortunate witness who was a 58-year-old Englishman living with his family in Bordesley Street.

Yet a feature of this riot was the involvement of many others who were not directly connected with the gang but joined in attacking the police. They included James Riley, a 64-year-old labourer from Allison Street who was handed four months as was 22-year-old George Davis. Nothing more is known of either man, or of thirty-year-old Charles Hemming. The final offender was fifteen-year-old Julia Giblin, an umbrella maker from New Canal Street, on the edge of the Park Street Gang's territory. Catherine Brampton, the wife of the hunted witness, said that eighteen panes of glass were broken at her house and that she saw Giblin carrying stones in her apron. She also identified three of the other prisoners as throwing stones and as she left court, Moran's mother, Mary, threatened to kill her. For that, Moran the elder was bound over to keep the peace. As for Giblin, she doesn't appear in any other records, although there were numerous Giblin families in Birmingham hailing mostly from Roscommon. Amongst them in the 1870s were Constable Edward Giblin and Sergeant Michael Giblin, who served with the police until the 1890s when a distant relative, Tommy Giblin, became notorious as a 'Professional Rough cum Peaky Blinder'.[141]

Responding to the ongoing disorder in Digbeth and Deritend, the Watch Committee convened a special meeting. The head of the police, Chief Superintendent Glossop, gave an assessment conflicting with the realities. According to him, many of the disturbances were caused by boys turned out to play on waste ground by the 'low Irish'. Playing quietly at first, when an opposite party appeared then the row began. The police could do nothing until these 'children' were caught throwing stones. By diminishing the slogging gangs to children's minor scuffles, Glossop blatantly ignored the involvement of older youths and men in the riots as much as he did the violence caused by English gangs like those from Barr Street and Milk Street. Inadvertently, however, he drew attention to sectarian conflict by producing a black and green paper flag decorated with emblems including a skull and crossbones and shamrock. Found on a railway bridge in Allison Street, it was connected with a party riot. Obviously, it was put there by the Park Street Gang to mark out its territory and warn off other slogging gangs. Glossop failed to recognise this even though he said that things went very well until a rival band came up, and there was very soon an outbreak. Of course, he blamed all these disturbances on the 'low Irish'.[142]

Glossop's inability to realise that Birmingham had a serious slogging gang problem was brought into sharp focus in September 1874 in another brawl between the Milk Street and Park Street/Allison Street Gang. A few months after the trial of Jacky Joyce, his older brother, Thomas, aged twenty, and another tin worker, appeared in court with Andrew Toy. Both had hospital bandages saturated in blood around their heads and were prosecuting William Smallwood for assault. An eighteen-year-old core maker from River Street in the

Milk Street neighbourhood, he was obviously in the local gang. According to Joyce, early the previous evening, he and Toy were on Deritend Bridge when Smallwood and a gang of about twenty wanted to know what they were looking at. As they tried to move on, Smallwood slashed them with his buckled belt, inflicting severe injuries. Claiming he'd never seen Smallwood before, Joyce denied he was known as the Captain of the Slogging Gang or that he was trying to throw Smallwood off the bridge into the River Rea. Toy said he'd also been belted, receiving two cuts over the eye and one on the head, adding that he was struck with a knife which he took from his assailant. For his part, Smallwood knew Joyce was the 'King' of the Allison Street Slogging Gang (the Park Street Gang) and he only used his belt when that 'lot' went to stab him. His story was corroborated by an independent witness, the son of a local factory owner, who saw Joyce and Toy wrestling with Smallwood and using filthy language towards him. It was only when both men took out knives that Smallwood swung his belt.

Soon after the fight, a constable heard Joyce saying to a pal that he'd go into Allison Street to rally his gang. If they didn't get together, he'd 'chuck them up' and have them 'sneaked' (put the police on them so they were arrested). The magistrates had no truck with Joyce and Toy. Defending himself, Smallwood gave them 'a good thrashing – a taste of their own medicine'. As a rule, there was no justification for someone taking the law into their own hands, but it was justified when a knife was drawn. The two sloggers brought the matter upon themselves, and it would probably be a lesson to them in future, teaching them that two could play at the game of assault.

It may well have been a lesson for Joyce as there is no evidence that he was involved in further brawls. He died in 1884 leaving his wife, Mary, with three children under six. She kept her family out of the dreaded workhouse by going out charring and taking in three lodgers in her two-bedroomed back-to-back in the Gun Quarter where she went to live. Her oldest son, Thomas, became a brass caster and was killed in action in November 1916 serving with the Lancashire Fusiliers. His wife, Mary Anne, had seven boys aged from a few months old to fourteen, descendants of whom still live in Birmingham. As for Andrew Toy, nothing more is known about him other than that he was baptised at St Chad's Cathedral. William Smallwood continued to live locally but there's no record of his involvement in any more fights or crime of any kind. The brief appearances of him, Toy and Joyce in slogging gangs emphasises that these bands were not organised criminal entities but shifting collections of fighting men from particular neighbourhoods, some of whom carried on brawling whilst others moved away from rowing and settled down.[143]

By the end of 1874, the Park Street Gang was notorious for its numerous struggles with other sloggers in and around the Park Street Burial Ground. No longer in use, this extensive space halfway along the street provided a plentiful supply of stones for ammunition in fights. The gang continued as a force until the late 1890s when it disappeared with the clearance of much of the street. By then it was no longer an Irish gang and nor were its rivals from Barr Street and Milk Street English gangs. From the late 1870s, the antagonisms provoked by the Murphy Riots waned and disappeared, whilst Irish migration to Birmingham tailed off. As the first-generation population declined, so too did their sons and daughters move away from labouring on the building to manufacturing work alongside the English, a trend facilitating close relationships. Writing about the Irish in Britain in 1891, John Denvir, an Irish nationalist, stressed there were few places in Britain where the Irish were more intermixed and intermarried into the general population than in Birmingham. This phenomenon meant that Park Street ceased to be seen as the Irish Quarter and its gang, like those of its rivals, became a neighbourhood band including youths and men of both English and Irish backgrounds.

Still, whichever gang a peaky blinder belonged to, those backgrounds remained important as noticed by Cecilia Costello, née Kelly. Born in 1884, she grew up in back-to-back housing in various streets around the Bull Ring, but her parents were from the west of Ireland. Her father, Edward, taught her the traditional songs he'd learned as a youngster and Cecilia was discovered by folk-music scholars late in life. In 1967, Charles Parker and Pam Bishop collected many songs and reminiscences from her. Pertinently, she recounted that in her day in the 1890s:

The young chaps'd have a pair of trousers . . . and the trousers used to flap like a woman's skirt see, them was bell bottom trousers. They used to have a cap to match, and they used to have a black silk scarf with a flower on. If they was Irish it'd be the green shamrock; if they was English it'd be the [?], all cut out, knitted like onto the scarf. And they never had them tied like they would today, they got 'em all loose and swinging out. A cap at one side, the bell bottom trousers and there you are.

Whilst ethnic allegiance remained an important marker of identity until the disappearance of the peaky blinders, ethnic antagonism disappeared. What didn't change was the capacity of the slogging gangs for rioting.[144]

THE ASTON RIOT 1884

The dominant political force in Birmingham, Joseph Chamberlain brooked no challenge to his fiefdom. As mayor and then a prominent Liberal MP from 1876, he was conspicuously silent on the pernicious effects of gang violence in the back streets but had no compunction with his lieutenants calling on those gangs when Lord Randolph Churchill dared to beard the lion in his den. The Conservative Party's rising star and a candidate for a Birmingham seat in the forthcoming general election, Churchill announced that on 13 October 1884 he'd hold a rally of his supporters at the Lower Grounds in Aston, now Villa Park and the home of Aston Villa Football Club. His bold move infuriated Chamberlain. Privately declaring that, 'The Tories will not be allowed to hold their meetings,' he predicted a blazing row. It was more than that. In what newspapers across the land castigated as disgraceful and extraordinary scenes, the meetings were broken up because of 'the disorderly conduct of certain Radical [Liberal] "chuckers-out" of the baser sort'. In a bitter Parliamentary exchange in the aftermath of the Aston Riot, those 'chuckers-out' were named as the Barr Street Gang, the Harding Street Gang, the Lench Street Gang and the Cecil Street Gang.[145]

Hiring roughs to interfere with political meetings was nothing new in Birmingham and was an especially disturbing feature of the parliamentary by-election of 1867. In that pivotal year of the 'crusade' against pitch and toss and the Murphy Riots, the use of rowdies by both the Liberals and Conservatives was another factor in the genesis of back-street gangs. On 19 July, the Conservative candidate Sampson Lloyd, of the banking family, held a packed and boisterous meeting in the Town Hall. His cheering supporters were countered by the cheers, groans and the other curious and indescribable sounds of his opponents. Merely a few weeks after the riots he'd provoked, Murphy's appearance for Lloyd signalled indescribable confusion in the volatile crowd filled with 'mischievously disposed roughs' from both sides. Four days later, a worse row broke out at the nomination event for the Liberal and Conservative candidates at the Town Hall. According to the Liberal-backing *Birmingham Journal*, it was 'created by an organised band of disreputable looking follows, who, if they were not "fighting men", have reasonable ground of action against Nature for libelling them, and who, if they were not paid by Mr. Lloyd's party, did that which men in their class have never done before, namely, work for a cause which they can have no possible interest in, for nothing'. As soon as the doors were opened, these 200–300 fighting men rushed in, denoting their allegiance to the Conservatives by wearing a piece of white material either tied around their necks or fastened in buttonholes. Decried as 'the vilest blackguards we ever had the misfortune to see' and unmistakably pugilists, they 'kept up an incessant series of yells, groans, shouts, cat-calls, and every species of noise which it is possible for human lungs to give utterance to'. Carefully drilled, they took orders from three recognised leaders themselves directed by one of the secretaries of Lloyd's committee.

The next day, a gang of these 'Tory Lambs', as they were termed, went up and down Birmingham's main central thoroughfare of New Street shouting for Lloyd. As a Quaker, he was committed to pacifism, yet his supporters were far from peaceful, striking anyone in their way with sticks, knocking down an old man and kicking him in the head, and stoning the police when they turned up. Wearing a piece of white ribbon in his buttonhole and wielding a thick stick with a large knob on the end, Thomas Cooke was the leader of these 'Tory Lambs'. A 26-year-old pearl button maker, he lived dangerously in Allison Street, filled as it was with Irish people hating the local Conservatives for championing Murphy. Charged with assault on the police, Cooke was given two months because he'd been before the court previously for stealing and drunk and riotous behaviour.

A year later, in April 1868, the tables were turned at a meeting in the Town Hall. Called in favour of ending the status of the Anglican Church in Ireland as the country's state church, it drew in 'Radical roughs' bolstered by a substantial force of Irish Catholics. Though there was also a large body of mostly Murphyite Conservatives, they were well outnumbered and were attacked as soon as the meeting began. Described as violent and vicious in the extreme, the fighting left several men with serious injuries. It was claimed that the uproar was a well-organised scheme and that afterwards, several men dressed like Irish labourers were each paid 2s beer money for kicking up the row. There was more trouble later that year in the build-up to the local elections with the Conservative-supporting *Birmingham Gazette* railing against Liberal's engaging roughs. In October, one Conservative meeting was disturbed and broken up by a mostly Irish organised gang of rowdies. Another had to be stopped after 'the ringleader, an Irishman named Mullins, flourished an instrument which appeared to be either a knife or knuckle-duster, and coolly defied any person to eject him'. He pocketed the weapon when approached by a superintendent but wasn't arrested as he and his band were 'masters of the situation'. With the police having no fancy for taking them on, the meeting ended in disorder. On a separate occasion, another Irishman was imprisoned for a month for beating a Conservative follower with a short, thick stick, whilst a gang of 'Radical roughs' fetched in from Birmingham and armed with bludgeons and knuckledusters battered two Conservative canvassers in Cheltenham.[146]

Well set as it was, violent electioneering marred the general election of 1880, by which time the franchise had been extended to include better-off working men. Both parties made a big play for their votes and in Birmingham, the Conservative candidate was the swashbuckling Major Burnaby. His big meeting at the Town Hall was ticket only and before the doors opened, a band of hired roughs took up position in the standing area facing the platform. They were supervised by a man taking instructions from a prominent Conservative. Although there was no trouble inside, outside a big crowd of Liberals hooted, groaned, hissed and jeered. Elsewhere, organised gangs of hired 'Radical roughs' systematically disturbed Conservative meetings, whilst during the voting, two gangs fought in the Summer Lane neighbourhood and 'Tory Lambs' intimidated Liberal voters at a nearby polling station. Four years later, the antagonism between Liberals and Conservatives in Birmingham exploded into a full-scale riot.[147]

On the afternoon and evening of Monday 13 October 1884, the Conservatives aimed to hold a series of simultaneous meetings at the Aston Lower Grounds drumming up support for Sir Randolph Churchill, their candidate for Birmingham in the general election. Then on the outskirts of Birmingham, this popular walled-in resort boasted the Holte Hotel, refreshment room, skating rink, great hall and sporting attractions. With thousands attending, the Conservatives made it clear they were going to take on Chamberlain and his people on their own territory. Outraged that their supremacy was under attack, the Liberals advertised an open-air counter-demonstration on vacant land outside the walls of the Lower Grounds. In a massive show of strength, their supporters gathered at three separate locations in Birmingham. Headed by bands and with banners flying, they marched to the meeting place where speakers blasted the Conservatives and resolutions were passed protesting against the 'Tory ticket picnic being considered an expression of the voice of the Midlands'.

In the hope of a morale-boosting big crowd, the Conservatives had handed out tickets indiscriminately, whilst counterfeits were printed by the Liberals. Realising that their objectives would fail if there were too many opponents in the audiences, the Conservative organisers 'engaged a number of stewards, of powerful physique and pugnacious disposition, who were instructed to eject, with or without force, as might be deemed necessary, the bearers of the forged tickets'. They did use force. When the gates opened at 3pm, those wearing Liberal badges had their tickets ripped and thrown in their faces and some were roughed up. Already highly strung, the crowd at the counter-demonstration was wound up even more with the arrival of the ejected and mistreated Liberals.

To the cry of 'Over the wall!', some of the protesters fetched a ladder and scaled it. Once inside, they grabbed planks, sticks and anything else to hand and began smashing down the wall. Thousands rushed through the gap into the grounds, setting off the fireworks the Conservatives had installed. Pouring into the skating rink, they caused so much noise and tumult that it was impossible to hold the planned meeting. Instead, there was a violent struggle with Conservatives in which chairs were brandished and blows struck.

The disturbance was even worse in the large hall where Churchill was to speak, and it seemed organised. As soon as the doors opened, there was a dreadful rush to get in and a large group formed up in front of the platform. With no police or officials to stop them, the few Conservatives and 'stewards' on the platform offered feeble and ineffective resistance. Even that maddened the surging multitude and in a determined charge, they swarmed upwards, hitting out with sticks and chairs. Screaming in terror, panicking women tried to escape as did many men. After the fighting died down, several thousand Liberal supporters possessed the hall and an hour later, when Churchill and the leader of the Conservative Party tried to speak, they were forced to give up by the cacophony of jeers and boos.

The next day, the Liberal-supporting *Birmingham Mail* blamed the 'Aston Fiasco' on the Conservatives for hiring roughs as stewards and for having the temerity to hold a big event locally. Unsurprisingly, Churchill took a different view, bringing a Parliamentary motion of censure against Chamberlain for instigating the uproar with inflammatory speeches and for tacitly approving of his subordinates' involvement in violence and mob law. They'd posted

Right: Back to back houses in William Street in about 1905 with a youth standing at the entry to a yard. To the right, notice the net curtains made by the wife/mother of the household to show her respectability and cleanliness. The teenaged women are wearing urden gowns indicating they're in industrial work and are standing outside a huckster's, a shop selling small quantities of sugar, cheese, canned food, and sweets as well as paraffin oil for lamps and tobacco.

© *Library of Birmingham MS 2724*

Left: Billy Kimber, the 'Birmingham Bulldog' and peaky blinder who rose from the ranks of violent petty thieves to lead the Birmingham Gang, Britain's first semi-organised criminal outfit, pickpocketing racegoers and blackmailing bookmakers. In the Racecourse War of 1921, he and his London allies lost control of the rackets in the south of England to the Sabini Gang. It was the first conflict in Britain between gangs from different cities. © *Juliet Banyard, Kimber's great-granddaughter*

Right: Edward Emanuel and his wife Elizabeth. Starting out as an unskilled hard man in London's Jewish East End, he became Britain's first major gangland boss. The power behind the Sabini Gang, Emanuel's machinations led to the defeat of Billy Kimber's Birmingham Gang and its London allies in the Racecourse War of 1921. Outwardly he became a legitimate businessman, but behind the scenes he remained the *éminence grise* of the Sabinis. This is the first photograph of him shown publicly.

© *Edward Becker, Kimber's great-grandson*

Left: People standing on the corner of Thomas Street before the area was cleared for the Birmingham Improvement Scheme and they were made homeless with no compensation. The photograph was taken between 1876 and 1885.

© *Library of Birmingham LS 2/1-134*

Left: Charles Bourton in 1891 when convicted of shop breaking. Aged sixteen, he's wearing the billycock of the first peaky blinders, with its brim shaped to cover one eye. A hawker from Nechells, he went on to do more time for thieving. © *West Midlands Police Museum*

Below: A yard of back-to-backs in Bagot Street in the Gun Quarter in about 1905. The woman on the right is outside the communal brew'us (wash house) with the miskin (rubbish area) beside it. Bagot Street's slogging gang was allied to the notorious Whitehouse Street Gang. © *Library of Birmingham MS 2724*

Tall and well-built Birmingham policemen at rest in 1912. They and their colleagues fought the peaky blinders and played a crucial role in putting them down.

© *BirminghamLives Archive*

Left: Jeremiah Corcoran in 1874 when he was eighteen and sentenced to twelve months for larceny. One of the Navigation Street Gang, the next year he was hanged for the murder of PC Lines.

Right: PC Charles Philip Gunter, killed by peaky blinders in 1901.

The funeral of PC William Lines in 1875, with his coffin in the middle of the mourners. He was the first Birmingham policeman killed by gangs.

Top left: David Cherry, in 1891 when sent down for three months for burglary. Wearing a daff round his neck, he has the cropped hair and donkey fringe of the later peaky blinders. © *West Midlands Police Museum*

Centre left: George 'Cloggy' Williams when discharged from house breaking in 1895. Two years later, he was convicted of the manslaughter of PC Snipe. He has the hairstyle of the original peaky blinders with a quiff across the forehead from left to right. To show it off, the billycock and later the flat cap was pulled down over the left eye, hence the peak was blinding it. © *West Midlands Police Museum*

Centre right: Henry Butterworth, one of the leaders of the Highgate Street Gang, in 1904 when sent down for assault and robbery. © *West Midlands Police Museum*

Top right: John McDermott, a ringleader of the Livery Street Gang, in 1875 when sentenced to six months for stealing a watch. Round his neck he's wearing a daff (silk-type scarf) twisted and then knotted. That fashion carried over to the peaky blinders. © *West Midlands Police Museum*

Below: An illustration of Birmingham Town Hall the day after the Lloyd George Riot. © *BirminghamLives Archive*

Left: The sons of Thomas Joyce, the captain of the Park Street Gang, John (left) and his older brother, Thomas, killed in the First World War.

© *Michael King, the great-great-great-grandson of Thomas Joyce the slogger*

Right: The English mob attacking the Irish of Park Street in 1867.

© *BirminghamLives Archive*

Left: A young woman enjoying the fair at the Aston Lower Grounds in the 1890s is wearing the flamboyant hat of 'the girl with the peaky blinder'.

© *Library of Birmingham, MS 2724*

Top left: Margaret 'Maggie' Williams, one of only three named female sloggers. She and her husband, Robert 'Bob' Scott, belonged to the Summer Hill Slogging Gang and both had numerous convictions before the two of them turned their lives around for the better. © *West Midlands Police Museum*

Centre: Agnes Cullis, girlfriend of William 'Bowey' Beard of the Digbeth/Park Street Gang, who was handed five years' penal servitude for her role in the manslaughter of the manager of the London Museum Concert Hall in 1890.
© *West Midlands Police Museum*

Top right: William 'Bowey' Beard (left) and Alfred Rutter of the Digbeth/Park Street Gang, each sent down for seven years' penal servitude for the manslaughter of Arthur Hyde, the manager of the London Museum Concert Hall in 1890. Both are wearing old clothes, undoubtedly bought second hand, with Beard wearing a billycock. © *West Midlands Police Museum*

The Black Patch Romany Gypsies in the 1890s, with Esau Smith holding the horse on the right and his wife, Henty wearing a white pinny, standing on her own on the left. They were neither peaky blinders nor gangsters. © *BirminghamLives Archive*

Above: Amid a crowd of men each wearing a billycock, Italian ice-cream maker John Lagorio stands in a Birmingham back street, like the one off Garrison Lane in which Italian barrel organ players were attacked. © *BirminghamLives Archive*

Below left: Frederick 'Satan' Timbrell of the Summer Hill Gang, killed by William 'Young Brush' Lacey in a gang fight in 1905. He's wearing the flat cap and daff of the peaky blinders and sporting their quiff. © *Evening Despatch 2 October 1905*

Below centre: George Simpson, 'the worst of the lot' of the Whitehouse Street Gang and one of several notorious brothers in 1904 when sent down for twelve months for stealing. © *West Midlands Police Museum*

Below right: Samuel Sheldon in 1907 when given five years' penal servitude for uttering false coins. Though he's nearly forty and his hair is receding, he still flaunts the quiff of the original peaky blinders. © *West Midlands Police Museum*

Right: My great-grandmother, Ada, on the right after she left her abusive peaky blinder husband, Edward Derrick. She's in uniform for a party in Studley Street celebrating peace after the signing of the Treaty of Versailles in 1919, formally ending the First World War. Sitting next to her is Mrs Waldron, who organised the street's parties and later day trips for its children. Standing on the right is Mrs Preston, whose mother, Granny Carey, lost five sons to the war. Standing on the left is my great-great grandmother, Granny Weldon.

© Carl Chinn

Below: The Birmingham Police photo sheet that some websites have used to incorrectly suggest that these four petty criminals were leaders of a non-existent Peaky Blinder organised crime gang. © West Midlands Police Museum

placards exhorting the men of Birmingham to invade the Lower Grounds and prevent the Conservatives meeting and appointed people to bring ladders for the storming party to scale. Worse than this, fumed Churchill:

> There is complete evidence to show that gangs of men known to the police were hired in Birmingham. There was the Cecil Street gang, and fifty pounds were paid to this body. There were the Harding Street gang, the Lench Street gang, under a man named Martin – I do not know whether the right hon. Gentleman [Chamberlain] knows him – the Great Barr Street gang, under the Brothers Reed, two notorious pugilists, each of whom received £20, and others . . .

Some of these sloggers were paid by councillors and members of the Liberal Committee, said Churchill. Their leaders were told that if they succeeded in breaking into the Lower Grounds, another 5s per man would be given, and if they broke into the hall and prevented the meeting, 2s 6d would be added. Stingily, though, the additional half a crown wasn't handed over in some cases. That allowed a Conservative-appointed solicitor to obtain useful and reliable information about the plans for the disruption of the meeting.

Another Conservative MP related that a colleague standing close to the wall inside the Lower Grounds 'saw a number of men come up in a body and heard some of the leaders say, "We are not in the right place; we ought to be 60 or 70 yards lower down," and they moved lower down.' Immediately, a respectably dressed man appeared on the wall and was joined by another in helping those outside to climb over.

Countering these assertions, Chamberlain announced that the Conservatives were at fault for the uproar by hiring roughs to vigorously repress Liberals. Switching the debate strongly in his favour, he produced sworn testimony from some of those roughs. One said that he'd broken up previous Liberal meetings and this time was told by a leading Conservative, 'If you see any Liberal badges on the people, tear them off their coats and destroy them.' Those who first came into the great hall were dealt with roughly and 'I must have knocked about 10 Liberals down. I used chairs, and broke two of them over the Liberals.' But when the Liberals got too numerous and strong, he 'hopped the twig' (left) along with several other roughs. Each was paid half a sovereign (10s). Another man paid to 'bear up' for the Tories engaged fourteen roughs but couldn't get any more as they wanted to know where the 'brass' (money) was coming from. On the morning of the riot, they went to a pub in the slogging stronghold of Barford Street where a Conservative shopkeeper bought them eight or ten quarts of beer before they headed to the Lower Grounds where they beat up Liberals.[148]

The motion of censure against Chamberlain was defeated by a small majority. It was fortunate for him that it was. Within weeks, three of the roughs who'd provided him with 'evidence' were charged with making unlawful statutory declarations and with libelling the leading Conservatives named as hiring them. During the proceedings, it was revealed that they and numerous others were paid for making their affidavits and that nearly all of them did so under false names. One of the trio was sent down for six weeks. He was Peter Joyce alias Larry Mack. Born in Mayo, he was a 41-year-old striker with a record of petty crime. He was clearly not in a slogging gang and nor were the other two men charged. In the court proceedings, it was revealed that shockingly all of those providing Chamberlain's testimony received their payments from a firm of solicitors engaged by the Birmingham Liberal Association. Moreover, they were brought to the law firm by men specifically employed for the task. One of them was the man Martin named in Parliament as the leader of the Lench Street Gang. Usually called McMartin, he was better known as 'the king of the roughs'.

THE KING OF THE ROUGHS & THE HARDING STREET BLACK BAND

There's no mention of a specific Lench Street Gang other than by Churchill. He called it that because Martin lived there but as it was in the small Gun Quarter, it's more likely that it was that district's gang. Martin himself was a repugnant character. Having spent five years in a reformatory and with convictions for begging and assault, in June 1874, he accosted a woman, ordering her to move on. When she told him to mind his own business, he insulted her with obscenities and hit her. Trying to get away, she ran across the road but was followed by Martin who struck her again, knocking her down and brutally kicking her. After serving six weeks for that assault, he was one of a gang of eight charged with violently assaulting and raping a married woman. At twenty-six, Martin was the oldest as the rest were teenagers. Late on a September evening, the victim was walking along a back street by St Chad's Roman Catholic Cathedral when suddenly, Martin grabbed her by the shoulder. Another man then punched her in the face and kicked her, knocking her out. Hearing a cry of murder, a watchman at a nearby works ran towards the sound and 'saw some fifteen or twenty boys gathered around a woman, who was lying on the ground across the kerbstone of the footpath'. In court, he described 'the details of the outrage, which he endeavoured to prevent, but the ruffians threatened him with violence if he interfered'. Moving away a little distance, he threw stones at the gang, but they didn't disperse until officers arrived. Found guilty of rape, one of the youths was sent down for fifteen years' penal servitude. Four others convicted of aiding and abetting were each handed seven years. Having already served time for throwing stones and assault, it was apparent that they were in the local slogging gang. Martin was lucky. Found not guilty of rape, he was discharged.

Ostensibly a file cutter, he wasn't keen on factory work, preferring to make money without too much effort. In 1882, he described himself as a betting man travelling around the country and as the right-hand man of a defeated Conservative candidate in a local election. A year later, and still living in Lench Street, he was with a group of reputed thieves from Birmingham arrested at Warwick Races for welching. Pretending they were bookmakers, they ran off before the end of a race to keep their takings and not pay out winning punters. One of the others was Thomas Matthews, revealed in *Peaky Blinders: The Aftermath* as one of the original Brummagem Boys, forerunners of the Birmingham Gang of racecourse racketeers.

It's apparent that intimidation at political meetings was another fruitful source of easy pickings for Martin. Initially supporting the Conservatives, over one period of twenty-seven weeks, he said they paid him 30s weekly. This was a very good income for an unskilled man who'd struggle to pull in more than 19s a week. It's probable that this was in the run-up to the 1880 general election contested by Major Burnaby, but such a large payment was unusual, and Martin fell out with the Conservatives because he didn't get enough for causing an upset during local elections. At the 1882 annual meeting of the Conservatives in the Gun Quarter, he took a gang to the entrance and demanded one of the organisers treat them with beer money. When this was refused, the gang went inside, and Martin shouted that he'd been given a paltry 2s 6d for six weeks' work at election time. His gang joined in yelling so loudly that the event was abandoned.

Having changed sides, Martin claimed to be 'a thorough going Rad' (Radical), but it's more likely that as the dominant political force in Birmingham, the Liberals paid him more. Though he denied it, he was regarded as the principal ringleader of the Aston Riots and in its aftermath, he was regarded as the 'manager' of the false witnesses. Noted as 'a gentleman who liked to take his politics hot', at another Conservative political meeting in the Gun Quarter, he kicked out and struck anyone he could reach, punching one man in the eye. A constable then heard Martin say he'd go into Lench Street and fetch seven or eight more people to disturb the meeting. Appearing in court charged with assault, it was clear that the Conservatives were fearful of him as their lawyer explained that whilst they didn't want him heavily punished, they did want him bound over to keep the peace for the next six months or at least until the forthcoming general election was over. As it was, he was fined 20s and costs.

His last 'appearance' as an enforcer for the Liberals was during the general election in the winter of 1885 when he turned up in Ipswich where one of the candidates was Jesse

Collings. A close friend of Chamberlain and a former mayor of Birmingham, Collings was defending the seat he'd won five years before in a tight contest and was re-elected with a small majority over his Conservative rival. However, the election was declared void because of illegal and corrupt practices by the Liberal agents. In the ensuing legal proceedings, it was disclosed that the day before polling, 'a certain McMartin, known in Birmingham as "King of the Roughs", arrived with a considerable retinue of roughs, and was received by others, to whom he distributed silver'. Wearing a brown hat, light overcoat and light suit, he displayed an enormous ring on his left hand. It turned out that Martin was employed to go to Ipswich by Francis Schnadhorst, the powerful secretary of both the highly successful Birmingham Liberal Association and the National Liberal Federation. Responsible for hiring Martin and the other gangs involved with the Aston Riot, Schnadhorst was also accused of arranging for a gang of Birmingham roughs to interrupt Conservative meetings in Brighton during a previous general election.

A fighting man clearly able to lead others, Martin was no thug to be dismissed as unintelligent. When charged with assaulting two bailiffs, he was called 'the king of the roughs' and 'the Womber Lane lawyer', after the street in the Gun Quarter where he also lived. Denying these labels, he wrote to the *Birmingham Mail* that when he supported the Conservative cause, he was known and spoken of as a gentleman and finished off by begging to say he no longer lived at Womber Lane but off Bristol Street. Martin had another letter printed in April 1886. Pronouncing that he'd never been to Ipswich in his life, he resented the injurious statements that he'd been seen performing illegal activities there. Lashing out at Birmingham's Conservatives, if he had any right to the title of the 'King of the Roughs' it arose from the work he'd often done for them locally and elsewhere, when he'd been well paid to provide the usual gang of roughs forming most of their audiences. Before signing off as William Martin, better known as McMartin, he felt he needed to 'scarcely say that I have never been asked to do similar work for the Liberal party in my life'.

A liar as well as a slogger, a year later, Martin's work for the Liberals was publicised when he sued Schnadhorst and W. B. Vince, solicitor to the National Liberal Federation, for an outstanding payment of £4 16s for his expenses when they sent him to Ipswich to act as a witness for Collings in the court case about his election. Although startling revelations were expected, there were none as the case was settled. It seems that the Liberals were not keen on what may have been revealed. Now a hawker making a precarious living traipsing the streets and selling fruit from a handcart, Martin was living in a back-to-back away from the Gun Quarter. He'd scuppered his relations with both political parties and thereafter, he disappeared.[149]

As for the Barr Street Gang named by Churchill, as discussed, it was one of the earliest in Birmingham. Throughout the 1870s, its territory was a dangerous place with the police stoned and outsiders passing through stabbed. Yet despite the supposed notoriety of the brothers Reed, its leaders at the Aston Riot, they are elusive. Nevertheless, Chapter 3 will show that the Barr Street Gang continued to be a fearsome force. There's no information on the Cecil Street Gang highlighted by Churchill. However, lying close to the Gun Quarter, it ran off Newtown Row in an area well known for sloggers and peaky blinders, and it was only a stone's throw from Harding Street, whose gang was also called out by Churchill. A long stretch going from Summer Lane to Newtown, Harding Street's roughs were well known by William McGregor, the Scot who, as a director of Aston Villa, founded the Football League and hence competitive football as it's played across the world. A draper in Summer Lane, he recalled that with 'the appearance of the Harding-street gang, ruffianism became so rampant that the bottom end of Summer-lane became a very dangerous quarter. It was no uncommon thing for the police to be stoned there, and often severely handled.' So bad were things that in 1869, law-abiding residents presented a memorial to the Watch Committee complaining of the disorderly conduct of a lot of roughs. One of the local superintendents reported that with so many of them assembling at the corner of Harding Street and Summer Lane, on Saturday nights he had to put two men on the beat and on Sundays, they were supplemented by five men in plain clothes. Because of its length, Harding Street was then split into two beats but as a former officer remembered, the most desperate ruffians infested the district.[150]

In 1868, one of them was responsible for a fatal stabbing, the first killing in Birmingham by a gang member. The unfortunate victim was Robert Davis. Known as 'Greasy Bob' because he was an oil refiner in a factory, late one night in February, he was drinking in the Swanpool Tavern on the Lichfield Road, Aston. Knocked down and rebuilt in 1898/9, it is Grade II listed and although now closed, it remains an outstanding example of late Victorian pub architecture. Leaving at midnight, Davis saw George Newey dancing about, offering to run against or fight anybody, and shouting, 'I am the leader of the Black Band in Harding Street, and I don't care a b– who knows it.'

Unimpressed, Davis said, 'You, the captain? A little fellow like you?' and pushed Newey, who did the same back. Davis pushed again and Newey fell. According to a witness, he got up and went into 'the horse road' followed by Davis. Catching hold of one another and struggling, they fell together with Newey underneath. Managing to roll Davis over, he took something glistening from his coat pocket and stabbed Davis with it several times. Somehow standing up, the wounded man cried, 'He's stabbed me.' Putting his hand on his thigh, he tottered to the door of the pub. Newey ran up the road followed by the witness who overtook him four times and on each occasion, Newey struck out with a knife. A policeman on duty nearby then cornered Newey crouching in an entry. He denied having a knife, but a dagger with blood on it found in a garden fitted a sheath he had on him. As for Davis, a sergeant saw him lying in a pool of blood on the floor of the bar. Blood was oozing from a cut on his left arm and there was an opening in his blood-saturated trousers corresponding with the wound to his body. A surgeon fetched to the pub said that Davis was unconscious, limp, pulseless and suffering from extreme loss of blood. He muttered a few unintelligible words and died within half an hour. The small puncture wound in the right thigh severed an artery causing fatal haemorrhaging and there were three other wounds all apparently done with a pointed, two-edged instrument.

A toolmaker aged seventeen, Newey was married with a child, as was nineteen-year-old Davis. At the inquest, Newey's father sat by him, whilst Davis's wife, mother, father and friends attended. After hearing the evidence, the coroner asked if anything was known of the Black Band in Harding Street. The attending superintendent replied that the street was 'a very low neighbourhood – in fact, a perfect den of thieves. They had had many stabbing cases from it, and the police were frequently assaulted there.' Because Davis was regarded as the aggressor and there was an absence of premeditation, the jury returned a verdict of manslaughter. Newey was later sentenced to five years' penal servitude, a more severe punishment than usual because whilst provoked, he carried the knife to use when the occasion arose rather than picking it up in a moment of passion.[151]

In the row before the stabbing, Newey boasted he was Claude Duvall, the French highwayman in Restoration England hanged at Tyburn in 1670. Obviously impressed by stories of the robber's derring-do, this moniker was also used by John Bolden Woodward, the real leader of the Black Band. In 1867, aged twenty-eight, he was injured in the election disturbances in New Street when the rampaging 'Tory Lambs' were attacked by a larger group of Liberal supporters. It's likely that Woodward was one of them as in October 1868, the 'celebrated Harding Street Black Band' was blamed for organising the disruption of a Conservative meeting in the Gun Quarter, paying each man involved 2s 6d. Earlier that year, Woodward came off worse in very rough, drunken horseplay with a hard man in a pub. Angered that he was bested, he went home and returned with a double-barrelled pistol. In a scrimmage in the street, the two men grappled and the gun went off twice. Taken to hospital, the injured man had a wooden plug taken from the chest. Brought before the court for unlawful wounding, Woodward was discharged because the gun may have gone off accidentally when the pair wrestled. He was fortunate as the judge told him that if the wound was three inches lower it may have been fatal and if so, he'd have been charged with wilful murder.

A month after the shooting, a 35-year-old man was arrested for assaulting his wife. Punched and dragged out of bed by the hair during a quarrel, she told the court he hadn't done any work for some time past, but went about collecting money for Claude Duval, meaning John Woodward. It's probable that his Black Band were blackmailing publicans and shopkeepers. If so, this was the first record of such an incident by back-street gangs, whilst the ages of the two men signifies that like the Navigation Street Gang, the Black Band was made up of older men as well as youths. A later conviction for Woodward demonstrates that from an early date, some sloggers were also thieves. In June 1875, 'John Woodward, alias Claude Duval, pearl-button maker, court, Harding Street', his wife, Jane, and two other men faced a serious charge of burglary after stealing five silk dresses worth £50 from a shop. Again Woodward was lucky. The case wasn't proceeded with because the items were returned, and the shopkeeper didn't turn up in court as his brother was one of the accused. Woodward's luck finally ran out in September 1876 when he was sent down for two months for violently assaulting his brother-in-law. Handed a month for stealing in early 1877, he then disappeared.[152]

Two years later, it was noted that Harding Street was 'famous some years ago as the headquarters of a gang of toughs known as the "Black Band" who gave the police a vast amount of trouble'. Yet whilst it was broken up and dispersed, a separate Harding Street Gang carried on battling the police. An old Summer Lane resident recalled that one officer in particular was 'of no little local fame and the subject of considerable affection'. James 'Jimmy' Walters was a familiar, popular and greatly respected guardian of the law, his wonderful pluck and fistic prowess was well remembered as were 'his numerous off-duty periods to heal his broken fists, and his unconventional shirt sleeve and hatless tussles round Harding Street'. One of Walters' colleagues emphasised that the most desperate ruffians infested the districts of Summer Lane, Newtown Row and Harding Street, whose slogging gang 'engaged in a sanguinary encounter with the notorious Aston gang. Many of the worst fights took place on Sunday afternoons after the closing of the public houses. Bitter antagonism between the rival sets was the cause of all the trouble.' That sanguinary encounter of the Harding Street Gang with the Aston Gang was one of many bloody combats between Birmingham's sloggers and peaky blinders.[153]

Chapter 3

MURDEROUS GANG ATTACKS

A MURDEROUS FIGHT: THE SUMMER HILL GANG

Blasted as rival hordes of desperadoes, Birmingham's peaky blinders and their slogging gangs baited the police, bullied the hard-working poor amongst whom they lived, and battled each other savagely. Born in 1871, Charles 'Pop' Inglestone grew up in the Barr Street Gang's territory and well recalled many rare fights between gangs of peaky blinders, roughs wearing caps with the peaks turned down over their eyes. Always at war with one another, it was nothing to see the members of one gang invading the territory of another, with many women among them too. Knives, cut-throat razors, clubs, stones, bottles, belts and anything that could be used as a weapon was utilised to hurt and maim. By 1901, however, the Birmingham press was reporting that happily the slogging gangs of the peaky-blinder type were long gone. It was an overly optimistic view. Less may have been heard of them but they weren't extinct, a murderous fight in 1905 indicating that the chronicle of Birmingham's gangs was not yet closed. Both the dead man and his killer 'belonged to a class of which no city could be proud, roaming the streets in gangs, constantly meeting rival gangs, and entering into conflict with them, more especially on Saturday nights. They were a body of men who were a very grave nuisance to the administrators of order in the city.' Indeed they were.[154]

The Summer Hill Gang on the edge of the Jewellery Quarter was responsible for the violence that led to the killing. A more recent slogging/peaky blinder band, it came to national attention in January 1899 when London's *Globe* newspaper was appalled when a man walking home from work was attacked by a gang armed with buckled belts. Beaten unmercifully and stabbed nearly to death, he was so terribly injured he couldn't give evidence at the first court hearing. Subsequently, two typical members of the buckled belt brigade were convicted. Edward 'Topsy' Arnold, aged nineteen, was given two months and Thomas Higgins double that for the assault and his insolent behaviour in court. Later that year, Arnold did another three months for two assaults whilst in 1902, Higgins was sent down for two months for kicking his girlfriend in the mouth and seriously injuring her. His excuse? He'd been at Wolverhampton Races all day and when he returned, Patty Simpson 'upbraided him till he could stand no more'. He was twenty-two.[155]

At that first hearing, both men were remanded for a week, at which James Lowe stood up and asked the magistrates for protection. As a witness, he was afraid not only of Arnold, who was a desperate character, but also his friends. Having already received threats, Lowe feared his life was in jeopardy owing to the tykes. He was right to ask for protection as on his way home from court he was punched and kicked by Albert Carter. Going to help her brother-in-law, Sarah Lowe was hit on the back of the head and knocked unconscious, whilst her daughter was hit by Margaret 'Maggie' Williams. A brass polisher, she was the oldest girl of seven children but none of the others seem to have broken the law. In court, both Carter and Williams were stated as belonging to a gang who didn't scruple to do anything to protect their own interests. He was given two months and Williams six weeks, but before she was sent down, she asked to be sent to Canada as she expressed a desire to reform. Told by the clerk he'd speak with the lady in charge of such cases, she said, 'Thank you; I am tired of my surroundings.' A local organisation did send children to Canada but at eighteen, it's likely that Williams was too old and anyway, she wasn't sincere.

One of only two named young women belonging to a slogging gang, she was the girlfriend of the thuggish Robert 'Bob' Scott. First sent down when he was thirteen for scrumping, he went on to do time for theft, burglary, warehouse breaking and several assaults. Described as a typical member of the peaky blinder class in January 1898, he and Williams were a perilous pair. When a constable arrested her for using obscene language, she lashed out at him and then Scott ran out of the watching crowd to smash a stone into the officer's jaw, knocking out a tooth and loosening others. He got two months for that and Williams a month. The next year, and now married, the two of them were at it again. Hearing a commotion outside, a woman went to look and seeing a row blew a police whistle. For her audacity, Williams threw her down and Scott kicked her, splintering a rib and damaging a lung. Scott wasn't arrested for a couple of days and that caused a ruckus with his gang. This time he got four months and his wife two. It seems that vengeance also played a part in their attack as the victim had barred them from the pub she ran. Then in 1902, Scott was one of five men charged in a revolting case when a courting couple walking on the canalside were attacked. The young man was beaten and robbed of his watch and his girlfriend was violently assaulted and raped. Three of the rapists were handed five years' penal servitude and a fourth, three years. Having an alibi, Scott escaped punishment.[156]

Then on Saturday night, 30 September 1905, he was an instigator in a brawl leading to murder. He and others of the Summer Hill Gang were drinking in a local pub. Now overshadowed by the Utilita Arena, a capacious venue for concerts and sporting events, it was a poor area, and members of the rival Camden Street Gang chose the wrong night to venture into the same pub. The interlopers were William 'Young Brush' Lacey, Harry Casey, George Hollins and another man. Sensing they were outnumbered, they quickly left but were chased by the Summer Hill Gang armed with knives and buckled belts. Anyone who's ever been run by rival fans at an away football match knows what it's like to be on your toes. It happened to me and my best mate in the early 1970s. Chased by a gang of home supporters, thankfully we got away, but you never forget that feeling of your heart pounding, your stomach churning, your nerves jangling and wishing your feet could move faster as you turned your head to see how far away they were – knowing that if they got you, you'd be punched, perhaps cut with a Stanley knife, knocked down, and kicked up and down the street. That must have been how Hollins of the Camden Street Gang felt when he heard Scott and the others shouting out what they'd do when they caught him and his pals. Scared as he was, he and another man fled for their lives, escaping a battering. Casey wasn't as lucky. The Summer Hill lot were led by Scott and Frederick 'Satan' Timbrell, who yelled, 'Come on. We've got something to do. Here they are; we'll lay into 'em.' The well-built Scott did lay into the slimmer Casey and floored him, but getting up, he kicked Scott, who threatened to kill him. With a surging crowd around him, Casey backed off as his attacker went for him again.

Lacey was nearby, with the Summer Hill mob shouting they were going to do him. He couldn't run fast as he'd been stabbed not long before and the wound still troubled him, but he was the one they were most after. There was bad blood between him and Timbrell, who'd had part of his ear bitten off in a fight between them a few weeks before. This was a chance for revenge and in the pub, Timbrell was heard saying he'd murder his enemy with something in his pocket and he was seen with a knife. Now, they were just a couple of yards apart and Lacey knew he was in for it. Looking at Timbrell, he bellowed, 'I will shoot you, you –, if you don't go away.' Timbrell shouted back, 'Shoot, then!' Pulling a revolver from his trouser pocket, Lacey did shoot. Falling, Timbrell cried out, 'I've got it!' Pointing the pistol at the Summer Hill Gang, Lacey backed up the steps to a shop where the bloodied Casey had just run in. Amelia Moseley ran it and after telling Lacey he'd no right to bring his bother there, he answered, 'I was afraid of having my head knocked in.' The courageous woman then went to her door with a weight in her hand, warning she'd knock down the first one trying to get in. Soon after, a policeman arrived and arrested

Lacey. Outside was an angry crowd, some of whom were yelling, 'Lynch him!' Consequently, the constable 'found it inexpedient to trust Lacey to its mercies' and instead waited for reinforcements before heading to the station.[157]

Shot in the abdomen and with his intestines perforated in seven places, Timbrell died in hospital. Aged twenty-five and a labourer, a newspaper sketch of him showed him as a peaky blinder and as his nickname of Satan suggested, he was violent. In 1895, he was given as one of two rough-looking youths unfavourably known to the police when he was handed six weeks for a brutal beating. Members of a gang causing trouble in a pub, they followed a customer outside and knocked him down. As he crawled across the road on his hands and knees, he was belted on the head by Timbrell, causing a wound so serious that the victim was hospitalised. Six years later, he threatened to 'put three inches' into a pub landlord refusing to serve him and then stabbed a customer. For that he did two months. Subsequently joining the Army as Frederick Kirk, in June 1902, he was court-martialled for striking a superior officer and served twelve months. As with many peaky blinders, Timbrell was also a petty thief with a conviction for stealing a tin of condensed milk and another for housebreaking, for which he was given nine months in October 1903. After his release, he was under police supervision for a year. He'd just finished that when part of his ear was bitten off by Lacey. In court, Timbrell's father said he'd last seen his son three weeks before his death when he'd advised him to come back home. His son replied, 'I mean to turn, Dad; I will keep away from them altogether.' Unfortunately, he did neither.[158]

Found guilty of manslaughter, Lacey was sentenced to

seven years' penal servitude. Like Timbrell, he flitted and flatted between addresses and was another violent petty thief with several convictions for theft and assault. A twenty-four-year-old general labourer, in common with too many other peaky blinders he abused his girlfriend. In September 1904, he went down for three months for aggravated assault on 27-year-old polisher Alice Lee, who'd deserted her husband for Lacey. After his release, they quarrelled and he left her but in in the misogynistic language of the time, it was reported that 'she, with that dog-like fidelity so inexplicable in the case of women who frequently are ill-treated by their male companions, besought him to make friends and live with her again'. He refused and seeing him in the street, she called out, 'There's the dirty dog,' and stabbed him through the ribs into the left lung, missing his heart by half an inch. Though portrayed as a jealous woman, Lee explained she was angry because Lacey was wearing a new coat, waistcoat and flannel shirt she'd bought him, and she wanted to rip them up. Although critically injured, Lacey recovered and was reluctant to give evidence as Lee had been very kind to him in the past. She was bound over to keep the peace, with the magistrate noting that Lacey had previously ripped up her clothes and that he'd treated her shamefully. Lee herself had fourteen previous convictions, including one for wounding when she'd stabbed a man who was fighting her husband. For that, she did eight months. As for Lacey, he remained a feckless, violent no-good. In 1914, he was sentenced to four years' penal servitude after biting a man seven times on the head and the hand for not giving him money. Fifteen years later, he and his brother attacked a man in a pub with glasses, a jug and stools, and bit him on the leg. Lacey died in 1938, one of the last of the real peaky blinders, whilst his enemy, Timbrell, was the last peaky blinder killed in fighting between slogging gangs. As for Scott and Williams, they had four children, the oldest of whom joined the recently formed RAF as a fitter a month after the end of the First World War.[159]

By the time of Timbrell's murder in 1905, most of the slogging gangs were gone, broken up by the police or the clearance of insanitary streets such as in the neighbourhoods of Lionel Street and lower Navigation Street/Green's Village. The ongoing effects of clearance were highlighted by the chief constable in 1908. Once infested by the worst type of ruffians, the Newtown Row district's character and reputation were improved because of the extension of Corporation Street. Elsewhere, an excellent result was brought about in the Floodgate Street area (including Milk Street) by the Housing Committee demolishing houses and the Licensing Committee removing some of the worst pubs. Things were also better in Gosta Green, where PC Gunter was killed just seven years before. It was an assessment supported by the informed Reverend Bass. Some of the houses where the worst people lived were pulled down, gangs of evildoers were broken up, and serious crime was diminished. There was more peace in the neighbourhood, but 'notwithstanding this, chronic and abject poverty is still with us, a high death rate, a heavy roll of sickness, sweating wages and want, common starvation, spiritual and material'.

Back-street violence was not eradicated, but whilst the throwing of bottles, brickbats and stones carried on, the use of knives was not so great. Importantly, though, the chief constable stressed that the ruffianism now prevalent was less serious than that of the slogging gangs and peaky blinders. No longer were they rampant and other than the reports on the Summer Hill Gang, the last mention of their clashes was in January 1905. Under headlines of 'Slugging Gangs' and 'The Peakies Feud', a dozen young men in court were depicted as never more typical specimens of the peaky-blinder fraternity. Belonging to the Bishopsgate Street/Communication Row Gang and Camden Street Gang, for several months they'd been meeting up in quiet streets to battle it out. However, their 'fists were not "weapons" calculated to do sufficient damage to please the sanguinary fighters, therefore hammers, buckle belts, and knives had been resorted to during the conflict'. In their final encounter, the Camden Street Gang mustered only nine against forty and were severely defeated. One was stabbed in the arm and beneath the eye with a fish knife, with his attacker calling out, 'That's done it, I think, lads. Let's blow [leave].' Appearing before the magistrates, the wounded youth was much bandaged as were others of his gang, with 'the scars upon their faces speaking to previous stirring encounters'. Two of his rivals were imprisoned. Neither had previous convictions.

Both these gangs were long established, but neither was regarded as amongst the most dangerous in Birmingham. Nor was the Summer Hill Gang. All three feuded locally in a relatively small area to the west of the city centre. There were numerous other gangs mostly operating in confined localities with Gooderson listing sixty-eight. Some were overlapping and most made only brief appearances in the local press, but their proliferation was emphasised in 1890 in the *Birmingham Mail*:

Slogging gangs are manifesting themselves in many quarters of the city; some of them are harmless enough, in so far that they confine themselves to the use of obscene language in the street, but the more notorious of the gangs are composed of youths who individually may be, the police assert, the greatest cowards, but who collectively are the most desperate of ruffians. The curious thing about these combinations of roughs is that they band themselves together without any definite intentions. Their only object is to form a mutual protection league. It is looked upon as the correct thing for each district to have its slogging gang, consisting of from 15 to 30 youths, ranging in age from 17 to 21 years. Those youths infest the street corners, if the police are on the alert they move into a low coffee house, where they decide upon their movements. A leader is appointed . . . and the grievances of each member against whomsoever they may be are heard. If the mob is of the opinion that it is a case worthy of their attention, the word is given forth that 'So and so has got to go through.' The time of attack is arranged, and even the men who are to lead off in the affray are decided upon.[160]

Of these many bands, a few were feared as really desperate. Amongst them were the Whitehouse Street Gang, notorious for its assaults on inoffensive people late at night on waste ground in Aston, and the Park Street Gang and Summer Lane roughs, both famed for their lawlessness and savagery. To their number could be added the Barr Street Gang, Milk Street Gang, Barford Street Gang, Charles Henry Street Gang, Highgate Street Gang, Rocky Lane/Nechells Gang, Ten Arches Gang and Sparkbrook Gang. Their favourite weapons included the cosh, a short, heavy stick, well loaded at the end and concealed up the sleeve; pieces of pokers; strong handkerchiefs with stones tied at the end; a piece of gutta percha (a plastic-type substance resembling rubber) or catgut with a stone attached to the end; brick-ends; buckled belts; and the big clasp knife, used by a chosen chiver to stab an enemy in the back but not fatally if possible. As well as free fights with each other, the gangs considered it fair game to wreck pubs where their rivals met, slogging all its customers whether or not they were sloggers themselves. Policemen were assaulted and beaten unmercifully, and civilians interfering with them were marked men. So too were music hall customers and workers, with one of the Digbeth/Park Street Gang killing the manager of the Canterbury Music Hall in March 1890.[161]

MUSIC HALL MURDERS: THE PARK STREET & BARFORD STREET GANGS

In his memoirs, Will Thorne recalled that in one of their 'games', the Navigation Street Gang went along to the nearby Theatre Royal when customers were lining up to go in. He was often in the crowd and just as the doors opened, he'd see members of the gang leapfrog over the waiting crowd, run to the gallery and take charge of the best centre seats to sell. Neither the police nor the theatre authorities could prevent these 'raids' until after the Riots in 1875. Yet if the antics of the Navigation Street Gang were stopped, those of the Park Street Gang at the Canterbury Music Hall weren't. Built in 1863 on the corner of Park Street and Digbeth it had various names, but colloquially it was called the Mucker, supposedly because of the mucky state of the customers in the adjoining

Royal George pub. According to theatre impresario Derek Salberg, the Mucker was the haunt of the local peaky blinders who, especially on Saturday nights, 'attended largely for the pleasure of throwing bottles around the auditorium, and pelting the audience with fruit they had snatched from the barrows in the nearby Bull Ring'. Female artistes needed a bodyguard to escort them from the theatre and fights were frequent. They were often involving men of the Park Street Gang like Stephen Murphy.[162]

A labourer aged twenty-two and the son of Irish parents, his father was a bladder dealer and greengrocer and his mother a lodging housekeeper. In 1877, after he was ejected from the Mucker's spirit vaults by a detective sergeant, he waited in Park Street with a gang. When the officer came out, Murphy lunged at him with a loaded stick, but after it was wrested from him, he was ordered to go home quietly. That was a mistake. Walking leisurely up the Bull Ring with his hands in his pockets, the officer was struck from behind by a violent blow to the back and his legs were cut clean from under him. Falling flat on his face, his nose was broken and three front teeth knocked out. Looking up, he saw Murphy making off, but half stunned, he couldn't follow him.

Eventually arrested, Murphy was sentenced to six months. He knew prison well, having previously done stretches for brutal assaults. The negative attitude locally to the police and law was highlighted upon his release when a grand concert was held at a pub for his benefit. A programme was even printed stating that a large and fashionable audience was hoped for and that the company of any lady or gentleman would be esteemed as a favour on behalf of someone who'd been in difficulties for a considerable time. Three years later, another

Park Street man and a companion were fined for hitting the manager of the Mucker and spitting on him when asked to leave for causing a drunken commotion. Then in 1886, another manager was involved in a fight with one of a gang of roughs who lounged around the Mucker. Scornfully described as pests of society and a source of considerable annoyance to honest people, their chief objective was extorting money by intimidating performers. Worse was to come.[163]

In early 1890, the specialist theatrical publication *The Era* revealed to a national readership that one of the slogging gangs, the terror of the respectable inhabitants of certain parts of Birmingham, was unexpectedly refused the privilege of free tickets to the Mucker. Under the dread of violence, these 'stiffs' were handed out in a block and the gang then blackmailed singers by yelling them into obscurity or applauding them into fame in consideration of payment given or withheld. Incensed that their enforced rights were stopped, the gang met up, vowing to cause a serious disturbance on the following Saturday. That they did. The music hall was filled to overflowing with young people maintaining the strictest order and decorum. Looking in shortly before 10pm, a superintendent saw nothing causing the slightest suspicion of a plot. Ten minutes later, the performance ended, the band played 'God Save the Queen', and the lights were lowered. That was the signal. Straight away, a policeman standing near the doorway was struck on the head with a bottle, tumblers were thrown at the attendants, and within a minute a raging row was kicking off. With the management probably expecting trouble, more police were at hand in the building than normal, and they bundled the offenders downstairs to the ground-floor vaults where the riot flared up again.

Ducking out of the way, a constable avoided serious injury when a heavy pewter tankard was thrown at him, but the ear of another was severely cut when he was hit with a tumbler. *The Era* fulminated that for this crime 'the offender received – what does the reader think? – *a fine of five shillings and costs!*'

Although the sloggers were named as the Digbeth Gang, it's likely that they were mostly the Park Street Gang and their associates, and they weren't finished. Early on the afternoon of 2 April, their leader, William 'Bowey' Beard, went to the main entrance of the Mucker looking for 'stiffs'. Of solely English background, his involvement emphasised that the Park Street Gang was no longer an Irish band. When a barman wouldn't hand out the free tickets, he was kicked and punched before escaping inside the building. A brief time later, he was again hit when ordering Beard out of the Mucker's liquor vaults where he was drinking with Alfred Rutter. That's when Arthur Hyde, the manager, came to help. Trying to calm things down, he said, 'Hold on. Be quiet, chaps.' They didn't go quiet, and instead punched him. Grappling with Beard, Hyde struggled to get him down a passageway into Digbeth but was then hit by Rutter. Together the manager and barman just about got their attackers outside but straight away were trapped by more roughs and a red-haired woman. Someone shouted at Hyde that they'd 'do for him'. Pushed against the wall, he was thumped and kicked by Beard, scratched on his face and kneed in the abdomen by the woman, and battered with his fists and a brick-end by Rutter. The woman then smashed another brick-end about the size of a man's fist on to Hyde's head and stabbed at him with a key. A witness rushing to help heard the woman yell, 'Kill him at once if you can, and if you can't we'll bring a knife down tonight and settle him.' The beating took only seconds, and the terrified barman was then attacked as a man bawled, 'We've settled one, and we'll start on t'other.' Scared for his own life, the witness fled but had hard work to get away.

With the police on their way, the gang ran off and Hyde was fetched to hospital. Though complaining of headaches and feeling sick, he later discharged himself and went home. His wife said that as he lay in bed with a severely scratched face, he uttered, 'I shall die. I'm going mad.' Late that evening, he became insensible. Never recovering consciousness, four days after the attack, he died from a large clot on the brain. Arthur Hyde was thirty-seven. A year after the killing, his widow, Annie, was renting a back-to-back in the same street as the sister of one of her husband's killers. The unfortunate widow was scratting a living as a charwoman helped by the earnings of her oldest daughter, a brass lacquerer. Her three younger children were at school.[164]

Found guilty of manslaughter in a most cowardly, brutal and cruel attack, Rutter and Beard were each sent down for seven years' penal servitude. The red-haired woman was Agnes Cullis, Beard's partner. Handed five years, she broke into a fit of hysterics and had to be carried from court. In the police photo taken of her, she looks mournful, with her eyes filled with melancholy. A nineteen-year-old hawker, she'd previously done seven days for fighting. Raised in Wolverhampton as one of seven children in a lodging house with many men from across Britain and Ireland, it might be wondered why she moved to Birmingham on her own, where at seventeen she married 'a Liverpool tramp'. Often seen begging in the vaults of the Mucker, she then picked up with Beard, another hawker. So too was his wife-beating father. One drunken night in 1881, swearing he'd break up the home, he took some furniture to sell. Coming back for more, his wife, Caroline, told him if he tried she'd rather smash them with a hammer. For her defiance, he hit her, knocked her down and kicked her unmercifully about the head and body. Appearing in court with her face shockingly disfigured, she said she'd been subjected to ill-treatment for twenty years, and asked for a separation. This was granted. The elder Beard was sent down for six months and ordered to pay his wife 4s a week. It was a pitiful sum.

Six years later, their son, William, was given two months for assaulting and robbing his 'poor old father' with the help of two or three other youths. It was a crime lambasted in the press as the limit of human baseness and brutality. Obviously, there was no awareness of the father's cruelty to his wife nor of his family's dire poverty caused by his heavy drinking. The hand-to-mouth existence of his children and their lack of proper nourishment made its mark on his son, William. His legs were bowed to an extraordinary extent through rickets, giving him his nickname of Bowey. With his parents separated and no home to go to, he went into a lodging house in Park Street. Joining the local gang, he was with some of them when they came out on top in a pub fight in December 1887. The next day, the defeated gang went mob-handed looking for revenge. Led by Edward 'Throttle 'Em' Dodd, they knifed one man before three of them stormed into Beard's lodgings. Dodd slashed him over the eye with his buckled belt, shouting, 'You are one of them, and have got to go through it.' Falling, Beard was kicked by one of the gang, whilst Dodd smashed a broom handle on his uplifted arm as he was trying to protect his head. Someone else bashed him with a bench, and after throwing a kettle of hot water over him, Dodd went to knife him but was stopped by one of his mates.

Glimpses into Beard's life were glimpses into society's shadowland. With no skills and no family support, he'd no hope. When released for killing Hyde, he went back to hawking but was fined £5 and costs for selling bad coalfish (coley). The equivalent of six or seven weeks' earnings for him, he'd have found it impossible to pay and it's likely he did a month inside in default. What happened to him then is unknown as he slipped out of sight. Another hawker lodging in Park Street, 23-year-old Rutter was as shiftless and lacking in hope. As a teenager, he sold newspapers on the streets, the resort of some of the most poverty-stricken youngsters, and was one of a group summoned for crying out the titles in attempts to sell them. This contravened a local by-law and was yet another example of the 'best governed city in the world' bearing down upon its poorest citizens. Rutter went on to do time for the minor offences of obstruction and vagrancy, but after doing his stretch for the killing of Hyde, he did another three years' penal servitude for grievous bodily harm. Afterwards and like Beard, he took up hawking fish, traipsing round the streets with a handcart, and living a single life lodging with others.[165]

The killing of Hyde unveiled the sloggers' 'reign of terror in Digbeth'. After finishing his witness statement at the inquest, Joseph Samuel Chinn, a local shopkeeper, spoke of the constant ruffianism in the area and of the concerns that offenders were dealt with leniently by the magistrates. His words alerted the *Birmingham Mail* to investigate. Its disclosures justified Chinn's assertions. Shortly before the fatal assault, members of Beard's gang went into a well-known pub in the Bull Ring and badly beat the landlord about his head after he insisted they pay for their drinks. Having appealed to the police about the actions of the gang, a grocer was targeted. Several hams hanging outside his shop were dragged down and dropped into the gutter and he was only able to rescue them by waving a large knife. Other shopkeepers had similar experiences. Chinn was a hairdresser and whilst his assistant was fixing the outside window lamps, the steps he was on were pulled from beneath him. The fall left him incapacitated for work and though the perpetrator was captured, he was sentenced only to seven days. Little wonder that there was a wholesome dread of sloggers amongst the public. A man simply blowing a policeman's whistle during a street row was attacked and had to run to Moor Street Police Station for safety, 'being pursued to the door of the lock-up by the members of the gang who had been deputed to stop his whistling'. Unless someone was singularly well versed in the art of self-defence and had a 'head impervious to hard knocks and heavy brass toe-capped boots, he stands little chance of being able to render the slightest assistance to the police, and runs the risk of becoming a candidate for admission to one of the hospitals'.[166]

Within four years of the killing of Hyde, the Mucker was the scene of another fatal assault, but this time one of the Park Street Gang was the victim. The man responsible was from the Barford Street Gang. First noted in 1868, two years later the police stopped a group of its rough boys armed with sticks, stones and other dangerous weapons on their way to an arranged slog with a rival gang. Originally drawing its members from in and around Barford Street itself, like the handful of the other most menacing gangs, by the 1890s its pull was wider. That created dangerously overlapping connections, exemplified by William Fallon, another young man with an unstable background. Aged thirteen, he took money from prostitutes for his brothel-keeping uncle. After his father objected, he and his wife were beaten up in their own home by his loathsome brother and his gang. It was too late, anyway, to save Fallon from peaky blindism. Although living in Communication Row, he didn't join the local crew, instead becoming involved with the Barford Street Gang. Yet that didn't stop him stealing some metal with one of the Park Street Gang. He was seventeen-year-old William 'Major' Bond, wittily nicknamed after Major Edwin Bond, a former head of the Birmingham Police. It was the follow-up to that theft that incited the killing.

Bond was the only one arrested and aggrieved, he demanded money from Fallon. Meeting up in the street, they quarrelled, and Bond was stabbed. Seeking revenge, he and his gang arranged to punish Fallon at the Mucker on Saturday evening 23 December 1894. Getting wind that William 'Diddy' Palmer especially wanted to give him a good hiding, Fallon left with two young women, but just as they were outside, he was rushed at by Palmer, Bond and others and knocked down by John Metcalfe. Getting up and swinging his buckled belt right and left, Fallon shouted, 'Come on; one at a time. I shall soon have you!' He wasn't on his own for long though as the Barford Street lot were there in numbers and ran to join in. Hearing one of them say, 'I have had it in for you for a long time,' a witness saw John Cherry stab Metcalfe in the right side of his neck. Cherry then launched himself at Bond, yelling, 'Take that, you –,' cutting his nose and cheek. Fatally wounded, Metcalfe staggered in the road for a few yards before falling in the gutter where he was kicked by four youths. As a concerned bystander picked him up, he moaned, 'I am dying.' As he held on to him, the witness was punched and belted before two policemen arrived and took Metcalfe into a shop. Muttering, 'I am choking,' he died. His jugular vein and the upper part of his gullet were cut. He was twenty.

The Barford Street tykes headed off. The next day, Fallon met Cherry, who said, 'That fellow that I "chivvied" last night is dead.' Fallon asked, 'How did you come to "chivy" him?' In answer, he pulled out a knife saying, 'I don't know how it could do it.' The blade had a small piece broken off the end and going into a pub, Cherry wiped it with his fingers. Soon after, he and four others were arrested. During the coroner's inquest, his behaviour was extraordinary, chewing tobacco and giggling continuously. When asked to stand up for the verdict, he stuck his hands in his pocket and laughed when told it was of wilful murder. With a confusing mess of evidence and contradictory statements as to who did what, only Cherry was finally charged. Born in Taunton, Massachusetts in America, he was the oldest brother of David and Frank Cherry, the assailants of PC Blinko, and like them was short at just under five feet one inch. Aged nineteen and a nailmaker, he had one previous conviction for assault. Before that, he'd been apprenticed to a barber who said at the trial that Cherry was a steady young fellow, whilst his former teacher stated he was always quiet and well behaved. Up to then, Cherry maintained a calm and motionless demeanour, but hearing these character references he broke down, burying his head in his hands and sobbing. Found guilty of manslaughter, the judge pronounced that 'A boy at the prisoner's time of life, in the heat of the moment, and using a knife which was an ordinary instrument for him to carry – that he might not from his knowledge of the human body and the probable result that would take place from his use of the knife, at all have anticipated the terrible results that followed.' The lenient sentence of five years' penal servitude was handed out. Disgustedly, it was reported that Cherry left the dock laughing, 'a strange contrast to the condemned man who a few minutes before had departed down the same way with faltering steps, and fear depicted in every feature'. Marrying after his release, he worked as a builder's labourer, remaining in Balsall Heath until he died in 1960.[167]

Having only one conviction for housebreaking, the deceased Metcalfe was from Bracebridge Street, Aston, a good distance from Park Street. It appears that he and the others involved were pulled into the Park Street Gang through regular attendance at the Mucker. Called a wretched fellow by the judge and named as one of the officers of the gang, Bond lived in Benacre Street, which was the territory of the Charles Henry Street Gang, whilst Palmer was from Trinity Street, on the Barr Street Gang's patch. By contrast, of the six named members of the Barford Street Gang, four were from that locality. They included George Cosier, a nineteen-year-old carter from the street itself, whose older brother, Reuben, was a leading member of the gang. In June 1889, when he was on his own, he was kicked severely and stabbed three times with a penknife by seventeen-year-old Patrick Joyce, the 'commander-in-chief of three or four dozen roughs of the worst type, who banded themselves together as a "slogging gang"'. It's apparent that this was the Park Street Gang as earlier Joyce was called 'a Park Street rough'. A notorious ruffian, he stabbed another youth in July 1891 and two months later, was himself stabbed in a row in the Gosta Green neighbourhood.[168]

Joyce wasn't involved in the fight causing Metcalfe's death and he steered clear of taking retribution against the Barford Street Gang. Instead that was taken by one of its own members against Fallon because he'd turned 'copper' by giving evidence against Cherry. Nineteen-year-old George Collett was the one who took matters in hand, and he wasn't someone to cross. Over the previous four years, he'd spent thirty-one months inside, including a stretch of twelve months for malicious wounding when he was sixteen. Leading a group of older youths, he was thrown out of a pub after striking someone with a beer jug and glass. Outside and with no provocation, he went for a man chatting with his mother, hitting him twice behind the ear and kicking him. His mates joined in and covered in blood, the victim was kicked unconscious. Collett then turned on the mother, chasing her with a knife and knocking her out with a punch. A husband and wife trying to help were beaten up and when taking refuge in a shop, men with knives tried to break in and get at them. Collett was inside again when Cherry was sent down, but within hours of getting out of Winson Green Prison, he came upon Fallon in the street. Grabbing his throat, he snarled, 'You'm the one as went against Cherry, warn't yer?' Fallon replied, 'Well, I had to.' At that, Collett caught hold of the handkerchief around his neck and struck him in the eye. Arrested in a pub soon after, Collett said to the officer, 'If you can square it for me I'll go and work for my father.'

In his defence, he said his friends told him that Fallon was going about saying that he'd serve him the same as he'd served Metcalfe, and that when they rowed, Fallon hit him first and then they had a seven-round fight lasting ten minutes. At the end of it, Fallon refused to give him the 'best man' and instead of acknowledging he'd lost, walked off to complain to the police. Under questioning, Fallon admitted that there was a fight but even so, Collett was given one month for assault. Within weeks, Fallon himself was sent down for two months for smashing up a pub and assaulting the landlord and his wife. He was still a marked man, though, for grassing on both Cherry and Collett, and in April 1895 he was in the Mucker when a bottle was thrown at him. Striking his head, it caused a serious wound. His attacker was fined 40s. As for Collett, he changed his life for the better. Marrying a woman from Barford Street, he went to work as a saddler with his father, moving back in with his parents after his wife died. Unlike Beard and so many peaky blinders, he did have family support, a skill and hope for a better life. During the First World War, he served with the Machine Gun Corps, dying on 23 November 1916 of wounds received in the Battle of the Somme. He's buried in the Martinpuich British Cemetery in the Pas-de-Calais, France.[169]

UNCHECKED VIOLENCE: THE MILK STREET & BARR STREET GANGS

The Park Street Gang's days were numbered. It soon disappeared through a drastic fall in the local population following clearance for a new railway line and station. Its enemy, the Barford Street Gang, carried on. Though last mentioned in 1900 (see Chapter 1), one of its members went on to join the Birmingham Gang. He was William Bayliss, a thug, abuser of women and, as will be seen in Chapter 4, racist. In 1897, he was one of a gang of drunken roughs standing at a street corner quarrelling and using bad language. A policeman ordering them to move on was violently assaulted as a crowd watched. The only person to help was a lady blowing the officer's whistle, for which Bayliss kicked her on the arm. He was sent down for three months. He carried on in the same vein, knocking about with some of the worst men in Birmingham, including Lacey, the killer of Timbrell. A brass polisher, or so he said, in 1909, Bayliss was handed three months for living off the earnings of prostitution. After hitting a policeman with the back of a chair in July 1914, he did another four months. A few years later, the police reported that he was only in intermittent employment and that he was 'addicted to drink and when under its influence is regarded as being very violent. He is constantly in the company of low class thieves and prostitutes.' In 1921, for his part in a murderous attack by the Birmingham Gang on Jewish bookmakers, he was imprisoned for twelve months.[170]

Doomed by the demolition of over sixty decrepit houses in the mid-1890s, the Milk Street Gang also disappeared before the Barford Street sloggers but until then, it remained a bane to the police and peaceful citizens alike. In May 1888, nineteen-year-old George Allen stabbed another young man in Digbeth. Alerted, two sergeants and a pair of constables went looking for him in Milk Street. They found him with Frank Nolan and a man called Clark heading a gang of about thirty, all of them ready and willing to resist arrest. Nolan and Allen each hit an officer with their buckled belts, and the conflict then began in real earnest. Bricks and stones were flung from all quarters, but keeping their ground, the police drew their staves and quickly made short work of their attackers. Allen and Clark were beaten down and a formidable-looking piece of iron was taken from Nolan before he could harm anybody. Allen was given two months, Clark six weeks and Nolan merely a 10s fine or fourteen days if he didn't pay.

Allen was a nasty piece of work. A hawker with a conviction for stealing seven dead hares, he'd also done ten months for stabbing someone else. He never changed. An irredeemable criminal, by 1904 he'd been sent down ten times for assault, including twice on the police, and six times for drunkenness. He'd also done time for neglecting his family. He married his wife, Catherine Burke, in 1900 and although her parents were Irish Catholics, the ceremony was in an Anglican Church. Better known as Kate, she was a flower seller and in 1913, they quarrelled after they'd been out all day hawking. She said she'd hit him with a basket and in retaliation, he struck her with a broken razor, cutting her face so badly she needed hospital treatment. Allen retorted he was cutting tobacco with the razor when she hit him, and she must have been cut when he put up his hand to ward off the blow. Like many other abused wives fearful of the consequences, in court Kate Allen played down the beating, saying they were both drunk and that she no longer wished to press charges. It was too late. Allen was sent down for one month for drunkenness and aggravated assault on his wife.[171]

Nolan was as bad. Not put off by his fine for the Milk Street Gang's attack on the police, he was at it again in February 1889 and was given a month for stoning officers with other rowdies. Two others of the Milk Street Gang were also soon imprisoned. Straying off their patch, William McCue, a filer aged nineteen and eighteen-year-old caster George Manders were seen 'maltreating' a man in a street on the edge of Small Heath. A concerned passer-by trying to pick up the victim from the floor was felled with a violent blow over the eye and kicked about the head and body with metal-tipped boots. He was taken to hospital unconscious with injuries so serious that he was treated for a month. Two witnesses, though, said the pair of sloggers hadn't carried out the assault. This was becoming a regular theme in such cases with pals turning up with alibis, but with three other independent witnesses testifying against them, McCue was given fifteen months. He'd spent much of the last three years inside for theft and assault and was unconcerned by the sentence. As he was taken down, he remarked, 'So long, Chicken.' Unlike McCue, Manders was a new member of the gang and with just one previous conviction for drunkenness, he received nine months. He avoided trouble after that, but McCue later did time for stealing a buttonhole worth just 4d, assaulting a constable in Chester and attempted housebreaking.

Though a habitual criminal, McCue moved away from the gang. So too did Nolan but he did something that riled his former mates in the Milk Street Gang – he joined their bitter enemies, the Barr Street Gang. He paid the price for his disloyalty. Both sets of sloggers were in Deritend: Milk Street ran parallel with Heath Mill Lane and Great Barr Street was its extension. The territories of both overlapped but their closeness did nothing to diminish their rivalry. Passing along a street one evening in April 1890, Nolan was attacked by some of his former pals. Defending himself with his fists, he was felled by Benjamin 'Block' Bloxwich who put one foot on Nolan's chest so he couldn't move. Bloxwich then beat him about his head with his buckled belt, swearing to knock out his brains. Kicked and belted unconscious, Nolan would have been killed without a woman gallantly lying her body across him. A constable coming to the rescue had to draw his stave and knock down the still fuming Bloxwich. Taken to hospital, Nolan had eleven scalp wounds, four of them exposing the bone, severe concussion and a terribly lacerated right hand where he'd tried to protect himself from the buckled belt. Told that it was evident that he belonged to a dangerous gang fighting in the street, the magistrates gave Bloxwich two months. They said they were determined to put a stop to that sort of thing and to the use of buckles. To those suffering the violence of the sloggers/peaky blinders, such sentences did nothing of the sort.

Two nights before Nolan was battered, one of the Milk Street Gang was so badly injured in a vicious slog with the Barr Street Gang that he was in hospital for a week. A total of five sloggers from each side were arrested and fined merely 20s. Bloxwich's brother, John, was also convicted but he was less fortunate. During the mayhem, somebody fired a pistol and as a constable approached the man, a bystander warned, 'Mind, policeman, he's got an axe!' Bravely, the officer grabbed the axe as it swung around him, but just as he went to make the arrest, Bloxwich threw half a brick at him from just three yards away. Though he ducked, the missile struck the policeman on the collar. For that assault, Bloxwich was handed three months. Aged seventeen and the son of an English father and Irish mother living in Milk Street, his real name was Blocksidge. Like so many other sloggers, he was a child when imprisoned for seven days for stealing coal. Within months, he was sent down for another fourteen days and given five years in a reformatory for intent to commit a felony. After coming out, he was quickly back inside for seven days for scrumping as he couldn't afford the 5s fine.

His subsequent crimes were mostly violent. They included the beating of a fourteen-year-old girl because she'd been given only fourteen days for pickpocketing whilst her accomplice, his sister, was sent to reformatory for five years. Finally, in 1898, he was given twelve months for unlawful and malicious wounding. After that, he stayed clear of the law, serving in the Royal Engineers during the First World War.[172]

What of Nolan? He was a friend of the notorious Sheldon brothers and in 1888, he, Samuel Sheldon and Edward Joyce were discharged for breaking into a shop. The involvement of all three emphasised the disappearance of sectarian gangs because Joyce's brother, Patrick, was one of the leaders of the Park Street Gang, whilst Nolan and Sheldon were in the Barr Street Gang. Their coming together also emphasised how some rogues intermingled between gangs when it came to thieving. Eight years later, Nolan was sent down for four months for passing bad coins with John Sheldon, Samuel's oldest brother. In between his arrests with the Sheldons, Nolan and an accomplice were charged with violently assaulting a man remonstrating with them when they were mistreating a little girl in Great Barr Street. Nolan, then twenty-six and of no fixed address, knocked down and kicked the victim, leaving him invalided and 'questionable whether he would ever be entirely himself again'. For this dreadful offence, he was fined merely 40s and costs, or one month. By 1913, he'd totted up eight assaults. That year, when recorded as a caster, he and two others were charged with making false coins. He got away with that one but was given an eighteen months' stretch for having apparatus for making bad coins.[173]

Slogging gang and peaky blinder violence seemed un-checked throughout 1890. Intimidation by the Digbeth/

Park Street Gang culminated in the killing of the Mucker's manager; the Milk Street Gang caused the Deritend Riot in January (Chapter 1), whilst for weeks afterwards they slogged it out with Barr Street Gang; and as will be seen in Chapter 4, across the city in Summer Lane, bullying peakies killed one man and maimed another simply because they'd crossed them in petty ways. Yet despite the facts staring him in the face, in mid-April, and like Glossop before him, Chief Constable Joseph Farndale announced that none of the recent violence could be traced to any organised combinations known as sloggers. In the Milk Street disturbance there was 'some trace of a quarrel between two opposite bodies; but they had no evidence of slogging gangs in the city for a very long time, and the superintendents reported that for years they had been decreasing in numbers and power.' His dismissiveness was matched by the chairman of the Watch Committee in effect blaming the Birmingham press for calling attention to one or two assaults in such a way as 'to leave in the minds of timid people some sense of alarm'. This downplaying of the gang problem contrasted starkly with the strong comments of the judge who'd recently passed heavy sentences on sloggers. Brutal assaults were becoming more prevalent and 'It was quite intolerable that gangs of young men should go about the streets and make it impossible for peaceable persons to walk about at night without being assaulted and knocked about.'[174]

PEAKY BLINDERS AND THE SHELDONS

Already notorious for its back-street gangs, Birmingham's unwanted reputation for thuggery was now reinforced nationally when, in a fortnight from 9 April 1890, almost 100 newspapers across Britain and Ireland carried reports of a letter from a Birmingham citizen on another callous attack. First published in a London newspaper, it threw some light on such outrages, the correspondent explaining that Birmingham and Aston had 'what are known as "Slogging Gangs", who delight in waylaying unsuspecting people in lonely roads and pouncing upon them unawares and brutally ill-treating them'. In a recent instance, these ruffians knocked down a man and were kicking him when a poor woman came up and begged them to desist. They replied by knocking her down. In another case, a young man named Eastwood was murderously assaulted by members of a gang known as the Small Heath 'Peaky Blinders'. According to the writer's testimony, the police appeared to come in for an exceptionally large share of these outrages. These revelations startled London's *Daily News*: 'Surely the Corporation of Birmingham, which claims to set an example of an enlightened and well-governed municipality, must be equal to the task of suppressing these scandals.' Unfortunately, the council made no efforts to suppress the slogging gangs and showed no interest in doing so. They didn't affect the city's middle-class electors living in their suburban security, only the poor who mostly didn't have the vote.

The murderous assault on the young man Eastwood was reported locally a fortnight before it was picked up nationally. His assailants were given as belonging to the peaky blinders gang with no district ascribed to them. It was the first time the term was mentioned in the press, suggesting that it was already used on the street. The connection between the name and a specific style of clothing was emphasised soon after by the first reference of bell-bottom trousers as the regulation cut of Birmingham's gangs in a report on the Highgate Street

Slogging Gang. That was quickly followed by a description of a noisy throng of youths as of 'that social status which is given by well-cut bell-bottom trousers and hard felt hats'. The hats were billycocks.

Like them, Eastwood's peaky blinder attackers were also sloggers, and it was late in the evening of Saturday 22 March that their unlucky victim went into the Rainbow pub. It's still there on the corner of Adderley Street and High Street Bordesley, the continuation of High Street Deritend and Digbeth and the main route into Birmingham city centre from the south-east. Sensitively restored to retain its late Victorian look, today the Rainbow puts on a wide programme of live music, club nights and live sports along with cocktails and 'a humane menu'. I drank there in the late 1970s and '80s when it was still a working man's pub in an industrial setting. My Great Uncle George Wood worked in the scrapyard next door underneath the first railway arch, and I'd often meet him for a few pints of mild after he knocked off work on a Friday. Our Georgie always drank in the short passageway leading from the door in Adderley Street to a small snug at the back. This passageway was what used to be the outdoor where beer to be drunk off the premises could be bought from the hatch at the end of the bar stretching along the main room. The Rainbow I knew then was how it would have looked in 1890 and it still retains that late Victorian feel.

Eastwood was a total abstainer from alcohol, but for some reason he called into the Rainbow between 10 and 11pm and bought a bottle of ginger beer. Shortly afterwards, several men of the peaky blinders gang came in. Eastwood knew them by sight as he lived nearby in Arthur Street, Small Heath. Straight away one of them said, 'What do you drink that tack for?' When Eastwood replied, 'Mind your own business,' Thomas Mucklow challenged him to a fight. Not surprisingly, knowing the evil reputation of the gang, Eastwood didn't take up the challenge. He must have been relieved when Mucklow and his two pals left. A little while later, Eastwood set off home. He had to turn left to go under two railway arches in Adderley Street before turning right to head home. He never made it. This was a lonely part of the street and he'd only got a few yards when Mucklow, the captain of the gang, roared out, 'Now, boys, give it to him hot.' Poor Eastwood did have it hot. As they pummelled him with their fists, he tried to defend himself but was overpowered by a terrible blow from a buckled belt swung by a man called Groom. Lying on the ground, he was kicked about the road and struck several times about the head with buckled belts.

Somehow, and it must have been the adrenaline pumping through fear and desperation, he regained his feet and ran off. Chased by the mob, he reached the back entrance of the local school and pulling himself over the wall, fled across the playground and scrambled over another wall into Allcock Street. Terrified, he banged on the door of the first back-to-back. Fortunately, Mr Turner let him in. Bleeding profusely from his injuries, Eastwood was exhausted, but his ordeal wasn't over. For almost an hour the gang hung around yelling, 'We'll kill him if we cop him!' Eventually they scarpered as the police approached and Eastwood was fetched to hospital suffering from severe wounds to the head and contusions all over both legs and body. On the right side of the forehead there was a wound an inch long, the frontal bone being badly fractured and splintered. The brain substance was also wounded and there was another serious scalp wound three-quarters of an inch long with the bone bared. These head injuries necessitated trepanning and Eastwood was in such a critical condition that he wasn't released for three weeks.

As there was insufficient evidence against Groom, Mucklow was the only one convicted. With no record, he was given nine months for inflicting grievous bodily harm. The judge also considered the good character given to him by the local detective superintendent, saying that Mucklow wasn't a street ruffian but a hard-working man. Unlike shiftless rogues such as Beard, Lacey, Bayliss and Nolan, or the many petty thieves who were also sloggers, Mucklow was like Collett – a man who enjoyed fighting. Their type was recalled by 'Bred and Born Brum' in 1936, who insisted that the peaky blinder was 'just an ordinary working man . . . He could always be found at work during the day in some brass foundry, doing his bit at the lathe or vice or perhaps as a polisher or in the casting shop.'

George Groom was of the same ilk. As revealed in *Peaky Blinders: The Real Story*, he was Mucklow's brother-in-law and he escaped scot-free. Mucklow lived with his wife's family in Adderley Street and both he and Groom were carters working for George Groom senior, a general haulier, whose premises and home were almost opposite the Rainbow. It's obvious that although Mucklow was hard-working, he had a vile temper as in 1902 in a bust-up over wages, he pushed old man Groom against a door and hit him twice on the head with a poker. Another relative grappled the poker away and after receiving first aid from a constable, Groom was rushed to hospital. Having a fractured skull, trepanning was necessary. Though he'd nearly been killed, Groom turned up in court and asked the judge to be lenient. He was, giving Mucklow six months for unlawful and malicious wounding. His wife stuck with him, and it seems he went back to work for his forgiving father-in-law.[175]

The attack on Eastwood was the only specific mention of the peaky blinders gang, and thereafter peaky blinders became the generic name for the hooligans of Birmingham. It overlapped with sloggers as most peaky blinders belonged to slogging gangs and whilst Mucklow's gang was given as the Small Heath peaky blinders by one letter writer, they lived in Adderley Street in Bordesley. This district blended imperceptibly into Deritend and Small Heath, much of which was countryside until it was developed with council housing during the interwar years, but its name was often extended to include Bordesley and Deritend. That overlap was highlighted in August 1894 when two leaders of a slogging gang were charged with violent assault. John Hemming was from Millward Street, Small Heath and Arthur Dolphin lived in Norwood Road in the newly developed Bordesley Green. When in Tilton Road, Bordesley with a gang of young roughs, they spotted someone they said was in another slogging gang who'd set upon Hemming previously. The rival was knocked down by a swinging stick and then kicked by both men. Hemming was sent down for two months and Dolphin for six weeks.[176]

Living in a better quality, newly built house and not a back-to-back, Dolphin was a rare example of a slogger from a more prosperous working-class district. There is no evidence that his victim was in a slogging gang, whilst neither he nor Hemming appear in any other records as sloggers. Their gang, in common with Mucklow's and numerous others, made only a fleeting appearance in the press unlike the long-established Barr Street Mohawks, as they were dramatically called by a London newspaper. Another original slogging gang, they were steeped with hatred of the police. Two constables knew that all too well. In 1888 when about to arrest a man in a street controlled by the gang, they were beset with stones and brick-ends. After heading off, the attackers were found by another officer under a canal bridge where 'they showed a desire to renew the affray, but the constables knocked one of them down and then pursued the rest and, with assistance, effected their arrest.' The local superintendent condemned the offenders as 'members of a gang of roughs who were a terror to the neighbourhood they infested. The scum of the more disreputable thoroughfares amalgamated, and marched about in such a menacing manner that people were positively afraid to appear in the streets after dusk.' Ranging in age from twenty-one to twenty-nine, four of the men were sent down for between one and four months. A fifth offender was Thomas William Clarke, who'd stoned the police in the first attack and again when his mates were arrested. Described as a member of the old firm, he was just that. An eighteen-year-old galvaniser, he'd several convictions for theft.[177]

With a bad reputation for assaulting police officers, the Great Barr Street neighbourhood was as dangerous for those living and working there, as the *Birmingham Gazette* divulged in August 1892 under the heading 'A Slogging Gang and Its "Captain"':

'Down him' is one of the unwritten commands of the leaders of the slogging gangs which exist in Birmingham. It is not necessary to do anything to offend the ruffians to have the order directed against you; all you have to do being to go about your business as a responsible citizen should. This, at all events, seems to be the lesson of a case heard yesterday. Frederick Moxon, a greengrocer of Birmingham, was driving along Great Barr Street . . . when a number of roughs 'formed into line' and 'down him' was shouted by their uncommissioned officer. The command was followed by a volley of brickends, and the ruffians commenced to interfere with the contents of Moxon's cart. Moxon got off his seat in order to remonstrate with his assailants, and the leader of the gang, Thomas Lett (30), Great Barr Street, knocked him down, and kicked him about the head and body, and his followers rifled his pockets.

Lett was fined the princely sum of 40s and costs, which he would have paid from 'donations' from local shopkeepers. Apart from this appearance, Lett was cute enough to avoid arrest, but Moxon was a marked man. His shop was actually in Great Barr Street and the next year his window was smashed by three women who then went inside to throw fish and other provisions about.[178]

The locality remained disorderly and in August 1894, two gangs fought in Adderley Street. Only nineteen-year-old Robert Jones was arrested. A worker on the brickfields now the site of St Andrew's, the Birmingham City football ground, he flourished a knife in one hand as he hit an officer with the buckled belt in the other. He was handed three months. Coming from Greenaway Street, he may have belonged either to the Barr Street Gang or another on the borders of Small Heath. Someone definitely a member of the Barr Street band was Samuel Sheldon, one of the brothers whose stories sparked the writing of the drama *Peaky Blinders*. Steven Knight, the creator of the series, has stated that 'my dad's uncle was from a family called the Sheldons, which in fiction became the Shelbys', but as the historical evidence makes clear, the real Sheldons had little in common with the fictional Shelbys. Samuel Sheldon especially was the antithesis of a glamorised gangster. Small at just five feet one and quarter inches, when arrested in 1907, he was photographed wearing a billycock and daff like the first peaky blinders. Sheldon was, indeed, one of them, and a slogger. In June 1886, he and another youth were described as a perfect nuisance in the streets when sentenced to three months for stoning a policeman. Having previous convictions for assault, he did the same stretch a year later for the same offence.

He was soon back at it, joining a gang of roughs in a fierce combat with two constables in Heath Mill Lane, close to the Old Crown pub. The oldest extant building in Birmingham and Grade II listed, now it is a focal point of the Digbeth entertainment and creative quarter, but then it was in the midst of 'sloggerdom'. Arresting some of the ringleaders, the officers were assailed more violently than ever with Sheldon following them and pelting them with stones. A day or so later he was prominent in another stoning of constables. Behaving with a violence which knew no bounds, he forced 'one of the objects of his wrath to seek shelter in a shop', which Sheldon strove to wreck, smashing the windows and doing a great deal of damage. Hunted down and arrested, it was disclosed that he'd already been convicted a dozen times for assault. Sentenced to four months, the *Birmingham Post* was pleased that such a rough was severely punished.

That punishment wasn't a deterrent. In August 1889, as one of a slogging gang that was the terror of the neighbourhood, Sheldon was given a very bad character when sent down for two months for yet another attack. The victim was severely assaulted with buckled belts, sustaining serious injuries. Within weeks of coming out of prison, Sheldon was one of a group of eight or nine committing a most disgusting assault on a sixteen-year-old girl. After they smashed the windows of her house, she must have gone upstairs to try and escape but they followed her. With no way out, she was trapped. It must have been a horrifying experience for her. At twenty-one, Sheldon was the oldest of the four despicable young men arrested. He was handed six months for aggravated assault.

Sheldon's mouth was as filthy as his actions were despicable and in January 1894, he used very bad language to a constable when drunk and disorderly. After he was arrested, he kicked the officer and another who came to help, whilst his mates tried to free him. In a desperate struggle, one of the policemen drew his staff, striking Sheldon on the head. After his wounds were dressed in hospital, he was handed fourteen days. Variously giving himself as a labourer, wire drawer, nailcaster and tube drawer, he made his money from thieving and in 1895, he was sent down for twelve months for shopbreaking, a stretch to run consecutively with six months for wounding the landlord of a pub when out on bail. The court was told that he was an associate of thieves and the maker of young thieves.

So too was his oldest brother, John Sheldon, who was just as vicious. A brawler, bully, lounger and criminal, on a November night in 1895, taking a dislike to an elderly man called Thomas O'Neill, he struck a vicious blow to his head as he left a pub. Trying to fight back, the victim was lashed on the head with a heavy buckled belt by Sheldon's accomplice. Seeing what was happening, Margaret O'Neill appealed to the pair not to beat her father. Instead, Sheldon's pal grabbed hold of her hair and pulled her to the ground where Sheldon kicked her, leaving her badly bruised. She was one of innumerable good people persecuted, threatened and assaulted by the slogging gangs and real peaky blinders.[179]

The youngest Sheldon brother, Joseph, was as bad. Named as one of a notorious slogging gang, in April 1899, he and two others were picking on some boys. A labourer tried to defend them but resenting his interference, Sheldon hit him over the head with a bludgeon. Knocked to the ground, a brick was thrown at him and he was kicked. Chased off by two policemen, the Barr Street sloggers threw bricks at them with Sheldon hitting one with a terrific blow to the head with a heavy buckled belt. Having previous convictions for assault, he was given four months. Out only a matter of weeks, he was described as a peaky type when charged with the burglary of a pub and for robbery with violence. After sitting down next to two ladies sitting on a bench, he punched one of them in the face and stole her purse. Pluckily the women followed him, but stormed with a barrage of stones thrown by his pals, they had to let him get away. Unknowing of his violent character, it was probably for the best that they didn't get to him. Sent to a higher court, he was given four and a half years' penal servitude, with the judge stating that it was apparent he intended to live a life of crime. Of no fixed abode, he was nineteen.

Samuel Sheldon's wife, Ellen, was also drawn into criminality. In 1900, she and two other women went for a neighbour who'd just given evidence against her husband. They abused the witness 'in every conceivable way, blackened her eyes, and disfigured her in other ways'. Ellen Sheldon was fined just 5s. In court, it was said that the three women came from the most lawless part of Birmingham. It remained so to the despair of its many decent residents, for though the Barr Street Slogging Gang was soon to be broken up, it was quickly followed by a vicious successor band that terrorised the neighbourhood in the Garrison Lane Vendetta. Made up of former sloggers and peaky blinders, this Sheldon Gang was headed by John Sheldon and included his brothers, Samuel and Joseph.[180]

PITCHED BATTLES: THE WHITEHOUSE STREET AND TEN ARCHES GANGS

The territories of the back-street gangs of Digbeth and Deritend were cheek by jowl south-east of the Bull Ring markets and their feuds were fought in a confined area. So, too, were those of other gangs like those in Adams Street and Coleman Street. Both were in Duddeston and were separated by only one street. Slogging it out in 1893, the bands of Cliveland Street and Weaman Street were also just a few hundred yards apart. Their battles were like those of twenty years before when the banging of tin kettles alerted the Sheep Street Gang to gather to take on an enemy in that they involved sometimes hundreds of young teenage boys throwing stones at each other from a distance. These encounters differed to the brutal brawls of gangs of smaller numbers of older youths and men inflicting serious injuries in close combat. Such was the case in a shocking stabbing affray between two gangs from Aston, one from the Lichfield Road and the other from a street running off it, Park Lane.

The antagonism between them boiled up from a fight at the Aston Theatre Royal. Opened in 1892, it later became the Astoria Cinema and then a television studio where The Beatles were greeted by screaming crowds of teenage girls in October 1963. Almost seventy years before, though, in 1895, the cries came from a young man thrown over the balcony in a brawl. In one of several subsequent hostile meetings between the gangs, Samuel Greer of the Lichfield Road Gang got a good kicking and was stabbed behind an ear. Intent upon revenge, on an August Saturday night, he went to the theatre and asked another youth to lend him a knife purportedly to peel apples. Greer was joined by six or seven others and after leaving they went hunting for revenge in Park Lane. Instead of the slogger they were after they found his friend, seventeen-year-old bottler William Latham, talking with a young woman. Albert Medlicott asked if he was 'one of the bleeding Park Lane Gang'. Though replying he wasn't, he was grabbed by Samuel Preece shouting, 'Here is one of the Park Lane sloggers!' He and Medlicott immediately lashed Latham's head with buckles. He tried to get away but within a couple of yards was caught by Preece and Medlicott who held him as he was stabbed in the left breast by Greer. As the three of them ran off, Preece boasted, 'We've done him, and we'll do the next one we catch.' Hearing that, the young woman ran towards the staggering Latham despairingly calling out, 'Oh, I'm stabbed!' As he fell unconscious to the ground, she unfastened his waistcoat, pushing her handkerchief tightly over the wound to stanch the blood pouring out.

Rushed to the General Hospital, Latham had a puncture wound on the left side of the chest between his fourth and fifth ribs resulting in an injured lung. Suffering severely from internal bleeding, his life was in great danger for several days. Hospitalised for six weeks, he was then sent to a sanatorium for another three weeks to finish his recovery. His three attackers were swiftly arrested. All were aged eighteen. One was a brass filer, another a polisher and the third a labourer. The local sergeant said though they were in a slogging gang they were hard-working, and none of them had any record of criminality. Neither of those considerations nor Greer's apology for what he'd done when he said he was drunk impressed Mr Justice Day. Referring to his judgements in Liverpool a decade before, he remarked that the prisoners belonged to gangs of ruffians infesting the suburbs of Birmingham and he'd dealt with offenders of the same sort previously, doing so with great severity. He sentenced Greer to ten years' penal servitude, and Medlicott and Preece each to two years.[181]

Neither the Lichfield Road nor the Park Lane sloggers were amongst the most feared unlike the Whitehouse Street Gang, which first came to notice after a brutal affair on the Old Pleck in 1882. Palled up with the gang from Bagot Street, on the edge of both Gosta Green and the Gun Quarter and now dominated by high-rise student accommodation, they badly battered one of the Harding Street Gang. After a fight between the bands the previous evening, Thomas 'Muff' Dan was walking home with a friend at about 10pm when John Adrian, a nineteen-year-old filer, aggressively came up to him saying, 'You were there last night.' Denying he was, Dan started to run. Hit in the back by a half brick thrown by sixteen-year-old caster, James Grindrod, he was slashed across his head by Adrian wielding a short, thick stick with a brass head loaded with lead. Knocked to the floor, he was struck with a pair of buckles by another man. Dan suffered three contused wounds on the scalp, a fracture of the skull and a compound fracture of the left thumb. Hospitalised for over three weeks, for a while his life was endangered.

After their arrest, Adrian and Grindrod were heard saying they expected to be 'fullied' (committed for trial) with one of them stating that, 'If they had "chivvied" [knifed] me I shouldn't have rounded [informed] on them.' An errand boy previously given an excellent character by his employer when fined for stealing from a boy, Grindrod was given three months for common assault and would later be convicted of assaulting a policeman. Found guilty of malicious wounding, Adrian received a harsher sentence of twelve months. A decade after his release, he joined a pal in a murderous assault on a mother and her son. Having a grudge with her husband, they broke into their house. Swinging a sword, Adrian cut the boy in the head before striking the woman. Lying on the ground petrified, as Adrian raised the sword to slash her again, she 'held her hands up, crying for mercy for the sake of her children'. Fortunately, her husband came in. A hard man, he beat up Adrian and his companion with a ginger-beer bottle. Each of them was sent down for three years.[182]

Before most of the Old Pleck was built upon and the remainder turned into a recreation ground, Superintendent Walker recalled that 'It was no unusual thing for rival gangs to arrive in battle array and headed by respective "captains" and armed with buckled belts, pokers, brick-ends, slings, life preservers and knuckledusters challenge their opponents to combat.' Invariably after the affray, a dozen or so needed treatment in hospital or at a nearby chemist. Another favourite 'battlefield' was the railway embankment on Holborn Hill where 'One gang would take charge of the summit of the bank while the other would seek to drive them from their position, and oftentimes while combat was in progress an approaching train has had to be brought to standstill in order to prevent loss of life.' Scarcely a day passed without the Whitehouse Street Slogging Gang holding a pitched battle with a Birmingham gang. So serious was the nuisance that in 1886 extra police were put on duty.[183]

That year, every Sunday the 'most disgraceful scenes' erupted in the vicinity of Aston's boundary with the town. One particular pitched battle between the Whitehouse Street Gang and the Nechells Gang was highlighted on Sunday afternoon 15 August. They clashed on Rocky Lane, a long road going uphill from Aston Cross and a 'fine' spot for a slog. With just a few houses at its beginning, for close to a half a mile it was dominated by works, open spaces, a canal and a railway line before entering the populated area of Nechells. The uproar that day raged along Rocky Lane with about 200 involved in the fighting at the outset, although Superintendent Walker reported they were gradually augmented until 2,000 boys ranging from thirteen to sixteen and men of mature age were taking part. Armed with heavy buckled belts, sticks, brick-ends, ropes and missiles of all kinds, they freely used them in all directions. So great was the disorder that the Birmingham police near the boundary had to be reinforced, while the whole of the available Aston constabulary was needed to end it. By then, several factories were badly damaged by missiles.

Despite the substantial numbers involved, only two

'rough-looking' men were arrested for disorderly conduct. Explaining that the scenes were becoming worse each succeeding Sunday, Superintendent Walker emphasised that unless an example were made of those who were captured, he was afraid the police would have great difficulty in coping. Agreeing that it was impossible for such a state of things to be allowed to continue, the magistrates decided to make an example of the pair, who had previous convictions. Each was ordered to find one security in £5 and be bound over in their own recognisances of £10 to keep the peace for twelve months, or in default two months. That was a big sum and as one of the convicted was a boatman it would have been nigh on impossible for him to raise it. Neither he nor his accomplice were from Aston. They lived in the Gosta Green neighbourhood and it seems they joined the Whitehouse Street Gang to get their own back. A few days before the Rocky Lane affray, forty to fifty of the Nechells Gang landed on Gosta Green, throwing stones and behaving so riotously that residents and shopkeepers had to put up their shutters to protect their windows. A solitary youth wielding a heavy buckled belt was arrested. As it was his first offence, he was let off with a fine of 2s 6d. He lived in Charles Arthur Street, the focal point for the Nechells Gang to the dismay of its residents. They dared not remonstrate with them for fighting and using the most obscene language because 'if we did, we should have our windows smashed'.[184]

Hostilities between the Nechells and Aston sloggers broke out again on a Monday afternoon in early December in Wainwright Street, on the edge of the Whitehouse Gang's territory. Once again, they were joined by allies from Gosta Green. Altogether 'about 150 men and lads from the Nechells district, including a respectable or disrespectable contingent from Aston' caused a great disturbance. Only one youth was arrested. He was fined 10s and costs, but unable to pay that sum, was sent down for seven days. The following summer of 1887 on yet another Sunday, the Whitehouse Street sloggers fought another enemy on the corner of Phillips Street. Like Rocky Lane, it was a well-chosen spot for a slog. Located right by the boundary of the Aston police with their fellows in Birmingham, it was often overlooked by both. The Whitehouse Street Gang came out on top and were seen thrashing a lone opponent in an entry.

After they moved off, a concerned passer-by went to see if the man was injured. It was a mistake. He was set upon by another section of the gang, lashed about the head and body with buckles and finally hit with a brick, fracturing his skull. The victim was in hospital for more than three weeks. Several men were arrested. Polisher William Newman and glassblower Walter Perrins lived close to Whitehouse Street, whilst painter Joseph Newman was from Bagot Street, indicating the ongoing alliance with its gang. Two other men came from Whitehouse Street itself. They were edge toolmaker Alfred Whitehouse and filer Benjamin Adcock. Both were discharged along with Joseph Newman. Perrins owned up to throwing the brick at the victim, saying, 'I mistook him for others. I was drunk at the time, and was knocked down myself.' He went down for eight months. Having admitted he'd struck the victim with the buckle, William Newman was sentenced to five months. The magistrates cautioned him they could have sent him to a higher court for a more severe punishment but didn't because of his youth. Although he was a very bad fellow, they'd decided instead to give him one more chance, not that they thought it would do him much good. It didn't and he went on to do two months for assaulting a constable. Thereafter he was another slogger who disappeared.[185]

The Nechells band didn't and in August 1888, nineteen-year-old filer William Emery led them in throwing stones at their Aston enemies. The self-proclaimed 'King of the Slogging Gang', 'it was only natural that his subjects should have entered into this sort of warlike festivities with unbounded energy while in his presence'. Continuing in the same sarcastic vein, a local newspaper reported that the internecine strife which had been waging amongst the roughs ceased instantly when two policemen appeared. Assuming command, Emery 'made it known that a terrible fate was in store for their opponents if the gang only possessed as much pluck as their leader'. Despite the stones falling thickly, the officers singled out Emery and chased him into the Lichfield Road, where a tram conductor took up the running and captured the fugitive 'king'. Meanwhile, the rest of the gang had scarpered pell-mell, bar for one 'faithful adherent' who hit one of the constables with a brick. He was given one month with Emery, an old offender who'd previously assaulted a constable, receiving three months.

The 'accolade' of king of the scuttlers was common in Manchester and Salford, but only one other person in Birmingham claimed such a 'royal' title. He was Emery's 'successor', Charles 'Chass' Frith, another filer aged nineteen. Later in 1888, he was called the king of the Charles Arthur Street Gang, as the Nechells Gang was also known. On a Sunday night in early December, he and four of his men were standing on a street corner when an inoffensive chap walked towards them. He heard one of them say, 'Here he is,' but didn't dream they meant him. Unfortunately, they did. As he reached them, Frith pulled out something which glistened like silver and struck him a blow in the face. Bleeding profusely, the victim was knocked down and kicked. The brave 'king' and his followers ran off, with him saying, 'We've done them properly to-night. We've put his light out.' Another one added, 'Wasn't he a coward when he was knocked down.' Taken to the General Hospital, the man mistaken for an enemy slogger had extensive and serious wounds to the right side of his face. The nose and lip were severed with the injury extending upwards towards the eye. A fortnight later, Frith was found by the police in a house at a festive gathering. As the merrymaking stopped, he bolted out of the back door, scaled a wall and dropped into the arms of two constables who'd been posted there for that reason. Charged with unlawful wounding, Frith was brought before a higher court at the start of January. His victim appeared with his head bandaged and upper lip strapped. Found guilty, Frith was sentenced to five years' penal servitude. His brother, John William, was another well-known member of the gang and was as obnoxious. Decried as a slogging husband, he was fetched before the courts for assaulting his wife. Not having worked for several months, one evening he pulled the bedclothes off his wife, Mary Ellen, hit her, bit her several times and then attempted to strangle her. He'd assaulted her before, and she told the court she was in danger of her life. Apparently, the life of an abused wife wasn't valued as her vile husband was fined only 20s or one month.[186]

The Nechells/Charles Arthur Street Gang wasn't mentioned after 1892 and it seems its members merged with the

Ten Arches Gang. First coming to notice as sloggers seven years before when the police chased youths throwing stones, six members of a Nechells slogging gang were later arrested for a similar offence in Thimblemill Lane. This was significant as the Ten Arches Gang, a 'detestable body of roughs', took its name from their meeting place under the arches of the viaduct carrying the railway over the Birmingham to Fazeley Canal at the lower part of Thimblemill Lane. Though just off the busy Lichfield Road, itself the extension of the Aston Road North, it was a lonely spot. Bounded by canal basins, a large engine shed and wasteland, few people lived nearby as no houses fronted lower Thimblemill Lane itself whilst it was a hundred yards to those in the adjoining Holborn Hill. Though in Aston, the arches were on the edge of Nechells and Astonians from nearby streets also joined the Ten Arches Gang. Said to be as well organised as a military battalion, it had a bitter enmity with the Whitehouse Street Gang whose 'manor' ended half a mile away. Retiring in 1904, Detective Sergeant Joseph Whitcroft recalled hectic days when ruffianism was rife at Aston and battles between rival slogging gangs often took place in the streets. In particular, when the Ten Arches Gang met the Whitehouse Street Gang, 'there was trouble, for they were armed with buckled belts, life preservers, iron tubes into the end of which molten lead had been run, and deadly weapons'.[187]

Still, after the initial incursions by Nechells sloggers into the borderland with Aston, it seems that the Ten Arches Gang stayed close to their own patch. The Whitehouse Street Gang didn't. Like other slogging bands, it was remorseless in its violence but unlike them, it was fearless in confronting others in their 'domain', no matter how far away and no matter how powerful. That was made plain on a Saturday night in February 1889 when they marched one and a half miles to the Park Street Gang's headquarters at the Mucker to settle old scores. Leaving the music hall, they chased some youths down Digbeth. Swinging their belts, they caught one by Allison Street and set about him. Two constables ran to stop them and seeing them, William Greening shouted, 'Whitehouse Street for them! Let them have it!' Fiercely resisting arrest, he was pulled into a baker's shop by one of the officers but from inside he called out, 'Now, lads, lay on; don't give over. We can lick these –.' Greening himself did lay on, hitting the policeman several times on the head. He was also kicked by Frederick Robinson whom the other officer was struggling to arrest. The rest of the gang started throwing stones at the shop, urged on by John Coley roaring, 'Now, Aston boys, we can give it these –.' Wielding their belts they turned on more police coming to help. They were led by Inspector McManus at whom Peter Ridding hurled a brick. Finally, some of the gang were overpowered. For deliberately using dangerous weapons, Coley and Frederick Gibbs were each sentenced to two months; Peter Ridding was given six weeks as he'd thrown missiles at the police before; and because they hadn't appeared previously, Greening and Robinson were each fined 20s and costs, or in default one month. Aged between seventeen and twenty, they were all factory workers. Other than Greening, none would commit further offences. They typified hard young men living harsh lives in communities where physical strength and fighting ability were valued by many. Joining a gang gave them both camaraderie and status, but unlike hardcore sloggers and peaky blinders, many of them moved away from the gangs and didn't become involved in criminality. Greening was the exception to them and in 1894, he was sent down for ten months for wounding with intent having hit a constable on the head with a hammer, fracturing his skull.

After their foray into the Park Street Gang's patch, in May 1889, the Whitehouse Street Gang next up strode over two miles to take on the Charles Henry Street Slogging Gang on its own manor. Pelting one another with stones and other missiles and swinging their buckled belts freely, somehow nobody was badly injured. But the next night, eighteen-year-old George Langford was taken to hospital, where the compound compressed fracture to his skull was so severe that he had to be trepanned. Although living in Charles Henry Street, he was from Aston and had backed up the Whitehouse Street Gang in the slog. He was an easy target for vengeance and Alfred Vincent, also aged eighteen and a polisher, was charged with violently assaulting him. Admitting that he struck Langford with a loaded stick, he insisted the injury was caused by others with their buckled belts. Said to be one of a gang of ruffians who assembled locally to make war against the rowdies of adjoining thoroughfares, Vincent was criminalised at thirteen when he was sent down for fourteen days for stealing 2s. This was followed by five years in a reformatory from which he'd just come out. Charged with grievous bodily harm, he was handed fifteen months. As he was taken down from the dock, he turned to the constable in charge of the case, swearing, 'I'll kill you, you – swine; see if I don't. I'll knock your bleeding head off when I come out.'[188]

Though ringleaders like the Simpsons, Casey and Newman were now often out of the picture because of imprisonment, it was obvious that the Whitehouse Street Gang was able to pull in new, younger and just as violent members. Amongst them was Charles 'Major' Bond who would help PC Leach when he was assaulted (Chapter 1). In 1892, Bond was an eighteen-year-old boatman when he and four others were arrested for a violent assault. One of them was Frank Medlicott, whose younger brother would be convicted for attacking Leach. A netting maker, also eighteen, Medlicott lived in Duddeston, just across the Birmingham and Fazeley Canal from Aston. The other three were all sixteen. Daniel Glynn, a wireworker, was from the Gun Quarter whilst both umbrella furniture maker George Cleaver and tube drawer John Taroni lived in the Newtown Row locality.

Descended from an Italian from Lombardy, today the family of Taroni's older brother are well respected owners of a recycling centre and scrap metal merchants in Aston. But then and like too many other young men, John Taroni was drawn into slogging and he and his pals were arrested after seeking vengeance with a rowdy crew from Summer Lane. According to Glynn, 'They stabbed one of theirs seven times in the neck, and threw him in the 'cut' (canal) a night or two afore and they were getting their own back.' They did just that when they met one of the Summer Laners on the Old Pleck in June 1892. Chatting with a girl, fifteen-year-old Albert Willock didn't stand a chance when he was stunned from behind. Taroni struck him several times on the back of the head with a double buckled belt wrapped around his wrist. Bond then ran at him with a brick, hitting him with that and a loaded stick. Falling to the ground, Willock was kicked by Glynn and Cleaver, who jumped on his chest.

To the astonishment of the press outside Birmingham, this happened in broad daylight and with policemen nearby.

MURDEROUS GANG ATTACKS

Just before the attacks, Superintendent McManus and an inspector spotted a knot of lads quickening their pace. Turning to follow, they saw them break into a run and disappear round a corner. Fortunately, to check the lawlessness locally, plain-clothes men were scattered about. Two of them were just twenty yards away from the assault but 'though they lost no time laying hands upon two of the young roughs, Willock was already unconscious'. Vomiting blood, badly bruised all over and wounded by a knife, he was also suffering from a concussion of the brain and was hospitalised for a few days. Glynn, Cleaver and Taroni were each given four months for malicious wounding. They had no previous convictions. Having done time for an assault on a constable, Bond was sent down for six months. So too was Medlicott, who handed himself in, saying, 'Take me as well; I was one on 'em. I threw the knife away that I stabbed him with on the Old Pleck where it was done.' He'd previously done time for stealing, assault and gambling.[189]

Early the next year, Cleaver was beaten up by three young men from the Summer Lane district in what looked like a tit-for-tat reprisal. Taking a belting, he was also hit with a poker and brick. He stayed clear of trouble thereafter, as did Taroni, Glynn and Medlicott. Unlike them, Alfred Simpson carried on fighting. Sent down for three months for assaulting a constable in January 1889 (Chapter 1), over the next three years, he served more time for assaults. In one of them, he knocked down and kicked a young woman passing him when he was quarrelling with some men. Then in April 1892, he, his brother, George, and two others badly beat up a policeman. Castigated as the worst of the lot, George Simpson was sent down for six months, with his brother getting four months.

Out of prison merely weeks, Alfred Simpson, the recognised leader of his slogging gang, went up against Michael Downey, the top man of the Newtown Row sloggers. After closing time on a Saturday night, about forty of both sides brawled in a free fight until the police arrived. Simpson had an ugly triangular wound on the forehead while Downey sustained an inch-long cut on the back of his head. Each alleged the other had stabbed him.

A year later, Alfred Simpson was fined for assaulting a sister-in-law when fighting her husband. Like the Sheldons he was also a thief and in 1894, he was handed twelve months for stealing gold from a small pile well behind the counter of a pub. He did so using a long stick, the end of which was smeared with bird lime to fasten on to each coin. Then in 1898, three officers were given a 'warm reception' when they went to his house after he robbed a glass jar from a shop.

He opened the ball by throwing a lighted lamp at them from the top of the stairs, with no worse result, fortunately, than saturating Evans's clothes. Simpson chose a hammer as his next weapon, and with this he hit Detective Hands, who attempted to close with him, several blows on the head, and their severity may be gathered when it is stated that his hat was cut and three nasty wounds inflicted. Police Constable Mills went to the assistance of the other officers. He went upstairs with a chair over his head for protection, but being overpowered, the prisoner succeeded in biting the constable's hand, in striking him over the head with a boot, and assaulting him with the stave of a chair. Mills had to use his staff and both he and

Detective Hands had to have their wounds dressed at the General Hospital.

Declaring he'd dropped the lamp by accident, Simpson complained he'd been treated roughly and acted in self-defence. This time, he was sentenced to four years' penal servitude in Parkhurst and then Dartmoor. He was thirty-six and at just over five feet five inches had a broken nose and scars on each eyebrow, several fingers and the back of his head. It was much too late for him to change and in 1904, he did a month for assaulting his wife, Mary. In court she had two black eyes after he'd punched her on the nose because she'd no chicken for him to eat.[190]

By then, the most dangerous of the brothers was the youngest, Charles 'Charley' Simpson. Born in 1874, after time in an industrial school, he became a fish hawker like two of his older brothers as well as a boxer fighting for money. A bantamweight at just under eight stone four pounds and with a long line of successes, he was known for slogging (hitting) of a fierce character. Nicknamed 'Navvy' Simpson because he'd attained certain fame as a 'bruiser', his slogging of the police was as fierce. With several convictions for drunkenness, he was on the Birmingham Police Black List for Habitual Drunkards but drunk or not, he was ever ready to have a go at officers and in 1904, he was responsible for an affray of 'Hooliganism run riot'. On a Sunday evening in December, PC Morgan ordered several men to move on for causing a disturbance outside a pub. With an oath, Simpson asked what he wanted there and then somebody else hit him between his eyes, blacking them. Despite the blow, the officer closed with his assailant. Both fell to the ground and being badly mauled and kicked, Morgan drew his staff but as he did, someone kicked him in the shoulder. Simpson followed suit with a blow to the face, knocking out two teeth and splitting the constable's lip. With fellow officers arriving, some of the attackers ran off, although they managed to arrest Simpson. When charged, chillingly he said, 'I didn't ought to have kicked him. I ought to have hit him with the chopper.' In court he sang a different tune, denying he was there and stating, 'I never done nothing.' Given in a rough and ready fashion, his evidence provoked some laughter, leading the Stipendiary to warn he wouldn't have such a serious and important case treated like it was theatre. Found guilty, Simpson was sentenced to four months. He disappeared from the dock shouting and threatening, 'I will do something when I come out. I will come on top yet.' He did do something when he came out. He went law abiding and in the First World War, he 'did his bit' on munitions work. Dying of cancer in 1921 aged forty-nine, the *Daily Herald*, a national newspaper, felt that followers of boxing would regret his passing.[191]

It was presumed that the Whitehouse Street Gang was broken up by the time of Simpson's sentence. Retiring in 1900 after eighteen years in charge of Aston, Superintendent Walker was praised for ridding its streets of its infamous slogging bands. That success, he said, was achieved gradually and it was not until after several desperate encounters with the police that the 'courage' of the sloggers was broken by measures soon to be followed in Birmingham: 'the adoption of vigorous tactics supported by salutary sentences from the Bench'. Inspector William Parkinson was especially remembered as a 'terror to the roughs'. An extraordinarily strong officer, he had a way of putting the sloggers completely out of action and somehow getting them to the charge room, where a colleague recalled that the floor was streaming with blood. Another policeman feared by the sloggers and peakies was PC James 'Big Jimmy' Hodson, 'who never hesitated to tackle the gangs, no matter how threatening their attitude'. He was a daunting character. In one violent row, a man hit a policeman on the head with a boot, threatened him with a kettle of boiling water and then picked up a poker, defying anyone to come near him. He only agreed to go to the station when PC Hodson arrived.

It didn't always go easy for Hodson, though. On the August Bank Holiday Monday of 1887, he was called to the Aston Tavern, where there was a fight between some of the Aston Slogging Gang and others. A major centre of the local community where inquests were held and dinners for local organisations were put on, it boasted extensive pleasure grounds and a bowling green. Today it's a superbly refurbished pub popular with Aston Villa fans and a boutique hotel catering for the entourage of performers at Villa Park such as Pink and Bruce Springsteen. That day, however, there was no pleasure. When the gang refused to be quiet, Hodson arrested one of them, but as he was taking him towards the door a glass was thrown at him, cutting his head. A jug was also flung, but seeing it coming, he ducked it. Succeeding in getting himself and his prisoner into the passage, the officer was again struck on the head and reaching the street, he was hit with three blows in the mouth by one of the gang. Two bystanders, a father and son, came to help, and in the ensuing struggle, Hodson was kicked in the mouth, loosening several of his teeth. Now backed up by another officer, the attacker was secured but one of the bystanders was hit with a violent blow on the back of the head. On the way to the police station, the two officers 'were followed by a great mob of youths and men – friends and acquaintances of the prisoners – who obstructed the police and threw stones at them'. Both were struck with the missiles, with one having his head cut with a stone.

Aggressive policing in Aston was matched by the strong actions of the magistrates. At the start of the 'crusade' against these 'street pests' as they were deemed, 'heavy fines were imposed in the hope that these would strike to the heart of the offender, but such an idea was altogether unjustifiable'. Neither did short terms of imprisonment have the desired effect. Sloggers flourished and the police were daily flaunted and frequently brutally assaulted. Not until the maximum sentence of six months for each separate offence was given out did the slogger 'begin to see that his day had gone and that the magistrates were determined that the dangerous combinations should cease to exist'. This campaign of repression extended over five years until it was pretty safe to say that slogging bands had ceased to annoy the residents.[192]

The drive against Aston's sloggers was undoubtedly successful but they hadn't quite been put down. In May 1900, three months after Superintendent Walker's retirement, newspapers announced a reminiscence of the slogging gangs when George and Thomas Hickling broke the windows of a pub with stones and brickbats. Described as two young men of the peaky type, they belonged to the Ten Arches Gang and flung their missiles because they disliked a man drinking inside the pub. Each went down for a month as they couldn't pay the damages, fines and costs imposed. Unusually, their father had a skilled job as a locomotive engine driver, but five of his six sons got into trouble. The one who didn't was William, recalled by relatives as 'a gentleman, very well dressed who owned chip shops, including Hicklings in Duddeston, and was also very involved in horse racing and making the billboards for the races'. By contrast, his oldest brother, Edward, did a month for a savage and unprovoked attack on a woman in the street, whilst Robert was another slogger. With a conviction for assaulting the police in 1901, when fighting in Rocky Lane, he buckled a passer-by and was sent down for a month. He was thirty-two. His younger brother, Alfred, started out in the Ten Arches Gang but then went on to have 'a remarkable career' of crime away from slogging. It began when he was thirteen and sent to prison for twenty-one days followed by five years in a reformatory. His crime? He'd stolen two bottles and 2½lbs of sweets. After briefly working on the railways, probably in a job his father arranged, he joined the Army, but was discharged for striking an officer. Thereafter, he saw inside almost every prison in the Midlands. As one magistrate observed, Hickling seemed almost a case of insanity as he couldn't help thieving. He couldn't and by 1905, when he was thirty-five, he'd amassed fifteen convictions for theft, mostly for small amounts of shillings and paltry items like a wooden bowl.[193]

Ostensibly a tube drawer, George Hickling was another thief, although he also had convictions for assault, including one on a constable. So too did Thomas Tuckey, another one of the Ten Arches Gang. Unlike the Hicklings from Nechells, the Tuckeys were an Aston family but lived almost a mile away from Whitehouse Street and closer to Thimblemill Lane. Named as a slogger in 1886 when he was nineteen, the next year, Tuckey threw a glass at the back of the head of a detective called to a pub disturbance. He was sentenced to three months. A longer stretch came in 1889 following a savage attack on a plain-clothes policeman. Tuckey and a friend slogged and brutally beat him about the head with a heavy piece of wood. With his helmet smashed, the officer received a nasty scalp wound which bled profusely. The attackers escaped but after they were arrested, Tuckey was given six months.

His younger brother, Harry, was as violent. Aged eighteen in September 1894, he and a friend were involved in a dispute between rival slogging gangs on a field by the canal. Afterwards, they attacked a man but were each fined merely 10s with costs. Aged fifty-three in 1921, Thomas Tuckey was given nine months and Harry eighteen for their part in the Birmingham Gang's bloody assault on Jewish bookmakers after the Epsom meeting. They were two more who connected sloggers/peaky blinders with the Racecourse War of 1921 and the beginnings of organised crime gangs.

Harry Tuckey, along with his older brother Samuel, was also involved in the last attack by the remnants of the Whitehouse Street Gang. Contrastingly, Samuel had no record and when he was sixteen, he jumped into the canal to rescue a married woman trying to commit suicide. For that gallant conduct, he received a certificate from the Royal Humane Society, presented ironically by Aston's presiding magistrate who'd sentenced his brothers. Not a violent man, on Whit Monday 1904, Samuel Tuckey fell out with another drinker supposedly over a penny. Harry Tuckey then heard the man's relative say, 'I will fetch a clique [gang] and have your brains knocked in if it costs me £100 or £200.' Afterwards, Samuel Tuckey went into the Albion on the corner of Whitehouse Street where five friends of the man he'd quarrelled with rushed in at him. The main room today is as it was then – with the bar less than two yards from the main door. Drinking in such a narrow space, Tuckey would have had no chance either to get out of the way or into a fighting pose. Nor did he. Punched in the face and struck with a glass, he tried in vain to reach the door but was stopped by a blow on the head with a hammer. That was swung by that long-term Whitehouse Street Gang member, James Casey. Tall for a slogger/peaky blinder at five feet seven inches, he was tattooed and bore the marks of numerous fights, having a scar on his right cheek, a large lump on the back of his head, and a piece off the end of his right thumb. Despite having fifty-six previous convictions and the seriousness of the assault, he and the others got away simply with fines for what was deemed 'a Whit Monday brawl'.[194]

That was the final act of the Whitehouse Street Gang. Their long-term foes, the Ten Arches Gang, carried on as the last of the slogging gangs. In 1909, two of them were sent down for five years' penal servitude. Brothers Alfred and Walter Smith, both labourers from Nechells, were found guilty of doing wilful damage to the extent of £7 to the property of Sidney Jenney. On a Saturday night in April they burst into his house, attacked him with a knife, wrecked the furniture and pictures, and smashed the vases and chairs. Not done, they set fire to the place, with Alfred Smith hurling a lighted paraffin lamp at Mrs Jenny and shouting, 'I'll have the rope for you, for pressing the charge against my sister.' Having previous convictions, they were described as belonging to a dangerous gang of thieves and the worst class of roughs the police had to deal with. The Assistant Recorder said the case was so bad that it ought to have been sent to the assizes on a charge of arson. This bullying, intimidation and abuse of women typified the sloggers and peaky blinders. They were not men to be admired.[195]

Chapter 4

BULLYING, ABUSIVE AND RACIST PEAKY BLINDERS

WANTON ATTACKS

'Surely all respectable and law-abiding citizens are sick of the very name of ruffianism in Birmingham and assaults on the police,' so wrote a despondent 'Workman' just three days after the killing of PC Snipe in 1897. A rare voice from the decent majority of the working class whose lives were afflicted by thugs, he despaired that 'no matter what part of the city one walks, gangs of "peaky blinders" are to be seen, who ofttimes think nothing of grossly insulting passers-by, be it a man, woman or child. I venture to say that 99 times out of 100, they are not even brought to justice.' Unfortunately, he was right. By then, some of the worst slogging bands may have been broken up through long terms of imprisonment and housing clearance, but back-street gangsterism was as virulent as ever. According to another dispirited citizen, hardly a day passed without brutal, unprovoked and wanton attacks on law-abiding citizens. Gathering on street corners, peaky blinders were a disgusting nuisance across the city, and writing to the press, 'A Few Respectable Though Poor Tenants' in Ladywood declared their revulsion at the terrible language and loud singing of music hall ditties until late at night by peakies and their 'molls'. They encapsulated a wider aversion to peaky blinders amongst the poor. With their streets appearing in newspapers mostly because of violence, class-biased negative stereotypes were reinforced. A general resentment at this branding was highlighted by several residents of Latimer Street angered that the *Birmingham Mail* reported it as a poor neighbourhood with a certain proportion of its people consisting of the rougher element chiefly of the peaky-blinder class. Their response was instructive: 'You may or not know that peakies if driven from one corner will locate themselves in a similar position elsewhere. Therefore why should a neighbourhood suffer for what they neither encourage nor appreciate?' Apologetically, the newspaper emphasised that their description was not intended in any way to reflect upon Latimer Street's artisans, men of the skilled working class and their families. The respectable portion of its population weren't to be blamed but rather they should be commiserated with because of the peaky locating himself in their locality.[196]

With his father a skilled leather cutter and himself becoming a silversmith, Bertram Hildick belonged to an artisan family living in a prosperous part of Aston by Villa Park. It was one of a row of small, three-bedroomed modern houses identified by the novelist George Gissing as socially 'a step or two upwards in the graduation which, in Birmingham, begins with the numbered court and culminates in the mansions of Edgbaston.' Yet to get into town, Birmingham city centre, Hildick had to pass through poorer streets dominated by back-to-backs where peaky blinders gathered. He vividly remembered an occasion when one of them nearly killed him. Still a teenage schoolboy, he was with a friend when suddenly a rotten egg crashed in his face.

As I wiped myself clean I saw a Peaky Blinder roaring with laughter and lounging against a lamp-post. He was wearing the type of clothes that were the uniform of his gangs . . .

'Did you throw that?' I asked. 'What if I did?' he shouted back laughing.

I went for him and punched him on the jaw. He staggered back, and then I saw his hand flash to the back of his trousers.

With a sharp long-bladed knife he sprang at me. Luckily I ducked, for he might have killed me, and my friend ran to my aid. But at that moment another burly Peaky Blinder approached. Much to our surprise – and relief – he grabbed the other Peaky Blinder by the collar and dragged him away.

I was indeed lucky to get away unharmed but that incident was typical of the sort of menace these young ruffians were.

One of their chief hates it seemed was respectability and conventional clothes. If you passed them wearing a collar and tie you ran the risk of them spattering mud, rotten eggs or fruit at you.

Yet they themselves had an almost regard for their absurd dress which they displayed with pride and egoism.

Although they lived mostly in slums or near slums

they were very robust – perhaps because of their rough life. And they were very conscious of their physical fitness.

If they thought a passing man had a genteel manner or was physically their inferior, they would shout out: 'Sissy!'

If the man stopped they would draw closer to him, put two fingers of the right hand in a V-sign under his nose and mutter: 'If yer don't shurrup I'll gouge yer eyes out.'

Hildick recalled that one of their most popular places of amusement was a little theatre in Summer Lane known as 'The Blood Tub'. Its highly dramatic and sensational productions were advertised by large posters with scenes of strapped-down women having their heads sawn off, or of men with sea-green faces peering through windows. There were no queues to get in and to stem the rush of the crowds, the doorkeeper kept the folding door half-closed, admitting only one or two at a time. But if a peaky blinder arrived late and was at the back of the waiting crowd, 'he would use his own ruthless methods of jumping the queue. He would vault on top of the man in front of him and literally walk over the shoulders of the others, to drop finally in front and squeeze himself in.'

As a teenager, Arthur Matthison was also fortunate in escaping violence. Living in one of the few large houses in Summer Lane because his father was the local registrar of births and deaths, his middle-class family was a rarity in an area known as a peaky blinder rendezvous. According to Matthison, such a hooligan was the product of poverty, squalor and a slum environment. Though a terror to respectable people and the police, who went in pairs every Saturday night, 'he never molested any member of my family. Perhaps as we lived on his doorstep, we were treated as members of the gang by courtesy or adoption.' Often returning home from work late at night, the local bullies would always give Matthison curt nods of comradeship except for one occasion. It was about midnight and coming back from an amateur theatre performance still dressed in a cavalry uniform, he passed 'a brace of beauties lounging at the entrance to a notorious court'. One of them said, 'Let's knock the sodger's [soldier's] blinkin' spurs off,' when the other, taking a good look at me, said, 'Strewth, it ain't a sodger; it's only the registrar's barstard.' My presumed illegitimacy no doubt saved me from violent assault and battery on that occasion, but I felt quite proud at having been recognised as a man and a brother in crime.'[197]

Unlike the Matthisons, by the 1890s, the vast majority of Birmingham's middle class had fled from central Birmingham to Edgbaston, Moseley, Handsworth and further afield. As one informed commentator realised, this meant that 'In our suburban retreats, less disturbed by Peaky pranks, though now and again hedges, fences, and flower beds testify to a visit, we are too apt to think it is no concern of ours, or to assert, as regards Peaky Blinders at any rate, "I am not my brother's keeper."' The middle-class flight to the outer suburbs was matched by that of the skilled and semi-skilled working class to long roads of better-built and roomier terraced houses in developing areas like Sparkhill, Bordesley Green, Alum Rock, Bournbrook, King's Heath, Stirchley and Cotteridge. Socially and economically, shopkeepers mostly were on a par with the better-off working class but contrastingly, many remained in poorer neighbourhoods. Living above and behind their businesses either in the back streets or on main shopping thoroughfares, they too were victimised. As one concerned observer put it, habitually moving about in gangs of a score or more, each with their greasy curl patted on their foreheads, peaky blinders en masse were seen as a somewhat imposing army, a terror to the small shopkeeper. Seldom, though, did the travails of these tradesmen and women come to notice.

An exception was the terrorisation in Newtown Row by a gang of roughs in December 1902. In what was reported as an extraordinary state of affairs, they went into shops demanding articles without payment. Fearing for their lives, the tradesmen dared not refuse, handing over what was demanded. So bad was this extortion that the manager of one butcher's shop summoned up enough courage to seek the help of the police. Late on a Saturday night, two constables 'secreted' on the premises heard Samuel Davies demanding,

'Now, then, I want a joint. Sharpen your – knife, and cut me one.' A customer then coming in, Davies went out only to return a few minutes later to order, 'Come on; I want that – joint.' Further demands and refusals followed until the two policemen stepped out of hiding and arrested Davies. Straight after they'd gone, George Coleman bounced in, threatening the manager: 'I see you have had Fatty pinched. Give me some chops or I'll knock your brains in.' Afraid because the constables were no longer there, the butcher handed over three chops and was then told to give up a kidney. Coleman was subsequently arrested, and he and Davies were each bound over to keep the peace and pay costs, or, if in default, sentenced to one month.

Terry Proctor was told how his grandfather dealt with peaky blinders who came into his butcher's shop in Summer Lane demanding protection money. A tough, adventurous man, Edwin Proctor wasn't going to brook intimidation and ordered them to, 'Shift off quick, or else!' They didn't and so, 'Edwin grabs a large swivel meat hook of the back meat rail, swings it over the counter, hooks one of them around the neck, pulls him over the counter and beats the daylights out of him, then throws him through the open shop window. They never had any trouble with them after!' Others also fought back, with a local newspaper announcing that perhaps the most effective way of dealing with these 'cadgers' was to follow the example of one Newtown Row tradesman. When threatened, 'I picked up my knife and steel and asked the loiterer what he intended doing?' The would-be-blackmailer left suddenly, prompting the declaration that, 'There is nothing like presenting a fearless front. A little bit of courage will work wonders in dealing with folks of this type.' It was easy for the journalist to say that safely ensconced in his town centre office.

William Fisher was one of the few who did have more than a little courage. Starting out as a licensee in a tough quarter, he had to deal with cheats aplenty in his pub as well as tough customers ready to start a fight.

My first trouble came from one of the Peaky Blinder boys – in their long-peaked hats and bell-bottom trousers. Many of these lads thought they could be cock of the walk in any public house they visited, particularly in mine, kept by a raw beginner. This one swaggered in and started to walk behind the bar to draw his own drink from the beer engine.

Half the customers were afraid of him and there was a breathless hush as I barred his way. He lunged at me but did not reach me. By standing close to him, I backed him outside the door and stood up to him. Fortunately I was able to give him a good thrashing – all that my six brothers had taught me about fighting had not been in vain.

I was never worried by him again and word soon spread that the new gaffer knew how to use his fists![198]

Workers were another target for blackmailing. Julie Tims's grandfather, Thomas, was a skilled screw tool maker employed in Watery Lane in the Barr Street Gang's territory. Twice, he was one of several workers waylaid by gangs on payday and relieved of their wages. These 'muggings' precipitated him to take a new job away from back-to-back Birmingham and move his family to Bournville, the garden town laid out by George Cadbury in what was then rural Worcestershire. Tims's experiences were similar to those of a clerk working in Ladywood. In December 1896 and on his dinner break, he was accosted by peaky blinders demanding he give them tobacco. On his refusal, they rushed for him but obviously propelled by fear, he outran them back into the works. Armed with a whip, the manager went outside with the clerk to sort out the gang, but both were immediately set upon. The whip was wrested away, and buckle-ended belts and knives were used on them. Eventually, a strong force of workers from the factory came to the rescue, driving off the gang. The seriously injured manager was hospitalised.

Small-scale employers weren't exempt from the sloggers' 'tax'. Late one Monday night in June 1898, Arthur J. Archer heard shouts for help from close to his scale making works by the Bull Ring. Going on to the street, he saw his brother surrounded by youths from the local slogging gang. Terrors of the neighbourhood, they'd battered their victim's hat over his eyes and were punching him. Seeing Archer, they told him he could either pay blackmail or be beaten up. He chose the beating but managed to get back inside his workplace with only a blow to his chest. Deeming it unsafe to leave, he lit up the rooms in the hope that the local constable on his beat would see this as a sign that something was up. A couple of hours later the officer arrived and he and Archer went outside. Immediately, James Cueson loomed out of an entry. The leader of the gang, he said he'd done time before and was willing to do it again for someone like Archer. A 34-year-old labourer with several convictions for assault, Cueson was sent down for two months. He'd go on to do another nine months for robbing a man.

Though publicans, shopkeepers and the better off of the working class were sometimes subjected to brutal, aggressive and wanton attacks, it was the decent poor living in the back streets who mostly bore the malice of the back-street gangs for the seemingly interminable years they raged. Reverend Bass despaired that his parish was the home of the peaky blinder, and that the vengeance of this blackguard king was awful to those who refused obeisance. The back streets were his little kingdom, and the terror of his anger was manifest on all hands to those crossing him: a blow or stab in the dark; the total destruction of your windows; and a hundred petty tyrannies exercised in so ingenious a manner as to defy detection. Even if he were discovered in some illegal act, he'd make a rapid retreat to the intricacies of courts with which he was familiar, rendering pursuit not only difficult but practically unavailing.

Unable to afford higher rents, the poor couldn't move away. Trapped as they were, anyone trying to stop gang violence was endangered. James Clayton knew that. Two nights before Christmas 1876 when standing with his wife on a corner, he saw a young man knocked down and cruelly kicked on the ground. Venturing over, he accused nineteen-year-old Hugh Garrigan of taking part in the beating. The reply was chilling: 'Yes; and I will do you now.' Straight away, he charged at Clayton, stabbing him in the neck with a sharp object. With blood pouring from the wound, he was taken to hospital. There was a clear cut immediately beneath the chin which would have very likely proved fatal if an inch lower. According to the surgeon, stabbing cases were now so numerous that they were as common as smallpox. Appearing in court with his head bandaged, Clayton declined to give evidence and although he admitted that Garrigan struck him, he didn't want to press charges. Asked if he'd been intimidated or induced to hold his tongue by bribe, the obviously scared witness was told to remember that the magistrates were duty-bound not only to protect him but also society at large from such outrageous assaults. Finally, the evidence of the assault was drawn out and Garrigan was sent to be tried at a higher court. Found guilty of unlawful wounding, he was handed twelve months. One of the Park Street Gang, three years previously he and his associates assaulted a waggoner trying to stop them stealing turnips from the cart in front of his. For his trouble, he was stoned and severely cut. Having previous convictions, on that occasion Garrigan was given six weeks.[199]

The ire of the gangs was easily aroused as two terrified

families found out when a 'soft' answer to roughs incurred their wrath. Blacksmith George Turnbull, his wife and four young children lived in a back-to-back in Duddeston close to Thomas Fisher, a riveter, his wife and two children under five. Taking a walk together towards the countryside on a spring night in April 1889, they passed a gang who pushed rudely against Fisher. As the newspaper reported it, submitting to 'the incivility with exemplary forbearance', he simply remarked, 'It's all right.' This mild observation was too much for the irascible humour of Thomas MacCabe, who immediately turned upon Fisher, striking him a violent blow on the head, felling him. Their lust for violence unsated, the rest of the gang kicked him in the most brutal and wanton manner. Understandably distressed, his wife strove to protect her husband, imploring the attackers to spare him, but she, too, was hit on the head and knocked to the ground. Turnbull was a few yards behind Fisher's family. Hearing the screams of the woman and children, he rushed to protect them, but MacCabe threatened to 'cut his eyes out' whilst the rest of the gang 'greeted him with volleys of stones, which their recipient, with pardonable exaggeration, likened to flights of bombshells. Wisely shrinking from so unequal a contest, Turnbull made a strategic circuit in search of the police, and, having reinforced himself with a constable, presently returned to settle accounts with the roughs, who, in the meantime, had dispersed.' After a long and exciting chase, MacCabe was the only one arrested. For this gross and unprovoked assault upon two respectable men and the wife of one of them, he was sent down for two months. A tube drawer, he was of no fixed address.[200]

George Onions was another who found it a dangerous thing to cross peaky blinders. Having supposedly kicked a dog belonging to a Summer Lane gang, he was marked for retribution. On a Saturday afternoon in November 1889, he was threatened with a knife and a buckled belt by eighteen-year-old labourer Thomas Henry Everall, heard saying, 'I wish I had got two or three with me, I'd do him.' He did what he said. Going up Summer Lane, he gathered a dozen other roughs armed with belts and chains and went back for Onions. Seeing him, Everall called out, 'There he is, lads; knock him down; kill him.' Though assaulted, Onions managed to run away but was caught and tripped up. Shouting, 'Come on, lads; we've got him,' Everall hit him on the head with the buckle of a formidable-looking belt, whilst Albert Chaplin, a labourer aged twenty-one, struck him with an iron chain. As someone else cried, 'Don't let's leave him alive,' the unfortunate Onions was hit and kicked by the rest of the gang. Hearing a whistle blown they cleared off. A kindly bystander took Onions to the General Hospital, but on the way, he was again attacked by Everall. The case didn't come before the magistrates for several weeks, when Onions appeared with his head bandaged. Having suffered a fractured skull necessitating trepanning, he was still hospitalised and off work.

A witness testified that Everall offered to give him a sovereign and a suit of clothes to say that he'd struck out in self-defence, whilst the man who'd helped Onions at first refused to attend the court. When he was finally called to give evidence, he did so half-heartedly and very feebly. Asked why he didn't speak up, he replied he had the flu. His remarkable reticence and evasive answers provoked the Stipendiary to exclaim, 'Now you had better tell the truth. You have treated us in a very disrespectful manner, but now we mean to get the truth.' That admonishment failed, with the witness avoiding any answers incriminating the accused. Despite that, they were sent to a higher court where they were found guilty of unlawful wounding. Chaplin was handed fifteen months and Everall five years' penal servitude because he was the leader of the gang. Just over five feet five inches tall, scarred on the right of his forehead, and having the rose, shamrock, thistle and other tattoos, he had convictions for theft and would do more time for burglary. Passing sentence, the judge pronounced that if the spirit of lawlessness in Birmingham went unchecked it 'would lead up to something which would have a very sad and serious consequence'. So it proved and within days of that warning, a man was killed in Summer Lane.[201]

He was Daniel Grice, a 38-year-old painter. On Saturday 26 April 1890, he and a couple of friends hired a cab to drive them to various pubs. Just before eight in the evening and whilst it was still light, they came out of the Geach Arms 'half tipsy' and as they loudly disputed over where to go next, the cabman asked for payment. Several people gathered round the commotion, amongst them a broad and powerful young man named James Jones who said, 'Why don't you pay the man and let him get off?' Grice replied, 'Mind your own business: it's nothing to do with you.' Jones didn't like that. At first reacting with, 'All right, don't make a row,' he then snarled, 'I'll give you something before you go home.' Catching hold of Grice's collar, Jones punched him twice in the face. As he went down, Grice's head struck 'the horseroad just outside the kerbstone' with such force that one witness asserted that 'she never heard such a fall in all her life'. Jones then hit one of the other friends. As the third man started to go to see what was wrong with Grice, he was pushed back by some of the crowd with the warning he'd get the same if he didn't get off. A 'respectable' young working man saw someone jump on Grice's chest whilst he was lying on the ground, and the daughter of a local shopkeeper heard a crack as if his ribs had been broken in. Jones and two others ran off. Grice was carried unconscious into the cab and fetched to hospital where he died within five minutes. He had a wound to the back of his head, discolouration of the neck and blood was oozing from his nose.

Known as 'Big Jim' or 'Big Jonah', at five feet ten inches, Jones was tall for a peaky blinder. Broad set, he was powerful and feared locally. Six years before, he'd been shot in the side by one of his victims, who told the police, 'You would have done the same thing yourself if you had been in my place. He met me in the street, set about me and kicked me on the shins, and in the stomach, and I told him if he came at me again, I should shoot him.' The man was acquitted on account of great provocation. Purportedly a labourer, Jones seemed to have had no occupation, although he had convictions for drunkenness and obscene language. A 'street lounger', he was constantly seen leaning against the walls of the Geach Arms with other young men of 'his own class, which is mostly distinguished by trousers that are tight at the knee and amply bell over the boot, by bright mufflers, tight-fitting coats, and big belts'. When last seen, he was also wearing a billycock hat. This was the first detailed description of the peaky blinder fashion.

The *Birmingham Mail* quickly sent a reporter to try and find out more. However, there was a great reluctance on the part of those who professed to have seen what took place to make any statement. One woman said she did watch all that occurred 'but as soon as she began to speak, she was taken away by a man, who said that she would be "marked" if it became known that she had given any information to anyone'. This appeared to be the feeling amongst most of the people in the neighbourhood, who were 'too much under the influence of terror to make free communications of what they know'. Indeed, the reporter himself was cautioned that if he didn't take care, he'd be served the same as the dead man. After disappearing, Jones was swiftly apprehended in Sheffield.

In his first court experience, a female witness complained that she'd put her life in jeopardy. She was right to feel that as several men were summonsed for intimidation, such was the deepest sympathy for Jones amongst 'the rougher element' locally. He pleaded self-defence, saying Grice was about to hit him. Found guilty, the judge was persuaded to leniency, commenting that looking at all the facts, even though it was a cruel thing to knock a man down without provocation, the offence might be expiated without awarding any grave punishment. Jones got away with three months for manslaughter. It can only be wondered at what Grice's widow, Jane, felt at such a lenient sentence for the killing of her husband. They lived in a back house and as a forty-year-old charwoman picking up a pittance she had no chance of paying the rent without her husband's wages as a painter. The only way she could have stayed out of the hated workhouse would have been to find lodgings. Hailing from Leeds, she wouldn't have even been able to afford the train fare to go back to her home town. As it is, nothing more is known of her.[202]

Unhappily, the violent bullying of 'Big Jonah' wasn't isolated. A year later, Albert Glynn was had up for two stabbings. An eighteen-year-old general labourer, he was lodging with a family in Love Lane, in Reverend Bass's parish, when, on Saturday 21 March 1891, he stabbed a man in the back without any provocation. He then absconded but almost six months later, on a Sunday evening, he rushed from a gang at someone else, stabbing him three times in the face with a pocketknife. The victim said he barely knew his attacker. Reacting to the evidence, the judge pronounced he'd 'never heard before, in any town or city in the kingdom of gangs of roughs going about at night with knives and buckles and assaulting decent people'. Declaring that such a state of things must be stopped, he passed an exemplary sentence of five years' penal servitude. It made no difference to Glynn. In March 1901, he and his brother were each fined 40s and costs for attacking the landlady of a local pub. She wasn't the only woman he beat up as he was sent down for three months for assaulting his wife, Leah. Coming home from a football match, he was enraged that she'd gone to her mother's house and went after her. Finding her, he punched her in the mouth and kicked her. Then, when lodging with another family, they were rowing when the man renting the house became involved and hit Glynn over the head with a hammer. Finally in 1906, he was sent back inside for another six months for breaking into a warehouse. A photograph taken then by the Birmingham Police showed him with the peaky blinders' cap and daff twisted twice round his neck into a choker.[203]

'Peaky Outrages' continued to blight the people of back-to-back Birmingham as highlighted in February 1902. Amongst a litany of them, the worst according to a newspaper was that committed by the notorious Joseph Greatrex. On a Saturday night in Ladywood, he went for a man he had a grudge with, smashing a bottle of beer over his head and cutting it in a shocking manner. Appearing in court with his head swathed in surgical bandages, the victim pointed out his attacker, at which Greatrex turned to him with a 'savage expression in his face and exclaimed that it was a – pity it did not kill him – it was what the – lot deserved'. Having also stabbed a friend of the victim, he was sent to a higher court and returning from the dock after giving his evidence, he struck one of the witnesses. Sent down for two years, he shouted there would be another Blinko case when he came out. It was no idle threat. Though only twenty and just five feet three inches, he was a most dangerous man and three years previously, he'd done three months for intent to do grievous bodily harm. An associate of roughs and thieves, he'd fired a six-chambered revolver at a constable who'd arrested some of his friends gambling with cards in the street. Startled by the shot, the officer turned sharply round only to see Greatrex taking aim. Scarcely having time to take in the danger, the policeman ducked his head when there was another flash. Fortunately, the bullet missed, embedding itself in the boarding behind him. With Greatrex about to take aim again, the officer 'slipped to the back of one of the youths he had in custody, believing that the assailant would not jeopardise his "pal" by again firing'. He was right. Greatrex didn't and instead took to his heels. Letting go of his prisoner, the constable chased and just as he caught him, Greatrex flung the revolver at a companion, calling him to, 'Chuck it into the – cut [canal]' He was lucky not to be found guilty of attempted murder.[204]

GENDERED VIOLENCE

Though belonging to an English family, through living in Allison Street, Nathaniel Nock was an early member of the

Irish Park Street Gang. A nailer from the Black Country, his father's premises were damaged in the Murphy Riots, perhaps explaining why Nock joined the gang. Aged twenty-one and a tube drawer, in August 1874 he was involved in a drunken disturbance leading to savage assaults. He and labourers Thomas Foy, nineteen, and Michael Moran, eighteen, were going along New Canal Street when they came upon Mary Mason junior, standing with her husband at the top of an entry. Using 'beastly language', one of them put his arm around her. When her husband remonstrated, they set about him, making him 'retreat' from the kicking into his mother's house. The trio of ruffians weren't far behind and to the horror of the family, they burst the door open, forcing themselves inside. Moran knocked down Mary Mason senior, jumping on her and beating her with the heavy wooden line prop. Leaving her badly bruised, they smashed the windows and seriously damaged the furniture. Not done, they went upstairs where Moran kicked the cradle holding a baby. Having followed them, Mary Mason senior begged them not to injure her grandchild, and Foy said, 'No, don't hurt the kid.' They didn't but instead Moran savagely assaulted the baby's mother, even though she'd grasped her child in her arms. He then pitched her from the top of the stairs to the bottom.

Another sister was so frightened by what was happening that she jumped out of the sash window, severely injuring herself. Seeing what was happening, neighbours sent for help. Two constables and a sergeant arrived whilst the thugs were still in the bedroom. Crying out, 'Look up here's the police,' they chucked the line prop at them from the window. Coming downstairs, Moran and Foy attacked one of the constables with a poker. Drawing his staff, he defended himself by hitting their heads and was helped by neighbours shoving the line prop at the two men. After a great struggle, they were taken to the station and Nock was arrested trying to rescue them. As he didn't take a prominent part in the affray, he was merely fined 20s and costs for obstructing the police, or a month if he didn't pay. Moran, the worst of the three, was sent down for a total of thirteen months for three assaults and wilful damage. Foy was given nine months in all and would later do time for a shocking attack on a sergeant who was viciously beaten by the Park Street Gang. He followed that with another assault when it took ten policemen to arrest him. By 1880, when he was handed six months for yet another attack on a constable, he'd racked up numerous convictions. He was incapable of change.[205]

Mary Killcoyne, seventeen, was another woman who suffered from the Park Street Gang. Having taken the perilous decision to testify against some of them, she became their prey. On a Sunday evening in 1877 when standing at the top of an entry in Allison Street, she was spotted by brassfounders Thomas Moore, seventeen, and George Moore, fifteen. The sons of an Irish father and Welsh mother, they were with Joseph Matthews, a fourteen-year-old hawker whose father was from Liverpool and mother from Stoke. Branding her a 'copper', they warned they'd stone her and then picking up a brick, Matthews smashed it on her forehead. Shouting to the other pair to fetch more stones, he flung one at her but missed.

Hearing her screaming in fear, her father, Patrick, rushed to her. Threatening 'he would do for him and all belonging to him as they were all coppers', Thomas Moore struck Patrick Killcoyne on the back of the head with a knife, inflicting a severe wound. Falling to the ground unconscious, he was kicked by the brothers. Their mother then turned up, goading on her sons. In court, two witnesses stated that Mary Killcoyne started the fight by assaulting Matthews. Preferring to believe her and her father, the magistrates condemned the attackers as 'Three Dangerous Young Savages', sending each down for four months.

A bricklayers' labourer, Patrick Killcoyne's long journey to Birmingham exemplified the migration of many from Ireland's western counties of Roscommon and Mayo. Arriving in Liverpool, he met his wife; Mary, the oldest of seven daughters, was one of two born in Stourbridge on the edge of the Black Country; the next three were registered a few miles away in Bromsgrove; and the youngest pair were born in Birmingham. Mary did well in overcoming the disadvantages with which she was born. Despite the poverty of her parents and in defiance of living in an insanitary street haunted by sloggers, she found skilled work in the mostly male jewellery trade.[206]

Women were easy targets for bullying and abusive sloggers. On a Saturday night in September 1885, a drunken gang of youths swept the footpath of High Street, Saltley of every respectable person, using the most disgusting language to women. Rosanna Whale was one of them. John Allport went up to her, cursing that 'I've been watching you and your b– game.' Demanding sixpence from her so as not to say anything about it, he warned that if she didn't give it to him, he'd blow her brains out. Saying she had no money, he caught hold of her by the throat, hurting her so much with his fingernails that she screamed. A nearby householder heard one of the gang caution Allport, 'You b– fool, why don't you come away or else you'll be pinched.' They went off with the rest of the roughs, leaving their victim dishevelled with her hat on the ground. Fined 2s 6d for drunkenness, Allport must have been pleased that he only had to pay another 10s and costs for the assault. He'd get that from a whip-round from his mates. It can only be imagined what effect the attack and lenient sentence had on the unfortunate Whale. A hand press worker like so many young women in Birmingham's small metal goods trades, she was eighteen.[207]

Ada Berrow was two years younger when she was badly hurt in a slogging gang feud. One night in August 1892, sitting on a doorstep in a street close to the Bull Ring, she was chatting with a youth who'd given evidence against a local slogger. Half a dozen of his pals came up to them. Seventeen-year-old brass caster William Brown demanded to know whether the lad was in the slog the previous night. Although replying he wasn't, Brown threw a brick at him. It missed, hitting Berrow instead, knocking her out. Taken to hospital with a fractured skull, she developed a fever and was hospitalised for three weeks. Although admitting he threw the brick, Brown said he hadn't meant to hurt Berrow. In sentencing him to six months, the Recorder stated he'd have given an even heavier punishment if he thought there was intent to hit the girl. To cries of 'Hear, hear' from several members of the jury, he added that slogging gangs would never be put down till there was a flogging gang. His comments would have been little comfort to the poorly Berrow.[208]

Although the legal, social and economic positions of middle-class women were slowly improving in the later nineteenth century, life for poor women was harsh and they received little sympathy or support from either reporters or magistrates.

Infused with class bias, they regarded violence against poor women as their lot and attacks like those on Whale, Berrow and so many others elicited little notice. Classism was even more pronounced towards the girlfriends of peaky blinders, who were tainted by insulting terminology. Often slurred as 'molls' – women associating with low thieves, they were also degraded as 'donahs'. Originally slang for a disreputable woman, in 1870s Australia its usage changed, becoming the name for the girlfriend of a larrikin, one of a street gang. It was first noted relating to peaky blinders in 1896 when 'a singular duel' was reported between a fourteen-year-old 'lover' and his fifteen-year-old 'lass'. Headlined as 'Love's Young Dream' in one newspaper, the clash was reported facetiously. After a quarrel, 'the young lady challenged her quondam [former] lover to a duel to the death! The young lover promptly accepted the challenge, and they fought.' She wielded her hatpin, but his buckled belt proved superior and the fifteen-year-old 'Amazonian challenger was removed to the infirmary in a precarious condition'. The 'donah's' boyfriend was fined just 10s and his 'second' 6s for cutting open another girl's head with his buckled belt.

Such flippancy trivialised violence against women. According to the *Birmingham Mail* article, 'When the "peaky blinder" takes unto himself a wife the neighbourhood in which the parties reside generally know of it and look forward with pleasurable anticipation to the row which inevitably follows in the evening.' After one such wedding, attended by other members of the peaky's gang, they celebrated in a back house with bread and cheese and plenty of beer, paid for by all who had the honour of an invitation. After the meal, the bridegroom left his wife to enjoy herself with her female friends whilst he and his pals went to their favourite pub. Later that evening, 'the newly-fledged husband returned, and with the true instinct of a peaky kissed his wife, and then blackened her eyes, because she had mislaid his favourite buckled belt. The lady retaliated by striking her husband on the head with that useful adjunct of every household, the poker, and succeeded in nearly cracking his skull, after which she returned to her parents, who, after hearing of her ill treatment, went down, and "took it out" of the "blinder" in such a way that he has been in bed ever since attended by his forgiving wife.' This report finished with the supercilious comment that this little incident in the life of a peaky blinder was characteristic of the modes of matrimony among the lower classes of Birmingham.[209]

The relationship between peaky blinders and their girlfriends/wives was mocked in verse by the self-proclaimed 'peakie's poet'. This 'chevalier' (knight) lived well away from back-to-back Birmingham in pleasant, semi-rural, middle-class Sutton Coldfield and dubbed his disparaging poem, 'The Peakie's Bride':

Do I know Bella Blinder? I should rather think I did.
Why, old 'un, you are tryin' on a little bit o' kid.
Worn't I at her wedding when she married my pal Bill.
Lor' lumme we did 'ave a spree, a blow out and a fill.
Er's jist the sort o' gal yer know to stick up for a chap,
And fairly on the job she is at getting 'er own back.
Well I'll tell yer all about – I mean 'er wedding day.
For I was at the church, y'know, and give the gal away.
There was quite a party on us too, I couldn't name
     them all.

Hookey Smith, and Sally Jones, and Badger and Ted
    Ball.
Billy's father he was there, his Old Dutch too as well,
But Bella ain't got neither, it's a bad job for the gal.
Billy looked quite ikey, and was got up very smart,
As for Bella, why lor lumme, she could give 'em all a
    start.
And yer might have 'eard a pin drop, things was so
    very still,
When Billy popped the ring on, and Bella said, 'I will.'
An' didn't we just chuck the rice, and ease a boot or
    two.
One dropped on poor old Billy's head and made 'im
    look quite blue.
We 'ad the feed at Billy's 'ouse, I mean at his old man's,
Some brought him bits of presents, such as kettles,
    pots, and pans,
About a dozen on us set on the beef and beer,
Some 'ad to 'ave it on the stairs if they couldn't find a
    cheer [chair].
It was a bloomin' clinkin' spree, and when the booze
    got lower,
Billy parted like a trump, and set out for some more.
Teddy Ball was fairly on, and got in mess,
For 'e upset 'is blessed beer all over Bella's dress.
This led to words an' narsty knocks, an' ended up in a
    fight.
Then someone tapped poor Billy's nose and made
    Ted's eye a sight.
Then Bella seein' Teddy 'it, says, now I'll make things
    'um.

An' didn't she land right and left, an' show a bit o'
   Brum.
Do I know Bella Blinder? I think is what yer said;
I should rather think I ought to – feel the lump that's
   on my 'ead.

Commended sarcastically to theatres as 'Pantomimes are
coming on apace and the fair Belinda deserves to be
immortalised,' this 'little ditty' was a crass imitation of the
way Cockney characters were parodied in music halls. A
few of the words showed some awareness of how poorer
Brummies spoke, such as 'on' for of, 'um for home, clinkin
for really good, and ikey for a peaky dressed in his fashion.
Yet the use of 'o kid' for 'ar kid' (our kid) and the inclusion
of 'Cockney' music-hall speech like lumme, gal, jist and
Old Dutch emphasised the overall ignorance of the writer.
More disturbingly, this contemptuous 'poem' was written
in response to reports a few days before on the killing of his
girlfriend by a supposed peaky blinder.[210]

On Monday 14 November 1898, the *Birmingham Mail*
carried the headline, 'Tragic Death of a Birmingham Girl. A
Lover Charged with Manslaughter'. She was Emily Pimm, an
eighteen-year-old brass worker living in the Summer Lane
neighbourhood with her widowed father, a gun finisher, three
siblings and paternal grandmother. Her killer was eighteen-
year-old metal polisher James 'Jim' Harper from the same
street and a part-time soldier with the Militia. Standing a
little less than five feet three inches, the initials PEM and PIN
were tattooed on his left forearm along with the words 'True
Love'. Pem was the nickname for a woman called Emily and
Harper had been 'walking out' with Pimm until she broke it

off with him about ten weeks before her death. Her younger sister testified that since then, she'd been courting another chap but was frightened to leave the house on her own, fearful that the jealous and possessive Harper would 'catch her and set about her'. She was right to be afraid. On one occasion when her father sent her to fetch a jug of beer from the outdoor (off licence), he'd met her in her yard and kicked and punched her. Defending herself, she'd cracked the jug on his head, cutting it.

Not long after, she was walking along Summer Lane with Minnie Spalding who spotted the abuser and warned her, 'Mind, Pem, there's Harper.' They were both scared as he'd also assaulted Spalding because she wouldn't keep his company. Fearing what he might do, they ran off but were caught. In his rage, Harper punched Pimm and gave her 'a double kick, like they kick a football'. Bravely, Spalding told him to leave it off, but was herself hit. Then he struck Pimm. Falling, her head crashed against the kerb so hard that it seemed to shake the footpath. Still not satisfied with dishing out his punishment for turning him down, Harper stamped on her face three times with his heel. Pimm later told an older woman that he 'jumped on me and his boots come heavy on my head'. Army boots with metal tips on the heel and toes, they were heavy.

By now a crowd had gathered and someone shouted, 'You've killed her.' Harper ran off as the abused Pimm lay unconscious with blood gushing from her ears and nose. As she came to, the worried Spalding asked, 'Has he hurt you, Pem?' 'I think he's broke the drum of my ear,' she answered. Getting up, Pimm set off for home, but on the way fell into Spalding's arms as though in a fit. The next day, after explaining to her father she'd hurt herself falling, he told her to go to the hospital. She did with two other pals, but heading home, Harper confronted her. Terrified at what he might do, she looked like fainting. He threatened to give her some more if she didn't walk out with him and desperate to get rid of him, she promised she would the next night. At that, he said, 'I'm sorry for what I've done.' Yet like all abusive men, he justified his actions by blaming the woman: 'but you shouldn't have throwed the jug. If yer don't come I'll give yer some more the first time I meet yer.' He never got a chance to hurt her again as tragically, a couple of days after she was beaten, her father found her dead in bed. The postmortem revealed that her fractured skull and a blood clot resulted not from the fall but from a kick. Found guilty of manslaughter, Harper was sentenced to six years' penal servitude.[211]

The 'Summer Lane Kicking Case' attracted widespread publicity. Several newspapers affirmed that Harper belonged to the type of hooligans known in Birmingham as 'peaky perishers', deriving their name from 'their fighting propensities, and their peculiar style – bellbottomed trousers, small peaked cap, close cropped hair, and fantastic curl on the forehead'. Yet, he didn't fit this description at all. With unconscious irony, a Birmingham publication said he was of 'the respectable peaky class', something that didn't exist; whilst another stated his appearance was above the peaky class. Fair-haired and fresh-complexioned, in court he wore a grey tweed suit and not the peakies' bell-bottom trousers. Nor did he affect either the quiff or the new fashion of a donkey fringe, although he had a cap and grey checked neckerchief instead of a collar and tie. With no previous convictions, there's no evidence that Harper was a peaky blinder. As Andrew

Davies perceptively argued, though violence within courtship and marriage was far from universal, it was still customary and extended across the social classes; yet both gang membership and violence against women were denounced as problems of the 'slums'. That was made clear by a report declaring that whilst he was unmarried, Harper 'took a husband's precious privileges [according to the Summer Lane code] of violently thrashing her'. Though she objected, he treated her protests with lordly contempt. Nevertheless, Davies maintained, close inspection of the trial reports suggests that neither the perpetrator nor the victim conformed fully to the stereotypes applied to them of a gang member and his 'moll'. These stereotypes, however, performed 'an important ideological function, distancing the problem of violence from the mainstream of civic life and thus preserving the veneer of English civility, whilst masking the persistence of male violence within courtship as well as marriage'.

Descriptions of Summer Lane were as steeped in negative tropes about poorer neighbourhoods. Saturated with the prevalent racist attitudes and beliefs in eugenics and social imperialism, the *Birmingham Gazette* couldn't help thinking that 'Some of the excellent missionaries who risk their lives and spend an enormous amount of money in preaching Christianity to a casual Chinaman or Hindoo, might find the Summer Lane territory well worthy their attention.' Obsessed with the notion of urban degeneration, throughout the 1890s, the upper and middle classes looked down upon the poor as physically, morally and racially inferior. Not truly English, they were seen as a shorter, darker, noisier, more volatile and more violent people living in a nether world or abyss. Ignorant of the vital kinship, neighbourly and female networks in poor neighbourhoods, intrepid 'explorers' ventured into the strange, uncivilised 'dark continent' of 'Outcast London' especially, bringing back tales of depravity and deterioration to thrill and frighten a voyeuristic readership. These national fixations exacerbated the long-standing exclusion of Birmingham's poor from the city's political and civic life and their marginalisation in the workplace.

In detailing the 'peaky's courtship, a phase of Birmingham low life', the *Birmingham Mail*'s own 'intrepid explorer' to Summer Lane reflected deep-seated prejudices as well as the prevailing misogynistic attitudes towards poorer women. It was a notorious fact, he said, that the peaky's 'moll' measured her lover's affection by the number of blows she received, being a firm believer that 'a woman, a dog, a walnut tree, the more you beat them the better they'll be'. The undemonstrative lovemaking finding favour with ordinary young men and women did not suit the palate of the everyday peaky. He wanted something more exciting than kisses and caresses. To be able to decorate his 'moll's' physiognomy with a black eye added zest and variety to his love episode. And strange as it seemed, the lady was not averse to these displays of affection: 'If he don't knock you he don't love you,' said one young woman. A proud 'girl', she didn't care to be seen talking to another chap, as her 'man might come up and make it 'ot for the both of us'. Reassured that the reporter would make plain his mission if the peaky turned up, she expressed her willingness to talk of the methods of 'lovemaking' among the bell-bottomed fraternity.

'Yes,' she admitted, 'the perisher – if you like to call 'em that name – is a bit rough when he's very lovin.' He'll pinch you and punch you every time he walks out with you and if you speak to another chap, he don't mind kicking you. But still, that's only now and then, and it's all for love. No, I shouldn't like it as well if he didn't knock me about a bit. It's his way, and it makes you think of him when he's away. Why there's – [mentioning the name of a companion] – she's been a walkin' out with a chap I know and she's seldom if ever free from a bruise. At Christmas she always has a black eye or has got to go to the 'orspital. You know, her chap gets a drop to drink extra at that time and gets a bit rough and quarrelsome, like, but she never blows [tells] on him to the perlice. She don't go to the 'orspital if she can help it, as the doctors always want to know how she gets hurt. She never tells 'em the truth for fear she'd get her peaky into trouble.'

Continuing to emphasise the savagery of the uncivilised poor, the middle-class reporter noted that the peaky was an ardent lover, loving with all the fullness of his brutal nature and woe betide the rival attempting to supplant him in the affections of his 'donah'. Jealous to a degree, in such a circumstance it was desirable for a girl to leave the town or remove to another neighbourhood. Should she 'face it out', the probable consequence was 'a 'orspital job'. Taking the peaky's 'moll' as a whole, they were a long-suffering lot. Like a dog, the more kicks they had the more affectionate they became. Glorying in the scars adorning their lovers' closely cropped heads, they accepted every addition to them as evidence of the peaky's manliness. For his part, he regarded it as his lover's privilege to knock about the girl of his choice with kicks and blows.[212]

Without recordings, it's impossible to verify if the young woman's spoken words were as they were written. The reporter did indicate an awareness of Brummie speech with the spelling of ''orspital' for hospital and the use of chap and phrases like 'a-walkin' out', but her voice is strongly filtered through the prism of a middle-class man and his need to titillate his audience. That said, poorer working-class life was hard, physical, challenging and often violent. Alexander Patterson, a sympathetic observer writing of the Edwardian poor in Bermondsey, South London, was certain that most couples married for love but that a wedding ended all nudging and giggling. Poverty, ugliness and hard work were a taut strain on the marriage bond. It was pulled even more so by the grind of daily life, cramped, overcrowded and insanitary living conditions, and a lack of privacy.[213]

Assailed by want of every kind imaginable, tempers were frayed and fights were common, and whilst not acceptable at all to us today, a certain level of violence between husbands and wives was accepted in poorer neighbourhoods. Talking of his mother, my great uncle Wal Chinn told me that, 'Twenty-two black eyes the old girl had. She'd go up the pub, up the Duck Pen [where the married women sat] and her cronies used to look at her and say, "Blimey, Floss! You got another one?" "Ar." "Where'd you get that one from?" "Orf the old mon."' His older brother, Bill, was proud that their mother was tough: 'Her [she] could fight like a mon. When we lived in Queen Street, the woman that lived a little bit lower, her used to walk about and throw her chest out, you know. Went up one night, and mother . . . says this woman came out and said, "What a matter?" and one thing and another. The old lady put her fist up. Bump. Down her went.' On another occasion, my great-grandmother, Florence 'Brockton' Chinn, took on a gang in the George after they'd attacked her husband, a strong former soldier. Known locally as the

Wrexham, it was the same pub where the Cherry brothers were arrested after cleaving PC Blinko's skull.

> Tek anybody on. At the Wrexham, Dad'd bin to work one Saturday morning. He had his dinner then went up the Wrexham to have a drink. And he hadn't been out long when he come back and all his lip was a bleedin'. And the old girl says, 'Who's done that?'
>
> There used to be a gang in the Wrexham at that time, about seven or eight handed. Len Wells and Langford. So, Mom says to me, 'Come with me, son.' We went up to the Wrexham and when we got to the corner her opened the door and her looked in and her [beckoned]. This one bloke, there was two brothers in there, they was about seven handed in there. And this one brother 'as hit the old mon, he come to the door and he come onto the pavement and mother hit him. Bump. Down he went. And he wouldn't get up to have another one. And her went to the door again to pull his brother out. But he wouldn't come out when he could see what had happened. Her was never afraid of the old mon.[214]

Yet if a fighting woman was respected and if a certain level of violence between husband and wife was accepted, the extreme violence of many peaky blinders wasn't. What then attracted young women to them? The fashion was one thing and according to the *Birmingham Mail*, their own 'get-up' was similar to that of the peakies. There was the same lavish display of pearl buttons, 'the well developed fringe obscuring the whole of the forehead and descending nearly to her eyes, and the characteristic gaudy-coloured silk neckerchief covering her throat. Her head was hidden beneath an elaborate hat of considerable dimensions decorated with feathers and poppies.' This description is substantiated by rare working-class accounts. Bertram Hildick recalled that occasionally, peaky blinders would leave their usual haunts for a stroll with their girlfriends who had their special style of dress: 'large hats with wide, droopy brims and enormous feathers, great drop ear-rings and brightly-coloured scarves'. One couple in particular he often used to see walking out. She was plump, pretty, highly coloured and walked with her arms held out several inches from her hips. He was tall and strode along with the dignified air of a Guardsman but with his hands in his pockets and the back of his coat turned up. Now and then she would shriek with taunting laughter, and he would give her a powerful blow. But she seemed quite unhurt and would break out singing her favourite music-hall song, which she punctuated at the end of each line with a gasp.

A unique poorer working-class perspective was provided by Cecilia Costello. She stressed that, 'If we seen an ordinary man come down like you, we wouldn't dream of him looking at you – "Ain't he common?" and the woman as well. Ladylike with gloves on up to there, and her hat properly on. Whereas the girl with the Peaky Blinders, she'd have a great big hat on, and she'd have the bloke coming down the road with her. So they'd be singing:

My bloke's a Peaky, none the worse for that
He's got bell bottom trousers
and a Peaky Blinder's hat

Rings on his fingers and
round his neck a daff
So all you nosey parkers can take it out of that.'

A second verse in the English Folk Dance & Song Society's collection came from a Mrs Holden:

Never trust a Peaky an inch above your knee,
I've trusted one, and he's been the ruin of me,
He went away and left me with a babby on my knee,
My chap's a Peaky, Peaky Blinder.

Costello's memories highlight the appeal of the fashion, but undoubtedly, the fighting prowess of the peaky blinder was another attraction in a harsh environment where masculinity was valued. This gave status not only to him but also to his girlfriend. And as has been seen, some young women themselves were violent, attacking witnesses and assaulting the police. Others like Cullis and Williams joined in gang fights. In 1898, whilst noting that peaky blinders were a social plague spot, one commentator recognised that they were not confined to 'one sex, for as "Molls" their sisters too often go on the equally forbidding rampage, and are too often but "aiders and abettors" of their male companions of the street'. Mostly, as has been seen in Chapter 1, young women supplied stones for sloggers and peakies to throw, but there is some evidence of them joining in gang 'battles'. In early May 1897, police were sent to the Holloway Head district because of concerns of the resumption of hostilities between two local bands. Seeing the officers, the sloggers took to their heels. As they fled, they dropped a sword bayonet, whip, two heavy handcart handles and an iron bar loaded with lead. A few nights later, some of them again gathered for a fight. With them were about twenty girls, most of whom were armed with sticks. Once again, the police forestalled any violence.[215]

The outcry against the increase in crimes of violence in Birmingham reached a climax towards the end of the 1890s, with the manslaughter of PC Snipe, the murderous attack on PC Leach and the killing of Emily Pimm. Yet less deadly beatings of women drew only a little notice locally. As with Harper, there was no evidence that some of the abusers named as peakies in reports of assaults on girlfriends were peaky blinders. By contrast, twenty-year-old cycle worker Charles Beet was involved in 'a peaky's courtship'. Dressed in peaky-blinder fashion, he appeared in court in January 1899 for assaulting Emily Brown, a hinge maker.

She'd formerly kept company with him, but lately had resented his attentions. Determined not to be cast aside, he followed her about and then beat and kicked her. In the struggle, her hat came off, and he took it. Beet's defence relied upon justifying himself because of his wounded male pride:

It's like this. She has been a-going with me and promised to meet me on Saturday night at half-past seven. She dain't [didn't] turn up, and I never clapped eyes on her until Sunday afternoon, when I copped her with a soldier bloke. Says I, 'Do you want me or not' and she would not gie a straightforward answer.' Speaking vehemently he added, 'Do you think I was going to be made a fool of? . . . She made a fool of me. That's what sticks in me.

It was Beet's eleventh appearance, and saying he had no right to hit a woman who resented his attention, the magistrate gave him six weeks. Unimpressed, Beet warned his former girlfriend, 'I'll give you a bit more when I come out, and don't forget.' There's no evidence he carried out his threat.

Dennis Kennedy was another peaky blinder whose violence towards women gave 'sidelights into Birmingham's low life'. A habitual criminal, he did time for breaking into a shop with Billy Kimber, the peaky blinder who'd go on to lead the Birmingham Gang. Like Kimber, Kennedy was violent and a thief and in February 1900, he savagely assaulted eighteen-year-old brassworker Winifred Madden. In his defence, he said she'd slandered his mother and that he didn't strike her, only kicked her. Having previous convictions, he was given three months. He'd been out two nights when he came across Madden's older sister, Isabella. She accused him of calling her child a bastard, at which he attacked her with a file, inflicting several cuts needing to be stitched. When asked if she'd been keeping company with Madden, she answered, 'No; but he was always thick with the young man I walk out with. He always treated me well, I can't think what made him do it.' Annoyed and pointing to a thin red line down one side of his face, Kennedy responded angrily: 'Didn't you scratch me with a hair pin. And strike me with a hat pin?' indicating another scar between the eyebrows. Madden denied this, but then said she may have done. Feeling hard done by, Kennedy went on: 'May have done. She accused me of sending her sister to gaol for one month, gentlemen, and forgot that her sister gave me three.' Kennedy got another two months this time. Prison had no effect on him and in 1910 he was handed five years' penal servitude and five years' preventative detention for breaking into a counting house and stealing an iron safe and six stock books. He was twenty-eight. Winifred Madden was also a thief and at seventeen was one of 'the three graces' each receiving three months for stealing seventy-one yards of shirting from a shop. Already old offenders, they behaved impudently, going down the steps to the cells shouting and singing boisterously.

A month after Kennedy's assault on Isabella Madden, Caroline Bromwich was battered by eighteen-year-old polisher and peaky type Richard Burns. Though young, he was a menacing character having already served two stretches of a month each for assaults on constables. Bromwich kept company with him for a few weeks until she discovered he belonged to a gang. Meeting him on Hospital Street on a Saturday night in March 1900, she refused to have anything more to do with him. Infuriated, he knocked her down and kicked her about the legs, face and stomach. When arrested, Burns told the officer, 'It was a bad job he did not kill her.' He was sent down for three months for aggravated assault. Within weeks of his release, he was back inside for assaulting a constable. But Burns wasn't yet done. In November, he was handed two months for beating a man with a whip stock.

Marrying in May 1902, his wife soon left him and went to live with her sister and husband. Shortly before midnight on a Friday night in October 1903, Jessie Burns rushed into their bedroom and crawled under their bed, crying, 'He's a coming.' Immediately afterwards, they heard a noise at the door. The husband shouted out through the window, 'Who's there?' Burns called up, 'Is she here?' Told she was, he ordered, 'Turn her out.' Refusing, the husband went back to bed, but within minutes Burns burst through the door and ran upstairs into the bedroom looking for a fight. Fearful of what might happen, his sister-in-law pleaded, 'Oh, Dick, don't; think of my children.'

Going downstairs with a child in her arms, she was followed by her husband with a lighted lamp. Standing across from them in the tiny room and separated only by a table was Burns. Pulling a revolver from his pocket, he pointed it at his sister-in-law and fired, saying, 'I'll do for you.' Fortunately, the gun wasn't loaded, but when Burns was arrested it was found with five ball cartridges and one blank. Convicted of intent to do grievous bodily harm, he got only one month.[216]

RACIST ATTACKS

Girlfriends and wives were not the only women subjected to the fury of peaky blinders, so too were those in the Salvation Army. Beginning in 1865 on the streets of East London, this new Christian group abandoned traditional concepts to preach directly to the people. Such an egalitarian approach provoked antagonism both from senior figures in the hierarchical Church of England and well-known secularists opposed to what they saw as religious fanaticism. It also drew frenzied opposition from some working-class men aggrieved at the Salvation Army's message against drink, 'low theatres' and gambling. Emboldened, small local groups sometimes called 'skeleton armies' disrupted Salvation Army meetings by singing obscene versions of their songs, throwing rotten food and dead animals, daubing meeting halls with tar, breaking instruments and destroying flags. In many places, members of the Salvation Army were also physically attacked. Wearing a military-style uniform and gathering in groups, they were easy targets. Female Salvationists were more so as their radical equal status within the organisation incensed many men. In Birmingham, there was no need for a 'skeleton army'. Feeling they had a 'free hit' on Salvation Army soldiers, sloggers and peaky blinders were to the fore in assaults.

James 'Big Jonah' Jones, the manslaughterer, began his criminal career in 1884 when fined for using abusive language at the Salvation Army barracks in Porchester Street, Aston. Just before Christmas two years later, some of its female 'soldiers' passing along Summer Lane were insulted and assaulted by a gang. The only one arrested was seventeen-year-old caster George Hughes, who hit Mary Ann Stafford on the back with a stick. Although she was too scared to prosecute him, for what was deemed a most cowardly attack he was fined only 10s plus costs or fourteen days. Hughes was a nasty man who liked hurting women and in 1889, he was charged with brutally beating his wife, Mary. On the Saturday after Christmas, he'd fetched a dog home, threatening that if she let it escape, he'd kill her. Making sure that didn't happen, she tied up the dog and when Hughes came home drunk, she lay him on the sofa and put the dog in another room. Waking up a couple of hours later, he asked where the dog was. His wife picked up a lamp to show him, but he knocked it out of her hand smashing it. He then punched and kicked her, and dragged her along the floor by the hair. In court, the abused wife explained that he'd 'frequently beaten her when drunk, but she had forgiven him until it was impossible to do any longer'. After accusing his wife as the drunk, Hughes acknowledged he'd five previous convictions, but pleaded he'd been a teetotaller for eight months. Since then, he'd done no harm, but 'broke out' this Christmas and if he were given another chance he wouldn't offend again. After he agreed to sign the pledge giving up alcohol, the case was adjourned for a month when the temperance missionary would report upon his conduct. A 'penitent' Hughes left the court with his wife. It's not known if he kept his word.

The Salvation Army 'barracks' in Legge Street, Gosta Green was also besieged by youths who laid into 'soldiers' when they left. One of their victims was Sarah Smith. She 'was assailed so frequently that she had to seek an escort from the Army every night' and on one occasion was injured rather severely when struck with a stick. 'Hallelujah lass' Bella Donnelly was another who suffered for her beliefs. In the summer of 1887, the Floodgate Street Slogging Gang went to the 'barracks' intent on disrupting the meeting and so disgraceful was George Cane's conduct that he was ejected by Donnelly. He didn't go away, though, and instead waited outside to get his revenge. When she left, he beat her and made her nose bleed. That got him one month. An eighteen-year-old labourer, Cane and his gang later caused a row in the Sherbourne Concert Hall, Balsall Heath, breaking jugs and throwing them about the hall. A constable trying to stop them was knocked down. Behaving 'like a madman', Cane kicked him on the nose and called upon the rest to 'knife the –.' Thankfully, a sergeant arrived and Cane was thrown out. He was followed by the rest of the gang who threw stones, other missiles and a large piece of coal that hit the sergeant on the chest. This time Cane was sent down for two months.

One of the last peakies to be prosecuted for disturbing a Salvation Army service was Joseph Osborne, fined 10s or fourteen days in 1892. A nineteen-year-old labourer from Green Lanes, Small Heath, he had to pay up again, this time for 40s, as the only one of a gang arrested for attacking and kicking a man walking on the main Coventry Road late on a Friday night. Within days, he'd beaten up somebody else. Well known to the police as desperate and dangerous, in 1895 he did three months for assaulting a constable. Although married, he didn't support his family and by 1901 was living in a lodging house. One night, his wife, Amy, fetched him out of a pub but when she asked him for some money he kicked her. Sent down for two months, his wife was granted a separation order and he was ordered to pay her 8s a week. With convictions for the neglect of a child, vagrancy, drunkenness and theft, Osborne typified the bullying and abusive repulsiveness of so many peaky blinders.[217]

The disruption of Salvation Army services faded away with the nineteenth century, but the peakies quickly found other groups to persecute: Jews and Italians. Birmingham had a small Jewish community compared with Leeds, Manchester, Glasgow, Dublin and, of course, London, but it increased from the 1880s with Yiddish-speaking Ashkenazi Jews fleeing the pogroms in the Russian Empire. They settled in two small quarters: by the Grade II listed 'cathedral synagogue' at Singers Hill, close to the modern Mailbox and Cube; and at the upper end of Hurst Street, around what is now the National Trust Back-to-Back Museum on the corner of Inge Street, which became known locally as 'Little Jerusalem'.

Nationally, the large scale migration of these refugees from persecution aroused antisemitic diatribes. Reinforcing long-standing anti-Jewish prejudices infecting all classes, they provoked racist attacks in working-class areas on people like David Fiddler. Incorrectly named as a German Jew in the press, he was born in that part of Poland belonging to the

Russian Empire. A hawker aged twenty-three, he, another young man and a young woman lodged in cramped and overcrowded conditions in a two-bedroomed back-to-back in Inge Street with a tailor, his wife and their four children. Described as unoffending, in 1892, he fell afoul of two of Birmingham's worst and most dangerous peaky blinders: William Bayliss and David Cherry of the Barford Street Gang (see Chapter 1).

Early that year, the gang went in force to the George, a pub in Inge Street with a largely Jewish clientele. It was late on a Saturday night and though the door was locked the gang battered their way in. One man was hit over the head with a ginger-beer bottle and belted, and John Newport, a twenty-year-old brass caster, was given one month for the wounding. A reprehensible thug, he was later sent down for fracturing a man's skull with a pint glass.

Fiddler had the misfortune to be a witness in the case, cause enough for Bayliss, Cherry and a pal to form an intense hatred of him. After threatening they'd half murder him, they almost did. Coming across him on a February morning, Cherry grabbed him whilst the other two kicked him in the stomach. Bayliss followed up by striking him with his buckled belt. Menaced with serious injury if he gave evidence, the victim was so scared that he refused to identify his tormentors until the magistrates assured him, 'that the law in Birmingham was strong enough to protect foreigners, and if any attempt was made to continue the assault the Police should be communicated with'. Each of the assailants was handed two months. Unsurprisingly, Fiddler didn't stay in Birmingham.[218]

Older Jews were as likely to be racially abused and beaten.

In the summer of 1899, the *Jewish World* reported that two brothers, respectable Jewish shopkeepers, were charged with assaulting several youths with a buckled belt. In court, though, the evidence put quite another face on the incident. It was proved that a gang insulted and assaulted an elderly Jew as he was coming out of the synagogue. Remonstrating with them, one of the brothers was tripped up and kicked. Taking off his buckled belt, a rough was about to lash him when the other brother rushed up, seized the belt and 'dealt the cowardly rough such a blow that he had to be taken to the hospital'. The charges against the brothers were dismissed, and the slogger was fined with costs, with fourteen days if he didn't pay.

Jews living in the neighbourhood of the Singers Hill Synagogue were often waylaid and beaten by the local gang. One of them was 22-year-old Reuben Jacob. Like many others who'd fled from the Russian Empire, he and his family were tailors living in similar conditions to those described by one working-class Jewish Brummie of his grandparents: they had their 'workshop in the front of the house, they lived in the back, and slept in the bedroom on top' in what was remembered as 'a ghetto community'. Passing along the street in the summer of 1899, Jacob declined to give coppers (small coins) to three men demanding a 'toll' and was immediately hit over the head with a buckled belt. Frank North, 'a Thorp Street peaky', and one of his mates held their victim whilst he was struck repeatedly with the belt of the third attacker, cutting his head and face severely. A Jewish woman who witnessed the assault said they were shouting savagely, 'Kill the Jew.' Two of the youths were sent down for six weeks and two months respectively. It took a while to arrest North, who told the officer, 'I shall never wear the peaky's muffler any more.' In court he emphasised, 'I'm going to reform. I've had enough.' Denying he'd taken part in the beating, he was supported by the sworn evidence of some of his companions. Obviously fearful of what might happen to him, Jacob didn't press the charge so North was fined merely 20s and costs. Like Fiddler, Jacob disappeared from Birmingham.

Instead of showing concern for Jacob and other Jews attacked, the *Birmingham Mail* rejoiced at North's 'air of picturesque heroism'. Incorrectly assuming that 'Jew-baiting' was not a recognised recreation among the rowdies of Birmingham, it preferred to dwell upon the pathos of North's 'conversion'. Making his vow to change, he wiped a tear from the cuff of his well-worn jacket and his voice was tremulous with emotion when renouncing his badges of 'peakyism'. His apparently sincere change of heart was applauded: 'When the peaky forswears his muffler, neglects his donkey fringe, and becomes careless about the cut of his bell-bottomed garments, it is a welcome sign that he is on the way to respectability.'

Irrespective of the dramatic reporting, North did change his life. Unusually for a peaky blinder, he was the son of a butcher and went on to join the Army, serving in the Second South African War. As a reservist, he was called up to the Royal Warwickshire Regiment just before the First World War and went with the British Expeditionary Force to France. Aged thirty-one and married with five young children, he was wounded in the eye and knee by shrapnel at Ypres in April 1915.

William Lacey, the killer of Frederick Timbrell, was another slogger/peaky blinder who preyed upon Jews. In January 1902, he received two months for attempting to pick the pocket of a tailor's presser. He received the same sentence two years later for attacking a bookmaker's clerk, who appeared in court with his head bandaged and a dozen cuts to his face. Having refused to hand over money, Lacey swore he'd kill him and attacked him with a knife. With his own face bearing marks of severe ill treatment, Lacey said he'd been assaulted by three Jews. He wasn't believed. After then serving seven years' penal servitude for the manslaughter of Timbrell, in 1912 Lacey returned to a Birmingham no longer plagued by peaky blinders. They may have gone but still he was sullied by their violence and racism, for which Eli Jacobs suffered. A Birmingham-born electroplate worker, he was the son of tailors with his father from Poland and his mother from the Jewish area of Whitechapel in London. Back to his old bullying tricks, Lacey demanded money from Jacobs, who took no notice of him. Lacey again called for him to pay up and then hit Jacobs, who tried to defend himself. He was no match for a dirty street fighter like Lacey who bit the little finger on Jacob's left hand to the bone, bit his head and throat, and chewed a piece out of another finger. In the face of all the evidence against him, Lacey said that it was a fair fight and Jacobs injured his hands by knocking them on the ground during the struggle. The Recorder wasn't taken in. Announcing that his conduct was more like that of a brute than a man, he handed him four years' penal servitude. Whilst Lacey did his time, Jacobs fought for his country in the First World War, receiving both the British War Medal and Victory Medal. He continued to serve and in the Second World War was a First Aid volunteer with Air Raid Precautions.[219]

Late Victorian and Edwardian Birmingham was an overwhelmingly English city with a Jewish population at little more than 3,000. Although they numbered only a few hundred, apart from the Irish, Italians were the only other noticeable non-British community. The great majority of them were connected by a striking chain migration from villages in the Comino Valley, close to the town of Sora between Rome and Naples. Arriving from the late 1870s and getting by as street musicians and ice-cream sellers, they settled in that part of Bartholomew Street known as Catchem's Corner, where there was a large lodging house and back-to-backs. Now beside the modern Millennium Point and the planned HS2 station at Curzon Street, it was near to St Michael's Roman Catholic Church, which became known as the Italian church, and the Bull Ring outside market with its opportunities for street traders. By the 1880s, the city's small Italian Quarter had emerged as a distinctive locality with families bonded by their shared background but embedded in an English and Irish descent population.

Birmingham's Italians feature strongly in the *Peaky Blinders* series, with the Changretta Gang feuding with the Shelbys. However, as emphasised in *Peaky Blinders: The Real Story*, there was no such gang in Birmingham. Honourable, hard-working and law-abiding, the real Changretta family were nothing like their fictional namesakes. And in reality, the Italians of Birmingham were also subjected to racist attacks by real peaky blinders and sloggers. Living as they did on the edge of the Park Street Gang's territory, the Milk Street Gang's patch wasn't far away and nor were the sloggers of Gosta Green and the Gun Quarter. In the spring of 1886, one of these gangs attacked the big yard in the Italian Quarter where about twenty-five to thirty men lived with their wives and children. The local roughs took 'a special delight' in going there and insulting the Italians, but on one Sunday night things escalated into a serious affray. Wanting the intruders to go away, Giuseppe Delicata, the *padrone* (leader), placed his hands on the shoulder of a woman with the roughs. Fuming at this affront, they went off for reinforcements, returning with brick-ends and other missiles to smash up the Italians' property. Alerted to the danger, Delicata gathered his men at the top of the entry leading into the yard, where anything that could be thrown was hurled at them. Though suffering a few injuries, they succeeded in holding off the gang, one of whom was taken to hospital with a skull fractured by a brick-end, presumably thrown by his own gang. He was 22-year-old George 'Dodger' Lines. Scarred on his arms, hands and forehead, he was a habitual criminal who would later do seven years for larceny. Racist tropes were to the fore in the *Birmingham Mail*'s opinion piece on the attack on the big yard.

On several occasions during recent years, the Italians who colonise this neighbourhood have indulged in violent squabbles amongst themselves, and in most of these disputes the knife has played a more or less prominent part. Nor was it absent from the lawless scene last night, though it would appear from the newspaper report of it that the visitors from the sunny south, whose characteristic impetuosity and hot-headedness generally make them the aggressors, were this time themselves the object of aggression, and did not stand alone in the use the knife... One at least of the Italians last night found that the English rough is not above adopting the same cowardly method of warfare.

Altogether things appear to have been made pretty lively for a quarter of an hour. The latent lawlessness of both the rough clement and the Italians was fully roused, brickends being hurled about, skulls fractured, knives drawn and used, windows smashed, and other dangerous diversions indulged in; and the frequency of such rows in this neighbourhood would seem to require the adoption of special police precautions at exceptional times.

Knives may have been deemed as the 'national' weapon of the Italians, but it was one of them who suffered a large cut on his hand from a knife, whilst knife crime by sloggers and peaky blinders was rife.

Although not as populous as Summer Lane, Garrison Lane was another neighbourhood tormented by peaky blinders. Rising uphill from Great Barr Street, it was within the bounds of the feared Barr Street Gang. Others were drawn there to play pitch and toss and rough sports away from prying eyes on its expansive clay pits and brick works. According to the brick manufacturers, by 1902, there was 'such a state of terror and lawlessness as to constitute a scandal to the city. Every night, and Saturdays and Sundays, the place was a veritable pandemonium, the peaky blinder and the rough reigned supreme.'

Machinery was broken, clay wagons thrown into the pits, and enormous amounts of damage was done. On one occasion, the managing director of one brick firm found about fifty roughs pelting the huts and the pumping house. Seeing him, he became their target and he had to flee for his life. Garrison Lane was as dangerous for Italian barrel organ players.

A decade before, on a summer's night in 1891, Angelo Arpini, Giovanni Ledeso and Luciano Pecchia were playing their barrel organ outside a pub in Garrison Lane. As usual, a small crowd gathered, but finding that their music wasn't too well appreciated, they moved to another pub in a side street. The pickings there were even worse with only a ha'penny collected, but just as the three men made to head off, one of the crowd tried to take hold of the handle of the instrument and play it. Pushing the man away, Arpini started to walk off with his pals, but within a few yards a gang of about twenty attacked them. In self-defence, Arpini drew out a small penknife, stabbing someone in the hand or arm. Taking to his heels, he managed to get away, but his two friends were beaten with buckled belts, with such a violent blow striking Pecchia's head that trepanning was carried out on him after he was taken to hospital. His condition was so serious it was thought that he'd die, but fortunately, he recovered slowly. Two men were arrested for unlawful and malicious wounding, but both were discharged in separate trials because of a lack of evidence.

Thomas Macdonald was another racist thug. A 25-year-old labourer with a previous conviction for unlawful wounding, in 1907, he was one of a dozen men playing pitch and toss openly in a Summer Lane street. When two policemen came along, they ran off, but one man was caught. A large crowd gathered round and pushing his way through, Macdonald hit one of the policemen and urged an accomplice to get hold of him and kick his brains out. With the constable falling to the ground, Macdonald stepped back a few yards before taking a running kick at him. The officer was so badly injured that he was off work for months. Macdonald also attacked the other officer and was given nine months and six months for each charge of inflicting bodily harm. Two years later at midnight on a March Saturday, he and two others crossed over the road to beat up Angelo Castiluci, someone they'd never seen before. Insulting him, Macdonald punched him to the ground, where he was kicked so badly he had to be taken to hospital. Ethel Edwards was with the young man and said that before they attacked the men called out, 'Oh, Oh, Antonio.' This was a reference to a popular music hall song:

Oh, Oh Antonio, he's gone away.
Left me on my ownio, all on my ownio.
I'd like to see him and his new sweetheart,
and up would go Antonio and his ice cream cart.

When arrested, Macdonald remarked, 'Oh, is he an Italian? I thought he was a Jew. If I had known he was an Italian I would have killed him.' He was handed two months.

In the television drama, one other ethnic minority has a key role, not as victims of peaky blinders but as gang leaders, for the fictional Shelbys appear to be of Irish Romani descent. However, there is no evidence that men from this ethnic minority were either in Birmingham or notorious peaky blinders. Nor is there any evidence of the involvement of Irish Travellers in the real gangs as they didn't move to the city in significant numbers until the early 1960s. There were Romany Gypsies in the late nineteenth and early twentieth centuries, but far from being gangsters they strove to survive honestly whilst battling racism and social exclusion. The biggest group had their winter base at Black Patch Park, an inhospitable and desolate spot on the borders of Birmingham and Smethwick where the waste from nearby furnaces was dumped and through which the filthy Hockley Brook flowed. Having to cook on open fires and with no sanitation, most lived not in colourful vardos (caravans) but in transportable dome-shaped bender tents made of a sheet draped over arcs of hazel rods pushed into the ground. Though unfairly castigated as criminals simply because of who they were, the men and women of the Badgers, Davises, Claytons, Loveridges and other families earned their livings by dealing in horses, labouring, hawking pegs and fortune telling. Led by their 'king' and 'queen', Esau and Henty Smith, they were honourable people and many of their descendants remain in Birmingham. Forcibly evicted by the police in 1905, their camp was destroyed and they were made homeless. Charlie Chaplin was one of those believed to have been born on the Black Patch and in 2015, his son, Michael, unveiled a memorial there to the Romani Gypsies.[220]

THE LAST OF THE PEAKY BLINDERS

Macdonald was imprisoned during the Garrison Lane Vendetta that had erupted in the old Barr Street Gang's territory. The worst gang war in the city's history until a drug-driven feud in the late twentieth century, it pitted a hard man called Billy Beach and his pals against the Sheldons and their mates. At just over five feet six inches, well built and strong, Beach was remembered as always wearing a white silk scarf around his neck in the fashion of the peaky blinders' daff. A polite man who'd touch his hat to women, he was recalled as all right when he hadn't had a beer but a bit nasty if he had. With several convictions for assault, he was a 27-year-old tough when he fought 42-year-old John Sheldon in a straightener over a betting dispute early in 1908. Beach won but Sheldon wasn't going to let anyone best him. Scarred from previous fights on his forehead, under his left eye and on his left eyebrow, violence was a way of life to him, and he would do anything to get revenge. Several 'meetings' between the gangs caused 'considerable turbulence and disturbance' culminating on the afternoon of 21 June. It was unheard of for firearms to be used in gang battles in Birmingham, but shots were fired in Watery Lane, and it was said that two men had faced each other with revolvers like something out of the American Wild West. One of them was Beach. Though grazed on the neck, he refused to name anyone to the police, but proudly boasted he'd given his opponent a good thrashing and was well satisfied with taking the law into his own hands.

It's apparent that Sheldon was the beaten-up shooter. He'd now been bested twice and, enraged, his gang quickly sought vengeance. The next week, 46-year-old Charles 'Coaly' Jones and Beach shot at each other with intent to murder. Unlike Beach who was an industrious tube drawer, Jones was a thief and loafer. A foul man with convictions for assault on the police, in 1900 he was depicted as a jilted lover when he violently assaulted Florence Noke. They'd walked out but according to the press, she'd given him his *congé* (unceremonious dismissal). Aggrieved at this insult, on several occasions he kicked her, once so badly that she was fetched to hospital. Having just come out of prison, for this assault he was sent back inside for six months. Like the Sheldons, Jones always had back-up in a fight and there were two others with him at the shooting with Beach. All four of them were charged with a breach of the peace and were bound over to keep the peace. It didn't last.

At 2am on 1 January 1909 and after a night's drinking, Beach went to the door to empty the leaves from the teapot when he saw the Sheldon Gang coming into his yard. One of them said, 'That's him; there's the – on the steps.' A shot was fired at Beach and in defence, he flung a paraffin lamp at the group. A bullet then hit the back of his ear. Hearing a crash of glass, his wife ran upstairs to find it was smashed by another bullet which grazed her ten-year-old daughter's head. The child was crying, 'Oh, Mommy, something's 'it me.' She was so traumatised by this frightening event that her grandson was told that she slept with a lump hammer under her pillow for the rest of her life. Despite his injury, Beach ran into his enemies, hitting out with his fists as Sheldon belaboured him with a pickaxe. When asked in court if it was a free fight, Beach replied, 'If you call ten to one a free fight.' As this was going on, his wife ran to fetch the police and the Sheldon Gang ran away. The yard was a shambles with blood everywhere, and in the snow, officers came across a revolver with six spent cartridges, a pickaxe, a coal hammer covered with blood, another hammer and broken bottles. They also found one of the attackers unconscious on the ground, having been knocked out by Beach. Sheldon and Jones were arrested but Beach was set on vengeance. Five nights later, he was joined by Arthur 'Nugget' Morris, who'd done five years for the Watery Lane Affray, and nine or ten others.

Marching to Glover Street, they smashed their way into the house of Edward Pankhurst, a friend of Sheldon. Later known as Edward Banks, in 1921 he was the leading figure in the Birmingham Gang's Epsom Road Ambush on Jewish bookmakers. Brandishing revolvers, the gang demanded that Pankhurst's wife tell them where he was. Bluffing he was out, one of the men vowed, 'When we catch the – we will kill him.' Crossing the street, they violently knocked at Sheldon's house. Getting no response, they forced their way into Jones's neighbouring home. He was in bed with his wife. Shots were fired up the stairs and throwing up the bedroom window, she shouted, 'Murder,' at which another shot was fired, smashing a pane of glass. Hearing police whistles, the men ran off. Beach was arrested and on the way to the station, he said to Inspector Bennett:

> I wish Sheldon would fight me and settle it. It's killing me going on like this. The quarrel's between me and him, and I should like to fight him even if I get put through it. Sheldon always wants to win. He does not back losers and will win at any price. I sent a pal round to get the whole dispute settled but Sheldon only wanted me to apologise, which I would not do.

Whilst all the arrested men awaited trial, Beach was seriously assaulted by Jones in a melee in the Crown public house opposite Birmingham's Law Courts. Soon after, he was stabbed close to the Lock Up in Steelhouse Lane, probably by Joseph Sheldon. Refusing to 'grass', Beach declined to give any information to the police. However, hostilities ended with the imprisonment of the leading protagonists. Sheldon and Jones were each sent down for twelve months as was Morris, whilst Beach was handed eight months. Unhappily, the fighting flared up again after they were released. In September 1910, Beach was walking along a lonely part of a street when suddenly, he was surrounded by about fifteen to twenty men. Five had revolvers, including John and Joseph Sheldon, and Jones. Several shots were fired but with them missing him, Beach dashed through the crowd to get away. As he did so, he was struck on the shoulder with a large knife by Joseph Sheldon. Beach ran for a house with a man on the doorstep, but just before he got there the door was slammed in his face. Cornered, he turned round to fight as best he could with his raised fists. Slashed across the face twice by John Sheldon wielding an old sword bayonet, Beach suffered two bad wounds. One extending from the nose over the lips to the top of the chin cut right through to the bone, whilst the other was a cut to the wrist as he tried to ward off a blow. He was then struck on the head with a hammer and shot in the shoulder by Jones. Found almost unconscious by a constable, he was fetched to the General Hospital where he was treated for several weeks for a fractured skull and severe scalp wounds as well as the shoulder wound.

Found guilty of feloniously and unlawfully wounding with intent to kill, the judge emphasised that John Sheldon was the captain of the gang and that the murderous weapon of the old sword bayonet was found in his possession. Although Beach was as bad, Sheldon was a dangerous man and his brother, Joseph, had made himself a prominent member of the gang. Jones too was dangerous and had openly boasted that he would not work for his living. Each of them was sentenced to five years' penal servitude. The Sheldons were now severely weakened, even more so as throughout this time, Samuel Sheldon was serving five years for uttering (circulating) false coins.[221]

Beach was also soon back to prison. In January 1911, in a

drunken row with three women in a pub, he was found guilty of wounding them with a penknife. Before sentencing, Detective Inspector Moran said he'd known Beach for many years. He bore a good character from his employers, was honest, and fought only with his fists even though the Sheldons used weapons. Despite this, he was sent down for fourteen months. He came out of prison early in 1912, as did Samuel Sheldon. That signalled more trouble. Beach accused Sheldon of cutting him on the cheek with a chopper and others of stamping on him. In a tit for tat, Sheldon said he'd been assaulted by Beach. With no witnesses, it was a perplexing case and wasn't proceeded with, although the court was told that as Beach was going to Canada, the strife between gangs would end. He did go to Canada but that didn't end the Vendetta. Instead, it made national news after another shooting. In the autumn of 1912, in reporting on a serious wounding, the *Manchester Guardian* reported that people in Deritend and Bordesley lived in a state of terror, and it was impossible to persuade them to give evidence against the offenders.

Although Beach had emigrated, he'd left behind lieutenants and early in October, they went into the King's Arms pub in Great Barr Street, the main meeting place of the Sheldon Gang, and fought with Samuel Sheldon and Thomas Ingram, another violent man. A couple of days later, Charlie Franklin confronted Sheldon with a revolver, saying, 'I hear that you and Tommy Ingram are going to set about me. I have a shooter here and I thought about blowing your – brains out.' Sheldon wrestled the gun from Franklin, whose face was slashed by Ingram. Seeking revenge, Franklin went back into the pub later and shot at Ingram. The next night, at about 9.30pm, Franklin and three others confronted Samuel

Sheldon in the pub. He was drinking on his own as Ingram had just left. The ensuing fight again attracted national attention with the *News of the World* reporting that Charlie Connor warned another drinker, 'You had better clear out; it's going to be on.' Turning to Sheldon he said, 'Hello, Baggy. We've got you now.' Sheldon replied, 'You haven't come here for a row, have you?' At that, Connor hit him on the head with a metal cosh. As Sheldon fell forwards, Franklin fired two shots. One bullet went through Sheldon's billycock, and another struck him in the side of the head but didn't kill him. The four attackers then ran out, leaving Sheldon in a pool of blood on the ground before he was rushed to hospital.

His assailants were swiftly arrested and at their trial for intent to murder, Detective Collins spoke of the periodical outbreaks of shooting between the gangs, all of whom lived close to each other. He added, though, that the defendants had 'the best of characters as regards to their work'. Franklin, whose only previous offence was fourteen days for burglary, was imprisoned for ten years. Two others of Beach's Gang were given four and three years, respectively. Between them they'd just one conviction for obscene language. Connor, who had no previous convictions, was sentenced to five years, although on appeal it was reduced to three years for wounding. He wasn't unblemished. A few years before, he was found not guilty of intending to cause grievous bodily harm after he'd shot at a man. Described then by the police as 'a steady, sober and most respectable young man', on another occasion he'd been shot in the neck.[222]

So ended the notorious Garrison Lane Vendetta. It was also regarded by some as the end of the peaky blinders. It was. Pushed away from Birmingham by strong policing

305

and severe sentences, the most vicious peaky blinders like Kimber found easier pickings by pickpocketing punters and blackmailing bookmakers at racecourses, where there was little security and few policemen. Their story is told in *Peaky Blinders: The Aftermath*. As for those former peaky blinders who stayed in Birmingham, they were ageing men whose lives were transformed by the First World War. John Sheldon came out of prison amidst it. Like others, he found munitions work, as did his wife, Ada. In common with so many, they lost their jobs with the economic downturn soon after the coming of peace and Sheldon reverted to type. In 1919, he was given as a racecourse pest particularly known to the police when fined 40s for fleecing punters at the Derby races with a rigged game. He was fined the same amount in 1928 for operating another fixed game at a park in Smethwick. It was his last offence. He was sixty-two. Still living in a back-to-back in what had been the Barr Street Gang's patch, he was much older than the fictional Shelbys and unlike them, he was a petty criminal.

Sheldon's brother, Samuel, lived nearby. Aged fifty-three in 1921, he was making a meagre living as a hawker whilst his wife was out of work. A few years later, they moved to Charles Henry Street, once noted for its slogging gang. Having been one of the most feared men in Birmingham, he and his wife must have been struggling as they had two lodgers. The youngest brother, Joseph, did better. After his release, he also went into munitions work before joining the Mechanical Service Department Army Service Corps as a heavy lorry driver. He was almost thirty-eight and the father of a recently born boy. After serving in East Africa where there was fighting with German forces, he returned to his wife, Sarah, in Blake

Lane, Bordesley Green. Entitled to the Victory Medal and British War Medal, he was a different and better man to the peaky blinder he'd once been and made something of his life. Later working as a printer's labourer, he and his wife raised a hard-working and decent family. He died in 1950, followed seven years later by his beloved wife. Joseph Sheldon was one of the last who'd lived the life of a real peaky blinder.[223]

HISTORICAL REALITY

Myths and misconceptions abound about the real peaky blinders, the back-street hooligans in late Victorian and Edwardian Birmingham who didn't stitch disposable safety razor blades into the peaks of their flat caps and were not around in the 1920s. In their heyday between 1890 and 1905, they belonged to numerous back-street gangs and were motivated by fighting and not by making big money illegally. Contrary to the claims of some websites, there wasn't a single Peaky Blinder Gang operating as a well-organised criminal operation controlling protection rackets and illegal bookmaking and engaging in fraud, land grabs, smuggling and hijacking. The most powerful member of this non-existent gang is said to have been Thomas Gilbert, whose photo taken by the Birmingham Police in 1904 has been widely shared. But the notion that he was a major organised crime boss is ludicrous. Why? Because he was actually a cadger, taking small sums of money from folk who felt sorry for him because he'd lost his right leg below the knee.[224]

Aged thirty-seven, Gilbert was first mentioned in 1903 as a one-legged man who'd recently obtained money by false pretences. A publican gave him 2s after he said he'd lost his leg in an accident at Ansell's Brewery and that he'd been given £10 by Mr Ansell himself towards the cost of an artificial leg. It was all a lie, and with Gilbert having similarly tricked others before, he was sent down for a month. This would have been a gruelling experience for anyone, let alone someone who was physically disabled but it didn't deter Gilbert from his cadging. In October 1904, just over a year after his release, he was denigrated as a rogue who'd obtained money by taking advantage of the kindness of a poor couple in Ladywood. He'd told them that he'd been a barman until a poisoned foot meant that part of his right leg was amputated. Taken in by his story, the good-hearted husband and wife gave him 3s 6d to fetch his shirts out of the pawnshop. Coming back the next day, Gilbert said he'd found a job at an Aston brewery and was given food and another 10s to get his overcoat and suit out of pawn so that he could go to work decently clothed. In court, it was revealed that Gilbert had never worked for the brewery whilst a detective made it clear that he'd enjoyed a great run amongst poor people through spinning yarns to get them to subscribe towards paying for a cork leg. Disgusted by the way he was deceiving folk who had little, the magistrates sentenced him to three months – although they regretted they couldn't punish him more severely.[225]

The police photo of Gilbert in 1904 shows him looking nothing at all like a peaky blinder, with him wearing a suit, collar and tie. It also indicated that the second, third and fourth fingers on his left hand were missing. He appeared on a sheet with three other offenders, all of whom have also wrongly been named as prominent members of the non-existent Peaky Blinder Gang. One of them was Ernest Haynes, misnamed as Bayles on several websites. Wearing what looks like a decent quality suit including a waistcoat, he had a flat cap, but by then, this was the headgear of most working-class men and youths. Aged nineteen and a barman, he was sent down for two months for stealing a bicycle. That was his only offence. His accomplice in the theft, Henry 'Harry' Fowles, is next to him on the photo sheet. Another barman, also nineteen, he was handed one month as it was his first offence. Yet despite all the evidence he was a petty thief and not a major personality in an organised crime gang; he's been fancifully called 'Baby-faced Harry' as if he had something in common with the infamous American bank robber, gangster and murderer 'Baby Face Nelson'. A year after stealing the bike, Fowles was reported as a smartly dressed and intelligent-looking youth when sent down for another three months for an impudent fraud. As with Gilbert, he preyed upon the poor, obtaining money by pretending that he was a collector for the Birmingham General Dispensary, which provided basic medical services for a small annual fee. When arrested, Fowles had a book containing many names and addresses of those who'd handed him money. There was no doubt that he'd been carrying out his fraud for a long time and that he'd used his intelligence and education to lead a life of crime.

Although Fowles wore the peaky's choker, he had no convictions for violence, unlike his older brothers, George and Frederick. By 1901, George Fowles had numerous convictions for burglary, vagrancy, obstruction and the theft of goods like a piece of mutton, three cloth caps, twelve cigars and twelve cigarettes. That year, however, he became infamous as one of three peaky blinders guilty of the manslaughter of PC Gunter. Younger than George Fowles by two years, Frederick Fowles was nineteen in 1898 when convicted for two separate assaults and then in September 1900, he was arrested for housebreaking. Taken four years later, a police photo shows him wearing a daff with the close-cropped hair and donkey fringe of a peaky blinder. Described as the ringleader of a gang of thieves, he was sentenced to three years' penal servitude for having housebreaking instruments in his possession with no lawful excuse.

Frederick Fowles was a habitual criminal and in 1914 he was sent to prison for fifteen months for passing and possessing counterfeit coins. Yet he was another one-time peaky blinder who turned his life round for the better during the First World War. After his release from prison and living with his wife and daughter, he worked as a metal turner in munitions before joining the Worcestershire Regiment in 1916. Later attached to the 2/9th the Durham Light Infantry, in October 1916, Fowles went with his battalion to the Greek port of Salonika to guard buildings, bridges, transport stores and supplies. He was discharged as medically unfit for war service in March 1918 and awarded a gratuity of £10 down and £1 a week for fifty weeks. A peaky blinder transformed, his service for his country gave him the right to the Victory Medal and War Medal. On the evening of 22/23 November 1940, he was killed during the Blitz on Birmingham in the Second World War. His name is on the Roll of Honour of Birmingham citizens who died in the bombing of the city.[226]

The final man on the 1904 police photo sheet who was supposedly a major player in the imaginary Peaky Blinders gang was Stephen McNickle. Aged twenty-five, he was taken wearing a rough-looking jacket frayed on the end of one arm. Guilty of shopbreaking, he was given eight months. Five years previously, he went down for three months for unlawful wounding, the same charge he faced in 1906, when he claimed he'd only hit out because he was sneered at and that the victim's injuries were caused by his fall on the pavement. His plea was heeded. Treated leniently, he was fined 20s. McNickle got into no more trouble and having served in the Militia with the 3rd Battalion South Staffordshire Regiment, he joined up in October 1914 at the start of the First World War. Going on to serve with the 18th York and Lancaster Regiment, he was so badly wounded in the Ypres sector in September 1918 that his right arm was amputated. Later discharged as medically unfit for active service, he died in June 1920. His widow, Louisa, was left with seven children, four of whom were under fourteen. Her war pension of 33s 4d a week wasn't enough to keep her family but fortunately, her two oldest sons were in work.

One of the younger boys, Joe, married Lizzie Astle, the half-sister of the father of Ian Moseley, who remembered:

Their daughter, my cousin Maureen (who is sadly no longer with us), had exactly the same face as Stephen. In fact, it is quite uncanny . . . Joe unfortunately died of cancer while he was still young and Lizzie was remarried to a veteran of the Battle of Ypres who was always a dear uncle to me. But Joe's brother Horace McNickle lived into the 1980s and we have fond memories of him. He was a very upstanding man – married at Aston Parish Church during the last war and lifted off the beaches at Dunkirk, also later wounded in Italy. They

were a lovely family, and we think that Stephen got a
bad press, having only committed a minor offence and
was made an example of by the police.

Stephen McNickle has had bad press, undeservedly so. He
wasn't a major gangster but a poor working-class man who
fought and died for his country and left behind a fine family.[227]

Sensational stories about him and the other three as leading
figures in a non-existent Peaky Blinder Gang are just that –
unsubstantiated stories. The real peaky blinders weren't an
organised crime gang. Nor, as has been claimed, did they wear
tailored suits with wealthier members boasting silk scarves
and starched collars with metal tie buttons, whilst their wives
and girlfriends weren't known for wearing lavish clothing
with pearls, silks and colourful scarves. This spurious Peaky
Blinder Gang didn't fight the 'Birmingham Boys' and having
lost out, didn't move to the countryside. Only one former real
peaky blinder became involved in organised crime and made
a lot of money. He was Billy Kimber. Unlike so many other
peakies, he deserted in the First World War, after which he led
his Birmingham Gang into a war with the Sabinis. Defeated,
his gang of former peaky blinders and sloggers gradually
disintegrated. None of them became wealthy, unlike Kimber
who became a racecourse bookmaker living in Torquay.

Alfred Stevens captured the feelings of many relatives of
the worst real peaky blinders, emphasising that 'they weren't
good people to know'. And he knew because his mother
was the daughter of Arthur Gardner, a violent rogue who
abandoned his wife to live as a travelling thief. The son of a
gun finisher and purportedly a gun polisher, he was a habitual
criminal. With previous convictions for assault and jostling

people in queues to pick their pockets, in 1907 he was put inside for eighteen months for thieving pennies from a gas meter in a poor person's house. He followed this up with stretches for housebreaking and failing to report for police supervision. Then in 1917, he was handed four years' penal servitude for actual bodily harm. A deserter from the Army, after refusing to pay for his drinks in a pub, he threw glasses at the publican, with two smashing in his face and cutting his right eye very badly. Attacking someone else in 1924, he served another two months. He then left Birmingham. The family were told that 'there was a murder around a bridge at the top of Sparkbrook/Bordesley towards the Blues ground and that's when he vanished'. His disappearing act was to America. After a few years away, he returned and in 1938 was given three months for loitering with intent to commit a crime (pickpocketing) at Bromford Bridge racecourse on the outskirts of Birmingham. In court, it was revealed that he'd been deported from the USA and a list was read out of his numerous convictions for theft and pickpocketing whilst he was there. Suntanned, unshaven and unfazed, he boasted, 'Those weren't crimes. They were drunken feats.' A persistent pickpocket, he was back in prison a year later for loitering with intent at Wolverhampton Racecourse.

Gardner married Minnie Smith in 1913. Both were living in Great Barr Street, in the midst of the territory of the Barr Street and Sheldon gangs. She didn't see much of him because of his time spent inside and on the road thieving. With little or no support from him, she must have had it rough raising a family on her own. But she did so successfully, working as a soft solderer and taking in lodgers. After coming back from the USA, occasionally Gardner would land at his daughter's house, visits that his grandson loathed, telling his own granddaughter Lucy Scott that 'he HATED him, said he stank and used to beat him up. He wasn't a very nice man, he was almost "snubbed" and even on his death certificate it says occupation unknown because no one really connected with him, and his own daughter was only doing her duty.'[228]

Living a miserable life, Gardner made the lives of others a misery. That was the reality for too many peaky blinders. They weren't anti-heroes to be looked upon with respect and envy. One day, perhaps, a film or television series may be made not about glamorised, mafia-style gangsters but about the real heroes of the back streets: women. Women like Minnie Gardner and my great-grandmother, Ada Derrick, who endured years of abuse from my great-grandfather, Edward Derrick, another petty thieving and violent peaky blinder. She fed and clothed her daughter with her earnings as a solderer and with the support of her mother and sisters living in the same street. Resenting her, he'd come home drunk, smash up the furniture, punch her about and threaten to kill her. Somehow, she found the strength to break away from him and forge a new life for herself and her daughter with a better man. This book is dedicated to women like her and Minnie Gardner, women like Mary Killcoyne and Polly Mullins who bravely gave evidence against sloggers and peaky blinders, and the countless back-street women who strove for decency against poverty, male violence and a class-biased society, hoping one day that their children and grandchildren would have a better life with days to come and not just a day to get through.

ENDNOTES

INTRODUCTION: BEST-GOVERNED CITY IN THE WORLD & CITY OF PEAKY BLINDERS

1   Carl Chinn Bookmaking Archive, US39, Cadbury Research Library, University of Birmingham, & Carl Chinn, *Better Betting with a Decent Feller. Bookmakers, Betting, and the British Working Class* (1992), pp. 199–206.

2   A. W. W. Dale, *Life of R. W. Dale of Birmingham* (1899) p. 412; Julian Ralph, 'The best governed city in the world', *Harper's New Monthly Magazine*, 81 (June 1890); & George Dawson speech, 'Opening of the Reference Library', *BP* (27 October 1866).

3   'The New Municipal Buildings. Laying the foundation stone by the mayor', *BM* (17 June 1874); Joseph Chamberlain to Jesse Collings (6 June 1876); Chamberlain Papers, JC 5/16/54; & Chamberlain to the town council, in John Thackray Bunce, *History of the Corporation of Birmingham*, vol. 2 (1885) p. 465.

4   Carl Chinn, *Homes for People. Council Housing and Urban Renewal in Birmingham, 1849–1999* (1999) pp. 1–32; V. W. Garratt, p. 3; *A Man in the Street* (1939); 1901 Census, TNA, RG 134, Piece 2832, Folio 58, p. 11; & Kathleen Dayus, *Her People* (1982) pp. 3–4.

317

5   J. C. Walters, 'No. 1. A First Glance Around', *Scenes in Slumland. Pen Pictures of the Black Spots in Birmingham* (1901) p. 3 & T. J. Bass, *Down East Amongst the Poorest* (1904) p. 22.

6   Wallace, Edgar. 'Plight of Birmingham's Idle Thousands', *Daily Mail*, 23 December 1903, p. 5. Daily Mail Historical Archive, link.gale. com/apps/doc/EE1862904059/GDCS?u=bham_uk&sid=bookmark-GDCS&xid=1c282614. Accessed 25 October 2023.

7   City of Birmingham Health Department, *Annual Report of the Medical Officer of Health* (1899) p. 8, & *Report of Medical Officer of Health, the Floodgate Street Area* (1904) pp. 7–8.

8   https://www.sundayworld.com/crime/world-crime/ex-new-york-mafia-boss-says-cillian-murphy-perfect-mob-guy-in-peaky-blinders-role/1152211799.html Accessed 28 October 2023.

9   'Ukraine's 'Peaky Blinders' drone unit defending the north-east frontline https://www.bbc.co.uk/programmes/p0j0g4bj;

10   'The Arrested Man in Birmingham', *BM* (21 October 1898); 'The Origin of Slang', *Folkestone Express, Sandgate, Shorncliffe & Hythe Advertiser* (14 October 1899); FB, 'Peaky Blinders', *Huddersfield Daily Examiner* (11 May 1966); 'The Romance of Words', *Devizes and Wilts Advertiser* (5 October 1899); 'Table Talk', *BM* (26 February 1898); & Carl Chinn, *Peaky Blinders: The Real Story* (2019) pp. 67–72.

11   'Crown Court', *BP* (15 December 1897); Advertisements, *BM* (18 April 1885, 14 March 1889, & 8 March & 18 June 1890); Tom Golding, *The Brum We Knew* (no date) p. 13; 'The Peakies Bride', *BM* (26 November 1898); & Charles E. B. Russell, *Manchester Boys: Sketches of Manchester Lads at Work and Play* (first published 1905, 1984 reprint) p. 16.

12   '"The Peaky Blinders" What the Adult School Does for Them', *Batley Reporter and Guardian* (6 July 1906); F. Atkins, 'Letter', *BWP* (3 April 1936); & Arthur L. Matthison, *Less Paint, More Vanity* (1937), pp. 62–3. See also Garratt, *op. cit.*, pp. 65–6.

13   Ex-Detective Superintendent W. J. May, 'It was a tough spot in those days', *ED* (15 October 1936).

ENDNOTES

14 Arthur Morrison, 'Hooliganism', *The Pall Mall Magazine*, Vol. 23, Is. 94, (Feb 1901); 'Hooliganism', *Justice* (20 August 1898); 'Suppression of the Rough', *BM* (28 October 1898); *Portsmouth Evening News* (30 August 1899); 'Hooligans Abroad', *Manchester Evening News* (6 November 1908); 'Riot in Birmingham by the "Slogging Gang"', *BM* (8 April 1872); Slog, *V. Oxford English Dictionary*, Oxford UP, September 2023, https://doi.org/10.1093/OED/5133516336; & Carl Chinn, *The Real Story*, pp. 13–31.

15 T. E. Page, 'The Police of Birmingham', *The Times*, 26 November 1877, p. 10. The Times Digital Archive, link.gale.com/apps/doc/CS168606074/TTDA?u=bham_uk&sid=bookmark-TTDA&xid=a9f06731. Accessed 23 October 2023; 'Crimes of Violence in Birmingham', *BM* (27 November 1877); & 'News of the Day', *BP* (15 February 1876).

16 R. Dudley Baxter, 'Personal Ratepaying', *The Times*, 8 April 1867, p. 5. The Times Digital Archive, link.gale.com/apps/doc/CS85107848/TTDA?u=bham_uk&sid=bookmark-TTDA&xid=fa291ac0.

17 C. A. Vince, *History of the Corporation of Birmingham, Volume 3* (1902) p. 226.

18 'Notes and Comments' & 'Brummagem Beauties', *Sheffield Daily Telegraph* (10 June 1882 & 29 July 1897); *The Wellington Journal & Shrewsbury News* (26 August 1899); & 'Topics of the Day', *Coventry Evening Telegraph* (11 October 1895).

19 'Street Ruffianism', *Globe* (21 January 1899).

20 *BG* (13 September 1905); 'Street Ruffianism in Birmingham', *BM* (1 May 1908); 'Night Adventure', *BG* (19 November 1912); 'The Disappearance of Tramps', *BM* (4 December 1915); Jon Wilks·Tradfolk 101 (8 March 2022); & http://www.planetslade.com/broadside-ballads-peaky-blinder.html); Chinn, *The Real Story*, pp. 141–3; & Carl Chinn, *Peaky Blinders: The Legacy* (2020), pp. 34–47.

21 See, for example, Sangimino, Marissa. 'Rewriting the Mafioso: The Gangster Hero in the Work of Puzo, Coppola, and Rimanelli', Boston College, 2015. http://hdl.handle.net/2345/bc-ir:104214 Accessed 26 October 2023.

22   Louise Mellor, 'Steven Knight Interview', https://peakyblinders.tv/
exclusive/steven-knight-interview/ Accessed 27 October 2023;'More
Persecution of Witnesses', *BP* (19 July 1875); 'Intimidation of Witnesses.
Police Protection Needed', *BM* (1 December 1898).

23   'The Peaky Blinder', *BG* (9 May 1929).

CHAPTER 1: CONSTABLE BAITING

24   Walters, 'No. 1. A First Glance Around' & 'No. 2. A Second Glance
Around', *op. cit.*, pp. 4–5 & Rev. T. J. Bass, *Tragedies of Life – A Fragment of
Today* (1903) p. 69.

25   'A Cheltenham Man Injured', *Cheltenham Chronicle* (30 April 1898) &
'Childhood at Play in the Birmingham Slums', *Empire News & The Umpire*
(31 August 1902).

26   'Murderous Attack on a Constable', *BP* (18 May 1898); & *BG* (21
January 1908); & 'Alleged Outrage by a Slogging Gang', *BP* (10 October
1895).

27   'Sentences', 'A Fitter's Revenge', *BM* (9 October 1901) & 'Major Bond in
Trouble', *B&AC* (16 June 1894).

28   WMP Record, '6735, Leach, Herbert' (1922) & 'Birmingham Watch
Committee', *BP* (11 May 1898); 'Ruffianism in Birmingham', *BM* (1 May
1908).

29   See Geoffrey Alan Foy, 'Policing Birmingham. A Study of a Borough
Police Force, 1839–1914' (University of Birmingham M.Phil., 1997).

30   'A Batch of Gamblers', *BM* (12 May 1868); 'A Gang of Gamblers', *ABG*
(30 September 1865); 'Gambling in a Churchyard' & 'The Police Running
the Blockade', *BM* (3 May & 15 May 1871).

31   1881 Census, Class RG 11, Piece 1040, Folio 10, P. 16; 'A Riot' & 'A
Case of Mistaken Identity', *BP* (4 May & 5 July 1871); 'Violent Assault',
BM (22 June 1872); 'Another Alleged Robbery with Violence', *BM* (20
December 1873); & 'Violent Assault on a Policeman in Weaman Street',
BM (21 April 1875).

32   Bunce, *op. cit.*, p. 300; Barbara Weinberger, 'Law Breakers and Law
Enforcers in the Late Victorian city: Birmingham 1867–1877'.

ENDNOTES

33 'Young Rioters Well Punished', *BP* (9 April 1872) & Weinberger, *op. cit.,* p. 125.

34 1881 Census, TNA, Class RG 11, Piece 2152, Folio 107, p. 23 & 1861 Census, TNA, Class RG 9, Piece 2155, Folio 108, p. 8.

35 'A Warning to Birmingham Roughs', *BP* (25 March 1873); & 1871 Census, TNA, Class RG 10, Piece 3115, Folio 43, p. 24.

36 'News of the Day', & 'Brutal Assaults on Birmingham Policemen', *BP* (25 March 1873 & 23 June 1874).

37 Bunce, *op. cit.,* p. 294; & Weinberger, *op. cit.,* p. 77.

38 'The Watch Committee', *BG,* (8 May 1867); & *The Town Crier* (September 1874).

39 *BP,* 4 May 1872.

40 'News of the Day', 'Ruffianism in Birmingham. Dastardly Assaults', & 'A Caution to Street Roughs', *BP* (11 April 1873, 24 June & 18 October 1873).

41 1871 Census, TNA, Class RG 10, Piece 3102, Folio 69, p. 8; & 'A Riot in Navigation Street', *BP* (13 March 1873).

42 'The Birmingham Roughs on Saturday Night', *BM* (30 June 1873).

43 Gooderson, *op. cit.,* pp. 63–4.

44 'Forty Years of Prison Life. Experiences of Charles Reade's Warder Evans related by Himself. Chapter X, The Last of the Birmingham Roughs', *Nottinghamshire Guardian* (8 February 1896) & 'The Navigation Street Murder', *BG* (29 March 1875).

45 Will Thorne, *My Life's Battles* (1925) pp. 13–29.

46 1861 Census, TNA, Class RG 9, Piece 2243, Folio 104, p. 9; William Lines & Elizabeth Barrett, Leamington Hastings, Warwickshire, Marriage 12 October 1864; Birmingham City Police Ledgers, 'Warrant 4107 William Lines'; 'Affray Between Policemen and Housebreakers', *BP* (6 November 1865); 'Assaulting the Police', *BM* (16 November 1871); 'The Navigation Street Riot. Death of Police-Constable Lines,' *BP* (25 March 1875); 'A Dangerous Character', *BP* (2 April 1872); 'Discontent in the Birmingham Police Force', *BP* (8 February 1875); & 'The Birmingham Police Force', *BM* (13 January 1875).

47   'RIOT IN BIRMINGHAM. A disgraceful riot', *The Times*, 8
March 1875, p. 7. The Times Digital Archive, link.gale.com/apps/doc/
CS119059560/TTDA?u=bham_uk&sid=bookmark-TTDA&xid=c984b1ff.
Accessed 14 November 2023; 1851 Census, TNA, HO 107, Piece 3112,
Folio 23, p. 12; & 'Two Policemen Stabbed', *BM* (8 March 1875).

48   'The Outrage in Navigation Street. Depositions of Policeman Lines',
BP (15 March 1875).

49   'The Navigation Street Stabbing Case', *BG* (15 March 1875); 'Two
Policemen Stabbed', *BM* (8 March 1875); & 'The Navigation Street Riot.
Death of Police Constable Lines', *BP* (25 March 1875).

50   'The Murder of a Policeman', *IPN* (31 July 1875); 'The Wake', *BG*
(28 July 1875); HO 140, Birmingham Court (21 April 1873); &
Birmingham Gaol, Warwickshire: Habitual Criminals Register
(11 April 1874).

51   'The Navigation Street Murder. Inquest and Verdict of the Jury', *BG*
(29 March 1875).

52   'The Execution of Corkery', *BG* (28 July 1875).

53   'Table Talk', *BM* (24 & 31 July 1875).

54   HO 140, Birmingham Court (10 July 1875); 1871 Census, TNA,
Class RG 10, Piece 3102, Folio 101, p. 30; 'The Navigation Street Murder.
Magisterial Proceedings', *BG* (31 March 1875); 'The Navigation Street Riot',
BP (12 July 1875); & 'The Navigation Street Riot. Sentence of the Rioters',
BM (12 July 1875).

55   1861 Census, TNA, Class RG 9, Piece 2139, Folio 53, p. 1; 'The
Navigation Street Murder. Inquest and Verdict of the Jury', *BG* (29 March
1875); 'Release of Birmingham Criminals', *BM* (12 January 1886); 'Murder
of PC Lines', *BWP* (27 May 1955); & Carl Chinn, *Peaky Blinders: The
Aftermath* (2021) pp. 253–54.

56   'The Inquest on Police-Constable Lines', *BM* (29 March 1875) &
'The Navigation Street Outrage. Alleged Threats Against Witnesses', 'The
Alleged Intimidation of Witnesses in the Navigation Street Murder Case', &
'Threatening A Witness', *BM* (29 March, 1 April & 8 October 1875).

ENDNOTES

57   1871 Census, TNA, Class RG 10, Piece 3112, Folio, 20, p. 5; & 'Intimidating A Witness in Police Constable Lines's Case', *BM* (15 & 16 June 1875).

58   'Promising Juveniles', *BM* (21 February 1876); 'Inciting to Stab', *BG* (22 July 1875); & HO 140, Birmingham Court (8 April 1876).

59   'Birmingham Watch Committee', *BM* (15 June 1875) & *BG* (15 July 1875); 'News of the Day', *BP* (15 February 1876); 1871 Census, TNA, Class RG 10, Piece 3114, Folio 87, p. 16; & 1841 Census, TNA, HO107, Book 1, Folio number 15, p. 22.

60   1861 Census, TNA, Class RG 9, Piece 2153, Folio 87, p. 19; 1871 Census, TNA, Class RG 10, Piece 3106, Folio 100, p. 25; 'Riotous Proceedings in Lionel Street', *BP* (17 April 1876); 'A Street Riot', *BP* (17 April 1876); & 1881 Census, TNA, Class RG 11, Piece 2986, Folio 103, p. 51.

61   HO 140, Birmingham Court (15 April 1875); 'Birmingham Quarter Sessions', *BP* (7 April 1877); 'Disgraceful Assaults on the Police', *BM* (28 May 1877); & 'The Assault on Police-Constable', *BP* (10 August 1878).

62   Carl Chinn, "'Sturdy Catholic emigrants": the Irish in early Victorian Birmingham', in Roger Swift and Sheridan Gilley (eds), *The Irish in Victorian Britain: The Local Dimension* (1999) pp. 62–4.

63   'The Howard Place Riot', *BM* (10 August 1878); 'The Serious Charge of Assaulting the Police', *BP* (26 June 1878); 'Violence in the Streets', *BP* (20 May 1878); 'Savage Assault on Birmingham Policemen', *BP* (7 August 1878).

64   HO 140, Birmingham Gaol (12 April 1876); 1861 Census, TNA, Class RG 9, Piece 2150, Folio 94, p. 42; HO 140, 'Birmingham Gaol' (6 August 1878); 'Robbery With Violence – An Extraordinary Story', BP (13 May 1884);'Flogging Garroters', *BP* (29 December 1870); 'Flogging at Warwick Gaol', *BM* (20 May 1884); & MEPO6, Birmingham (1889).

65   1881 Census, TNA, Class RG 11, Piece 2979, Folio 73, p. 7; HO 140, 'Birmingham Gaol' (6 August 1878); & WMPP, West Midlands Criminal Registers (25 September 1911).

66 'Report of the Watch Committee', *BG* (4 August 1880); 'Assault' *BP* (24 February 1880); 'Sunday Gambling', *BP* (9 August 1880); & 'Sunday Gambling at Aston', *BP* (28 April 1885).

67 SUNDAY AFTERNOON DIVERSIONS IN BIRMINGHAM: A DISGRACEFUL SCENE. (1891, 31 March). *The Manchester Guardian* (1828–1900) Retrieved from https://www.proquest.com/ historical-newspapers/sunday-afternoon-diversions-birmingham/ docview/482886036/se-2.

68 Vince, *op. cit.*, pp. 218–20 & p. 232.

69 'Savage Attack Upon a Policeman', *BP* (31 August 1887).

70 'A Terror to the Neighbourhood', *BM* (29 October 1873); 'A Caution to Ruffians', *BP* (31 July 1889); 'Slogging in Kenyon Street', *BP* (5 November 1895); 'Balsall Heath Local Board', *Birmingham Journal* (5 May 1866); 'One Who Pays Taxes', *BP* (20 November 1879); 1881 Census, TNA, Class RG 11, Piece 3015, Folio 39, p. 18; 'Savage Assault on the Police at Balsall Heath', *BM* (27 January 1888); HO 140 (31 July 1891); & 'Savage Assault upon the Police' & 'Punishment Richly Deserved', *BST* (3 November 1888).

71 'Ruffianism in Balsall Heath', *BP* (3 December 1889); 'Ruffianism at Balsall Heath', *BST* (16 February 1889); '"Sloggers" Again', *BM* (9 May 1890); 'Moseley. The Highgate Slogging Gang', *BST* (10 May 1890); 'A Midland Savage', *Northern Guardian* (Hartlepool) (14 December 1895); & BCP, QS/B/20/72 (29 October 1907),

72 'Punishing Street Ruffians' & 'The Slogging Gang Again', *BP* (12 April 1890 & 10 May 1890); 'Assaulting the Police', *WH* (18 September 1890); 'Street Ruffianism', *BP* (1 August 1891); BCP, QS/B/20/121 (30 October 1903); MEPO6 (29 July 1891 & 10 April 1894); 'A Serious Stabbing Case', *BP* (26 January 1894); & 'A Christmas Night Stabbing Affray', *BM* (10 April 1894).

73 'The Sparkbrook Slogging Gang', *BM* & *BP* (21 March & 10 April 1890); 'How to Deal with Ruffians', *BM* (14 June 1889); & BCP, QS/B/20/69 (16 January 1894).

74 MEPO6 (16 January 1894); 'Alleged Fowl Stealing at Solihull Lodge', *BST* (20 October 1894); Library of Birmingham, Carl Chinn Collection MS1902, Interview William Chinn (16 October 1979); 'Unprovoked

ENDNOTES

Assault', *BP* (21 March 1893); 'A Cowardly Ruffian', *BM* (28 October 1891); 'The Consequences of Jealousy', *BM* (24 November 1894); 'Alleged Stabbing a Wife', *BM* (20 August 1881); & 1891 Census, TNA, Class RG 12, Piece 2395, Folio 87, p. 5.

75   'Breach of the Peace', *BST* (3 August 1889); 'Balsall Heath Police Court Yesterday', *BP* (14 February 1891); *Kelly's Directory of Birmingham* (1890), pp. 1850–51; 'Deritend Model Tavern', *ED* (20 June 1903); 'Military Funeral at Colchester', *Chelmsford Chronicle* (5 January 1900); Carl Chinn, 'Black Country Memories: Black Country Irish', *Express and Star* (14, 21 and 28 May 2009); 'The Perils of the Police', *BM* (12 June 1871); & Chinn, *The Real Story*, pp. 5–9.

76   'The "Slogging Gangs" and How They Were Broken Up', *BWP* (10 February 1900); & Library of Birmingham, Carl Chinn Collection MS1902, Lilian Perry née Wood Interview & George Wood Interview (15 November 1984 & 8 March 1986).

77   'Jim Brown Remembers When Birmingham was a Cesspool of Crime and Vice', *BWM* (13 March 1949); 'The Old Pleck', *BM* (7 May 1890); & 'Anti-Compensation Demonstration in Birmingham', *BP* (23 June 1890).

78   1861 census, TNA, Class RG 9, Piece 1998, Folio 74, p. 28; 1871 Census, TNA, Class RG 10, Piece 3156, Folio 146, p. 20; 'A Disorderly Character', *BP* (16 March 1886); & 'The Aston Slogging Gang at Work', *BM* (29 June 1886).

79   'Serious Outrage' & 'Breaking a Plate-Glass Window', *B&AC* (28 June 1883 & 23 August 1884)); 'Roughs at Aston', *BP* (30 June 1883); Chinn, *The Legacy*, pp. 18–20; 'The Street Obstruction Nuisance', *WH* (10 September 1885); 'The Slogging Gang', *BM* (30 April 1886); 'Ruffianism at Aston', *WH* (2 December 1886); 'Assaults on the Police', *BM* (12 August 1887).

80   'Assault on the Police', *BM* (25 May 1888); 'Where Are the Police', *BM* (26 October 1887); 'Stabbing in the Streets', *BM* (6 January 1888); 'The Aston Slogging Gang', *Leamington Spa Courier* (8 January 1887); MEP06 (30 October 1888, 30 October 1889 & 31 December 1889); & 1881 Census, TNA, Class RG 11, Piece 3042, Folio 37, p. 25.

81   'Bank Holiday Rowdyism at Aston' & 'Thursday', *WH* (24 & 31 May 1888).

82   'Crime in Aston', *B&AC* (23 July 1887); 'The Aston Sloggers Again', 'Disgraceful Rowdyism on Aston Road', 'State of Affairs' & Editorial, *WH* (26 January, 26 April, 3 May & 14 June 1888); 'How to Cool His Courage', *BM* (13 April 1888); 'Alfred Simpson Hawker', *BP* (1 September 1888); 'Another Slogger', *BST* (28 January 1888); 'Collecting Funds for the Aston Slogging Gang', *BM* (31 August 1888).

83   'The Aston Sloggers', *Daily News* (London) (4 October 1888); 1891 Census, TNA Class RG 12, Piece 2435, Folio 66, p. 4; 'The Fight Between the Birmingham Police and the Slogging Gangs' & 'The Aston Sloggers Punished' *BM* (3 & 30 October 1888); & 'The Affray Between the Police and the Aston Slogging Gang', *BP* (3 October 1888).

84   1881 Census, TNA, RG 11, Piece 2995, Folio 119, p. 33 & Piece 3002, Folio 112, p. 6; 1891 Census, TNA, RG 12, Piece 2995, Folio 119, p. 33; 'Old Offenders', *BST* (28 May 1887); 'Ruffianly Conduct', *BP* (18 October 1887); 'Assaulting the Police', *WH* (21 March 1889); & 'A Member of the Slogging Gang', (19 March 1889).

85   'A Member of the Slogging Gang', *BM* (22 January 1889); 'An Incorrigible Young Rough', *BM* (20 April 1885); 'Aston Sloggers on the Rampage', *WH* (21 February 1889); 'Stabbing Cases', *BP* (12 April 1893); 'Two Roughs', *BM* (8 April 1896); & BBCP, QS/B/20/114 (23 October 1902).

86   'The Dreadful Buckle' & 'A Juvenile Virago', *BM* (14 June 1889); 1901 Census, TNA, RG 13, Piece 2871, Folio 68, p. 7; 'A Ruffianly Fellow', *WH* (18 August 1887); 'The Aston "Slogging Gang"', *B&AC* (3 July 1886); 'Alleged Indecent Assault' & 'A Weak Case', *BP* (10 May & 1 July 1889).

87   'Serious Disturbance in Summer Lane', *BP* (20 May 1891); 'Assaults on Police Officers', *BP* (30 August 1893); 'Savage Assaults on Aston Constables', *B&AC* (30 December 1893); 'Assaulting the Police', *WH* (23 May 1895); 1901 Census, TNA, Class RG 13, Piece 2844, Folio 20, p. 31; & 'No Appearance', *B&AC* (13 March 1886).

88   'Savage Assault on the Police' & 'The Disturbance in Deritend. Clever Manoeuvre by a Policeman', *BP* (28 January & 7 February 1890); 'The Deritend Riot', *BM* (15 April 1890); *BM* (1881 Census, TNA, Class RG 11, Piece 2384, Folio 80, p. 33); 'Assaults on Policemen', 'A Frequent Offender',

ENDNOTES

& 'A Dark Outlook for Users of Buckled Belt', *BM* (10 October 1881, 3 May 1886 & 21 January 1889); 'White Savages', *BP* (14 August 1889), MEPO6, (15 April 1890); BCP, QS/B/20/49 (15 April 1890).

89   'What Shall We Do with Them?' & 'The Chief Constable and the Sloggers' *BM* (12 & 23 April 1890).

90   'Verdict of Manslaughter against a Policeman' & 'The Charge of Manslaughter against a Policeman', *BP* (7 & 18 April 1891).

91   Vince, *op. Cit.*, p. 229; 'Assaults on the Police', *BP* (29 October 1895); & 'The Bromsgrove Street Disturbance', *BP* (30 October 1895), BCP, QS/B/20/83 (1 May 1909).

92   'Assaulting a Policeman with His Own Staff', *BM* (23 January 1896); 'Summary', *BP* (3 December 1895); 'No Mistake', *BM* (8 September 1902); Chinn, *The Real Story*, pp. 179–82; & *Lloyd's Weekly Newspape*r (1 May 1898).

93   Corder, R. E. 'The Seamy Side', *Daily Mail*, 3 April 1929, p. 8. Daily Mail Historical Archive, link.gale.com/apps/doc/EE1865746004/GDCS?u=bham_uk&sid=bookmark-GDCS&xid=4c13b762. Accessed 12 December 2023; 'Topics of the Day', *Coventry Evening Telegraph* (30 December 1896); & 'A Volunteer Attacked by "Peaky Blinders"', *BM* (19 February 1896).

94   1871 Census, TNA, Class RG 10, Piece 3084, Folio 131, p. 24; WMPM, Birmingham City Police, 'Examination of a Candidate' (20 February 1890); 'The Benefit of a Good Character', 'Assaults on Soldiers', 'Savage Assaults on the Police', 'Cowardly Assaults on the Police', 'Assault on a Policeman', 'Assaults on the Police', 'Assaulting Neighbours and Police', 'Dastardly Assault Upon a Policeman', 'Assaulting Policemen', 'Violent Assaults on Policemen', 'Assaults on Constables' & 'Assaults on Policemen', *BP* (6 May 1890, 29 January, 21 April & 29 September 1891, 23 February, 26 April & 23 August 1892, 11 August 1893, 13 March 1894, 9 April 1895 & 12 November 1895); 'Local News and Jottings', 'Assaulting the Police', 'A Dangerous Ruffian', Assaulting the Police', *BM* (20 March, 15 June & 16 November 1891 & 12 June 1894); 'Savage Assault on a Policeman', *Huddersfield Chronicle* (4 November 1895).

95 See e.g. 'Reign of the Rough', *Dundee Courier* (22 July 1897), 'The Epidemic of Ruffianism in Birmingham', *Edinburgh Evening News* (12 August 1897); 'Editorial', *Redditch Indicator* (31 July 1897); & 'Tragic Death of a Birmingham Policeman', *Liverpool Weekly Mercury* (24 July 1897); & 'The Sequel to the Snipe Case', *BG* (14 October 1897).

96 BCP, QS/B/20/86 (13 October 1891); 1891 Census, TNA, Class RG 12, Piece 2386, Folio 145, p. 10 & Piece 2431, Folio 109, p. 1; 'The Case Breaks Down', *Warwick and Warwickshire Advertiser* (30 July 1898); 'The Murder of a Birmingham Policeman', *BG* (17 December 1897); 'The Murder of P.C. Snipe', *BP* (10 February 1898); 'Dramatic Arrest', *Reynolds's Newspaper* (4 September 1910); & 'The Killing of PC Snipe', *BP* (19 March 1898).

97 'The Murder of Police Constable Snipe', *Daily Argus*, (29 January 1898); 'Old Birmingham Crime. An Interview with George Williams', *ED* (5 September 1911); 'After Thirteen Years in Prison', *Dundee Courier* (5 November 1911; & 'Not "Cloggy" Williams', *BP* (12 September 1911).

98 'The Reign of Violence in Birmingham', *Lloyd's Weekly Newspaper* (25 July 1897); 'Birmingham Roughs and the Police', *Sheffield Evening Telegraph* (20 July 1897); 'Magistrates and the Police', *Globe* (28 July 1897); & 'In Defence of the Staff', *BM* (4 March 1899).

99 'Birmingham Roughs on the Rampage', *Leeds Times* (24 July 1897); *Manchester Evening Chronicle* (28 July 1897); 'Stabbing Affray in Grosvenor Road', *BWP* & 'Alleged Wounding', *Sutton Coldfield News* (17 February 1900); 'Sentences', *Leamington, Warwick, Kenilworth & District Daily Circular* (10 March 1900); & BCP, QS/B/20/178 (2 December 1920).

100 'Serious Affray in Birmingham' & 'Disgraceful Ruffianism in Birmingham', *BP* (27 & 30 June 1900); 'News of the Day', *BP* (2 July 1900); & 'Peaky Blinders', *South Wales Echo* (26 October 1900) & 'Birmingham "Peakies" and the Police', *BWP* (27 October 1900).

101 'News of the Day', *BP* (14 July 1900).

102 'Ruffianism in Birmingham', *Harborne Herald* (17 November 1900) & *BWP* (7 July 1900); & 'The Gunter Case', *BM* (14 December 1901); 1891 census, TNA, Class RG 12, Piece 4498, Folio 11, p. 15; WMPM, Birmingham City Police, Ledger 1, 6963 Charles Philip Gunter; 1901 Census, TNA, Class RG 13, Piece 2871, Folio 16, p. 23 & Piece 2861, Folio 140, p. 3.

ENDNOTES

103 'Cowardly Attack on a Birmingham Policeman', 'The Assault on a Police Officer', 'The Murderous Attack on a Birmingham Constable', 'The Attack on a Birmingham Policeman', 'Death of Police Constable Gunter', 'Death of Police-Constable Gunter. The Opening of the inquest,' *BM* (23 & 31 July, 4 & 21 August 1901, & 28 & 30 Oct 1901); & 'The Attack on Police-Constable Gunter', *BG* (25 September 1901).

104 'Burry Port Policeman Killed by Hooligans of Birmingham', *Llanelly Mercury* (7 November 1901).

105 'The Attack on Police-Constable Gunter', 'Death of Police-Constable Gunter', 'Death of Police-Constable Gunter. The Opening of the inquest', 'Birmingham Police Witness Assaulted' (15, 28 October & 30 October & 28 August 1901).

106 'The Murder of Police-Constable Gunter', *BM* (13 December 1901) & 'Summary', *BG* (14 December 1901).

107 'News of the Day', *BP* (14 December 1901); 'Midland Circuit', *The Times*, 18 December 1901, p. 7. The Times Digital Archive, link.gale.com/apps/doc/CS119335314/TTDA?u=bham_uk&sid=bookmark-

108 1891 Census, TNA, Class RG 12, Piece 2416, Folio 106, p. 8; 'The Gunter Case', *BM* (15 December 1901); 'The Lambeth Gangs', *Daily Telegraph & Courier* (London) (22 July 1898); 'Organised Ruffianism. The "Peaky Blinder" Brigade', *South Wales Echo* (15 August 1898); & 'Summary', *BG* (17 August 1898); 'Sentence on a Peaky Blinder', *Cheltenham Chronicle* (12 January 1901); & 'A Hooligan Sentenced', *Portsmouth Evening News* (9 January 1901).

109 'Birmingham's Oldest Chimney Sweep', *Erdington News* (13 August 1910); 'Assaulting the Police', *BP* (27 July 1900); 'Five Years for Stabbing a Policeman', *BG* (10 January 1901); MEPO6, Birmingham (1 November 1904); & 'Relatives Barricaded in a Bedroom', *ED* (28 October 1905).

110 'Ruffianism in Birmingham, the Stipendiary's Resolution', *BM* (5 November 1901); 'Uncivilised', *ED* (22 April 1902); Railway Employment Records, Station Birmingham, Company Great Western, Description Register of uniformed staff No.2 B 1890–1915 (September 1895); 1881 Census, TNA, RG 11, Piece 1517, Folio 50, p. 24; WMPM, Birmingham City Police, Ledgers, 6651 Ernest Blinko.

111 'Summary', *BG* (30 January 1902); 'Life Sentences on Birmingham
Peakies for a Murderous Attack', *Morning Leader* (15 March 1902); 'A
Murderous Attack on a Birmingham Constable', *BM* (28 January 1902);
'The Assault on PC Blinko', *BWP* & *BM* (8 March & 6 March 1902); & 'An
Echo of the Blinko Case', *BM* (24 October 1902).

112 'The Murderous Assault on a Constable', *BG* (7 March 1902);
'Terrible Assault in Birmingham', *Coventry Herald* (31 January 1902);
& 'The Attack on a Constable', *ED* (6 March 1902); & 'Police Constable
Blinko's Assailants on Trial', *BM* (14 March 1902).

113 'Violent Scene at the Lock Up', *BM* (7 February 1902).

114 MEPO6 (11 March 1902); 'Weekend Ruffianism in Birmingham', *BG*
(15 October 1901); 'Rowdy Youths in Calthorpe Park', *BWP* (29 September
1900); 1881 Census, TNA, Class RG 11, Piece 2951, Folio 101.

115 'Youthful Delinquents', *Harborne Herald* (5 November 1887); HO
140, Birmingham (14 March 1902); 'Saturday Night Ruffianism', *BM* (8
December 1891); 'Assaulting a German Jew', *B&AC* (13 February 1892);
'Rowdies Well Punished', 'Robbed by Roughs', 'Assault on the Police at
Balsall Heath', 'Brutal Assaults on the Police' & 'A Violent Character', *BP*
(4 October 1892, 1 August 1893, 18 October 1897, 25 July 1899 & 19 June
1900); 'Blinko Case Echo', *BM* (31 October 1945); 'Military Medal', *BP* (8
October 1918); 'The Clubman's Diary' *BG* (15 December 1938); & https://
www.cwgc.org/find-records/find-war-dead/casualty-details/35233/f-h-
cherry/.

116 'Police Constable Blinko's Assailants on Trial', *BM* (14 March 1902).

117 'Police Attacked at Key Hill', *BP* (27 March 1905).

118 'The Church in Birmingham', *BM* (16 February 1907); Vince, op. Cit.
Vol IV, p. 346; 'Birmingham Ruffians', *ED* (12 September 1909); 'Table Talk',
BM (24 July 1909).

119 'Night Adventure' (19 November 1912); 'The Disappearance of
Tramps', *BM* (4 December 1915); 'A Wave of Crime', *BWM* (29 June 1919);
'Preventer of Crime. One of the Hunters of the "Peaky Blinders"', *BWP*
(23 March 1919); & 'Libelling "Brum". No Modern Successors of the Peaky
Blinders', *BWP* (11 January 1920).

ENDNOTES

120   *The Moseley and Kings Heath Journal*, vol. 8 (August 1899), p. 114; 'Letter', *Westminster Gazette* (21 May 1910) & Chinn, *The Real Story*, pp. 123–36.

121   'Murder of PC Lines', *BWP* (27 May 1955); 'Memories of Peaky Blinder Gangs', *ED* (29 January 1930); 'Prisoners Severely Mauled', *BM* (10 February 1899), 'The Use of a Staff on an Incorrigible Ruffian' & 'Assaults on the Police', *BM* (7 March & 14 August 1899); 'More Peaky Blinders', *Sports Argus* (22 March 1902), & BCP, QS/B/20/71 & QS/B/20/113 (26 June 1894 & 26 July 1902).

122   'Obituary, Mr A. D. Penrice,' *BP* (13 January 1961); WMPM, Birmingham City Police, Ledgers, 7266 Arthur Penrice; & 'Savage Attack on a Birmingham Policeman', & 'Scene in a Birmingham Court' *BM* (10 & 13 July 1905).

123   'News in Brief', *BG* (21 November 1905); 'Assault on a Birmingham publican', *BM* (27 December 1902); 'Walked Off with a Cash Box', *BG* (1 March 1905); & 'The Weaman Street Stabbing Case', *BM* (30 April 1901).

124   Ex-Detective Superintendent W. J. May, *op. cit.*

125   'Hibernianising the Birmingham Police Force' & 'Police and Public', *BM* (27 October 1901 & 13 March 1905); & Library of Birmingham, Carl Chinn Collection MS 1902, Walter and William Chinn Interview (15 October 1979).

126   'Boys' Life Brigade', *BM* (26 October 1911); TNA, WO 97, Royal Hospital Chelsea Pensioner Service Records, 1760–1925.

127   'Birmingham Police Awards and Promotions, *BM* (23 November 1904); 'Birmingham Watch Committee Promotion List', *BM* (18 December 1912); 'Birmingham Watch Committee. Souvenirs for Army Instructors', *BM* (20 October 1915); 'Police Union Formed in Birmingham', *BP* (31 October 1918); 'Strike Sacrifices. What Policemen Gave Up for a Principle', *ED* (11 August 1919); Chinn Collection MS 1902, Stan Doughty, 'Interview' (1984).

128   'Ex-Police Chief', *BG* (13 February 1928); 'Presentation to Mr McManus', *BM* (3 July 1918); 'The New Acting Chief Constable. Some Exciting Adventures', *BM* (14 March 1899); 'A Kicking Case', *BM* (30 September 1874); & 'A Savage, Gross and Brutal Assault', *BM* (21 June 1875).

129 'Another Birmingham Policeman Stabbed', *BG* (13 September 1875); 'Courage and Ruffianism in Conflict', *Dublin Advertising Gazette* (25 September 1875); 'The Charge of Stabbing Police Constable McManus', *BG* (24 September 1875); HO 140 (27 October 1875); 1871 Census, TNA Class RG 10, Piece 3109, Folio 11, p. 15; PCOM 2, Birmingham Gaol, Habitual Criminals Register (31 July 1875); 'A Ruffianly Crispin', *BP* (8 April 1880).

130 'The Birmingham Fair: Then and Now', *BM* (15 June 1898); Pat Collins, Letter to T Murphy Esq, The Showmen's Guild (1935); Richie Calder, 'Showman's Life', *Daily Herald* (10 August 1934); 'Birmingham Gangs', *BM* (4 November 1939).

131 'Ruffians in Birmingham', *BM* (1 May 1908); '"Black Mask" Gang', *Derby Daily Telegraph* (30 September 1926); '"Black Mask" Gang Who Played at Thieves', *ED* (15 March 1932); 'Black Mask Gang', *Nottingham Evening Post* (9 February 1934); 'Black Mask Gang', *Leeds Mercury* (12 February 1936); Advertisement, *Athletic News* (24 July 1922).

CHAPTER 2: RIOTOUS GANGS

132 'Red Riot', 'Birmingham Disgraced' & 'Sub Rosa', *Morning Leader* (19 & 20 December 1901); 'Alleged Conspiracy', *St James's Gazette* (20 December 1901); 'Lloyd George Riot', *Westminster Gazette* (19 December 1901); 'Police Charge the Crowd', *Liverpool Weekly Courier* (21 December 1901); 'An Historic Riot Recalled', *South Wales Daily Post* (16 December1907); OUR, SPECIAL C. 'MR. LLOYD-GEORGE AT BIRMINGHAM: LIBERAL MEETING IN THE TOWN HALL AN EXTRAORDINARY SCENE THE MEETING BROKEN UP IN CONFUSION A BATON CHARGE BY THE POLICE MR. LLOYD-GEORGE AND THE MEETING', *The Manchester Guardian* (1901–59) 19 December 1901: 5. ProQuest. 12 February 2024; Birmingham Watch Committee, 'Report. Liberal Association Meeting', 18th December, 1901 (8 April 1902); 'Arrests by the Police', *BP* (21 December 1901); & BCP, QS/B/20/110 (5 February 1902).

133 Carl Chinn, '"Sturdy Catholic emigrants": the Irish in early Victorian Birmingham', in Roger Swift and Sheridan Gilley (eds), *The Irish in Victorian Britain. The Local Dimension* (1999), pp. 52–74.

ENDNOTES

134 'The Irish v the Police', 'The Park Street Riots', 'Mr Murphy in Birmingham', *BP* (20 June 1865, & 17; 19 & 22 June 1867); 'Mr. W. Murphy in Birmingham', *BG* (17 June 1867); & 'The Riots, the Committee and the Magistrates', *BJ* (6 July 1867).

135 T. Underwood, 'The "Murphy" Riots and Demolition of Park Street, Birmingham June 16th and 17th 1867' (1867) & 'How the Irish Fought in Birmingham', *The Nation* (6 July 1867).

136 'The Election for South Shropshire' & 'The Fatal Affray in Dale End', *BP* (24 August 1865 & 19 July 1867); 'Shocking Murder in Dale End', *BG* (17 July 1867); 'The Attack Upon Morris Roberts', *BJ* (10 August 1867); & *Coventry Standard* (28 February 1868).

137 'Continued Excitement in Birmingham' & 'Further Disturbances in Birmingham', *BP* (22 & 25 November 1867); 'The Rowdyism in Our Streets', *BG* (15 November 1869); 'Gambling in a Churchyard', *BM* (15 May 1871).

138 'Further Disturbances in Birmingham', *BP* (23 November 1867); 'Threatened Irish Riots', *BG* & 'Threatened Riot in Park Street', *BP* (28 December 1868); 'Threatened Riot in Park Street', *BJ* (2 January 1869); 'A General "Scrimmage" in Park Street', *ABG* (22 August 1868); PCOM 2 (28 April 1872); 'Breaking a Prisoner's Arm', *BP* (31 March 1884); 1841 Census, TNA HO107, Piece 1145, Book 2, Folio 41, p. 7; 'The Charge of Cardsharping', *BG* (3 October 1867); 'Monday', *ABG* (10 September 1870); 'Charge of Unlawfully Wounding', *BP* (7 July 1865).

139 1871 Census, TNA Class RG 10, Piece 3104, Folio 99, p. 28 & 1861 Census, TNA, Class RG9, Piece 2145, Folio 22, p. 37; 'Mr Murphy's Lectures in Birmingham', *BJ* (22 June 1867); Chinn, *The Real Story*, pp. 30–1; 1871 Census, TNA Class G10, Piece 3104, Folio 8, p. 41; 'Witnesses Censured by the Magistrates for Perjury', *BM* (3 April 1872); & 'Sunday Riots', *BP* (30 April 1872).

140 'A Caution to Rioters', *BP* (8 July 1874); 1871 Census TNA Class RG 10,Piece 2145, Folio 103, p. 30; 'Unlawfully and Maliciously Wounding', *BM* (18 February 1874); 'Shocking Murder of a Boy in Cheapside', *BG* (5 March 1874); 'A Boy Murderer', *Yorkshire Post and Leeds Intelligencer* (5 March 1874); 1871 Census TNA Class RG 10, 'Piece 2168, Folio 132, p. 18;

'The Alleged Murder in Cheapside', *BP* (9 July 1874); 'Warwick Assizes', *Coventry Standard* (10 July 1874); & 1881 Census, TNA, RG Class 11, Piece 2168, Folio 132; p. 18.

141　'Serious Rioting in Birmingham', *BM* (22 June 1874) & *Worcester Journal* (27 June 1874);'Our Roughs', *BM* (14 July 1874), 'News of the Day' & 'A Warning to Street Rioters', *BP* (15 July 1874); 1871 Census, TNA, Class RG 10, Piece 3106 – Folio 71, p. 24, Piece 3115 – Folio 24, p. 42 – Piece 3108, Folio 12, p. 1 – Piece 3107, Folio 65, p. 27 – Piece 3098, Folio 105, p. 41; BCP, QS/B/20/6 (20 April 1881);'Threatening a Witness', *BP* (16 July 1874); WMPM, Birmingham City Police, Ledgers, 3548 Edward Giblin & 3834 Michael Giblin; & 'Tommy Giblin and the Roughs Generally', *BM* (8 January 1896).

142　'Birmingham Watch Committee and Street Disturbances', *BP* (31 July 1874).

143　'Incidents of the Slogging Gang', *BM* (26 September 1874); 'The Allison Street Slogging Gang', *BG* (28 September 1874); 1881 Census, TNA, RG Class 11, Piece 2987, Folio 23, p. 39; 1891 Census, TNA, Class RG 12, Piece 2387, Folio 146, p. 28; WW1 Pension Ledgers and Index Cards, 1914–1923 (4 June 17); Michael King, email (2 March 2022); Sandra Fisher, email, 9 March 2023); Andrew Toy, Baptism St Chad's (24 January 1858).

144　'Black Spot in Birmingham', *BP* (17 November 1874); Carl Chinn, *Birmingham Irish Making Our Mark* (2003) pp. 79–92; Denvir, *op. cit.*, pp. 415–6; & 2–7; Musical Traditions MTCD 363–4 ('Old Fashioned Songs') (1967), https://www.vwml.org/record/RoudFS/S369588/

145　Peter Marsh, *Joseph Chamberlain. Entrepreneur in Politics* (1994), pp. 174–6; p. 268; *Cassell's History of England. Vol. VIII* (1910), p. 17. (https://api.parliament.uk/historic-hansard/commons/1884/oct/27/public-meetings-the-riot-at-aston-hall

146　'Disgraceful Proceedings', *ABG* (20 July 1867); 'News of the Day' & 'Tory Row', *BP* (23 July) & 'Tory Lambs in Trouble' (25 July 1867); 'Disgraceful Rioting in the Town Hall' & 'The Fighting at the Town's Meeting on Monday Night', *BG* (22 & 13 April 1868); & 'Cheltenham' & 'A Liberal Lamb in Trouble', *BG* (20 November 1868).

147   'Tory Meeting in the Town Hall' & 'St Stephen's Ward', *BP* (31 March & 1 April 1880); & 'Political Contrasts' & 'St Stephen's Ward' *BG* (24 March & 1 April 1880).

148   R. K. Dent, *The Making of Modern Birmingham* (1894) p. 516; 'Serious Rioting at a Conservative Demonstration', *Reynolds's Newspaper* (19 October 1884); 'The Aston Fiasco' & 'Rival Demonstrations at Aston', *BM* (14 October 1884); 'Peers and the People', 'The Aston Disturbances', *BP* (13 October & 13 November 1884); 'Drawing the Badger', *Shrewsbury Chronicle* (7 November 1994); 'The Aston Riots', *Lichfield Mercury* (5 December 1884); 'Conservative Demonstration At Birmingham', *The Times*, 14 October 1884, p. 6. The Times Digital Archive, link.gale.com/apps/doc/CS100845390/TTDA?u=bham_uk&sid=bookmark-

149   'A Conservative Meeting Broken Up', 'The Alleged Assault at a Political Meeting', 'The "King of the Roughs" and The County Court Bailiffs', 'The Assault on the County Court Bailiffs', & 'The Ipswich Election', *BM* (22 December 1882, 31 July 1883; 14 September, 2 & 4 February 1885, & 2 April 1886); 'Ipswich Election Petition', *Woodbridge Reporter* (11 March 1886); & 'Ipswich Election Petition' & 'Sequel to the Ipswich Election Petition' *East Anglian Daily Times* (9 March 1886 & 26 February 1887); DE WORMS., HENRY. 'The Brighton Election', *The Times*, 28 February 1884, p. 8. The Times Digital Archive, link.gale.com/apps/doc/CS134792796/TTDA?u=bham_uk&sid=bookmark-TTDA&xid=34c757dd. Accessed 12 February 2024; Carl Chinn, *Peaky Blinders: The Aftermath* (2021) pp. 247–8; & Marsh, *op. cit.*, p. 176.

150   'Stoning the Police – A Warning', *BP* (27 March 1874); & 'Ruffianism in Birmingham' & 'Disreputable Behaviour in the Streets', *BM* (1 February & 11 September 1875); 'Ruffianism in Aston' *B&AC* (27 May 1876); W. McGregor, 'I Remember', *Birmingham Gazette and Express* (19 September 1907); 'Nuisance in Summer Lane', *BG* (24 November 1869); 'Old Time Ruffianism', *BM* (1 May 1908).

151   'The Fatal Stabbing Case at Aston' & 'Trials of Prisoners', *BJ* (8 & 28 February 1868).

152 'Persons Injured', *BJ* (27 July 1867); 'The Gun Trade and the Conservative Candidate', *BP* (1 October 1868); 'The Case of Shooting in Harding Street', *BJ* (16 May 1868); 'Unlawfully Wounding', *BG* (29 July 1868); 'Assaulting a Wife', *BJ* (13 June 1868); 'Serious Charge of Burglary' & 'Peculiar Case of Housebreaking' *BM* (5 & 9 June 1875); 'Violent Assaults', *BM* (19 September 1876); 'The Aston Murder', *B&AC* (3 March 1877); 1881 Census, TNA, Class RG 11, Piece 2994, Folio 37, p. 27.

153 'Church Work in Birmingham. St Stephen's', *BG* (13 June 1879); 'The "Harding Street Gang"', *BP* (26 April 1880); 'Summer Lane Memories', *BM* (4 November 1939); 'Old Time Ruffianism', *BM* (1 May 1908); & 'A Little Colouring', *BM* (5 May 1886).

CHAPTER 3: MURDEROUS GANG ATTACKS

154 'Slogging Gangs', *Leeds Mercury* (14 October 1905); 'The Slogging Gangs', *BWP* (10 February 1900); '"Pop" Recalls the "Peaky Blinders"', *ED* (22 March 1948); & 'Ruffianism in Birmingham', *BM* (5 November 1901).

155 'Street Ruffianism', *Globe* (21 January 1899); 'The Buckled Belt Brigade', '"Topy" Punishment', & 'Violent Assaults', *BM* (16 January, 5 June & 20 November 1899); & 'An Unprovoked Assault', *BWP* (25 October 1902).

156 'A Witness Seeks Protection' & 'Assaulting a Witness', *BM* (9 & 10 January 1899); Valerie M. Hart and Rowena Lyon, *The Lost Children* (2020); 'Knocking a Constable's Tooth Out' & 'Results of a Street Row', *BM* (17 January 1898 & 25 July 1899); 1891 Census, TNA, RG 12, Piece 2396, Folio 89, p. 13; 'A Revolting Case', *BWP* (2 August 1902); & BCP, QS/B/20/113 (26 July 1902).

157 'Witness Assaulted', *ED* (6 May 1903); 'Shot in Street', *ED* (6 & 10 October 1905); & 'Birmingham Shooting Affray', *BM* (10 October 1905).

158 'Shot in the Street', *ED* (2 October 1905); 'The Use of their Belt', *B&AC* (21 September 1895); 'A Ruffianly Assault', *BM* (29 April 1901); & BCP, QS/B/20/121 (31 October 1903).

159 'Women's Jealousy', *BG* (16 March 1905); 'Hurst Street Stabbing Case', *BP* (30 March 1905); 'The Street Wounding Case' & 'The Heneage Street Stabbing Case', *BM* (2 May 1905 & 10 October 1899); 'Unlawful Wounding'

ENDNOTES

& 'Scene at an Inn', *BG* (7 October 1914 & 12 June 1929); MEPO6
(11 January 1938); 1911 Census, TNA, RG 14, ED 18, Piece 18006, p. 24;
& Air Ministry: Air Member for Personnel and Predecessors: Airmen's
Records, Pieces 2701–2850, File Number 2777, p. 205.

160   'Ruffianism in Birmingham', *BP* (1 May 1908) & *Down East Amongst the Poorest* (1904) pp. 3–4.

161   'Slugging' Gangs', *BM* (24 January 1905) & 'The Peakies Feud', *BG*
(11 January 1905); 'The Disturbance on The Parade', *BP* (23 October 1888),
'Street Ruffianism', *BM* (3 September 1894); G Gooderson, pp. 301–2; &
'Mob Law in Birmingham', *BM* (11 April 1890).

162   Thorne, *op. cit.*, p. 28 & Derek Salberg, *Ring Down the Curtain* (1980)
pp. 63 & 82.

163   1861 Census, TNA, Class RG 9, Piece 2146, Folio 9, p. 11; 'What
the Police Have to Put Up With', & 'Table Talk', *BM* (6 January & 7 July
1877); 'Violent Assaults', *BP* (11 June 1878); & 'Serious Charge Against a
Birmingham Concert Hall Manager', *BM* (24 December 1886).

164   'Rowdies at Music Halls', *The Era* (19 April 1890); 'Our Rowdies',
Daily News (10 April 1890); 'The Digbeth Gang', 'The Fatal Assault on a
Concert Hall Manager', 'The Digbeth Manslaughter Case', *BP* (9 & 11 April
& 8 & 11 August 1890); & 1891 Census, TNA, Class RG 12, Piece 2984,
Folio 66, p. 27.

165   BCP, QS/B/20/51 (2 August 1890) & QS/B/20/86 (14 October 1897);
1881 Census, TNA, Class RG 11, Piece 2804, Folio 39, p. 1; Anglican Parish
Records. Birmingham, Library of Birmingham (5 March 1888); 'Brutal
Assault on a Wife'; 'Local Notes and Jottings', 'Notes on the News' & 'Bad
Fish', *BM* (6 & 11 April 1881 & 2 August 1887 & 28 February 1896); 'A
Gang of Ruffians at Work', *BP* (29 December 1887); 'Newspaper Hawkers
and the Police', *BP* (1 February 1884); 1901 Census, TNA, Class RG 13,
Piece 2835, Folio 121, p. 41.

166   'The Fatal Assault on a Concert-Hall Manager', *BP* (9 April 1890);
'A Reign of Terror', *BM* (11 April 1890); & 'What Shall We Do with Them?',
BM (12 April 1890).

167 'Disorderly Boys', *BG* (29 April 1870); 'Brotherly Love', *BM* (3 February 1890); 'The Digbeth Stabbing Case' & 'The Alleged Murder at Digbeth', *BP* (16 & 28 January 1894); 'The Digbeth Tragedy', *BM* & *BG* (17 & 18 January 1894) & 'The Digbeth Tragedy: Sentence on Cherry', *BG* (19 March 1894); 1881 Census, TNA, Class RG 11, Piece 2352, Folio 66, p. 28.

168 'Young Housebreakers', *BM* (7 October 1890); 'Assault', *BP* (30 March 1894); 1891 Census, TNA, Class RG 12, Piece 2381, Folio 97, p. 24; 'Park Street Roughs on the Rampage', *BM* (12 November 1888); 'A Slogging Gang', *BP* (13 June 1889); 'Well Deserved Punishment', & 'Local News and Jottings', *BM* (30 June & 14 September 1891); 'Stabbed by a Slogger', *BP* (7 July 1891).

169 BCP, QS/B/20/68 (30 October 1893); 'Alleged Unlawful Wounding at Bordesley', *BM* (16 December 1891); 1891 Census, TNA, Class RG 12, Piece 2382, Folio 115, p. 28; 'Sequel to the Digbeth Tragedy', *BP* & *BM* (1 & 3 May 1894); 'No Character Wanted' & 'Assault with a Bottle', *BP* (15 August 1894 & 3 April 1895); Birmingham, St David (2 February 1902); England Soldiers' Effects Records, 1901–60. National Army Museum, Chelsea, 23105 (24 November 1916; & https://www.findagrave.com/memorial/56189339/f-g-collett.

170 'Lady to a Policeman's Rescue', *Central Somerset Gazette* (4 September 1897); 'Stabbed on a City 'Bus', *BG* (30 March 1905); 'Women and the Police', *BM* (20 July 1914); & MEPO 3/346, Birmingham Chief Constable's Office, Report (10 June 1921).

171 'How the Scheme Will Affect Birmingham', *BM* (23 July 1894); 'Housing of the Birmingham Poor. The Milk Street Scheme', *BM* (29 June 1899); 'Affray with the Milk Street Roughs', *BP* (8 May 1888); 'Sessions for Stabbing', *BM* (27 April 1886); BCP, QS/B/20/128 (4 November 1904); 1871 Census, TNA, Class RG 10, Piece 3107, Folio 111. p. 20; St Gabriel, Deritend, Birmingham, Marriage George Henry Allen & Catherine Burke (18 March 1900); 1911 Census, TNA, RG 14, ED 18, Piece 18165, No. 232; & 'Cut with a Razor', *BG* (7 August 1913).

172 'The Outrage by Militiamen at Small Heath', (2 July 1889); BCP, QS/B/20/45 & QS/B/20/96 (1 July 1889 & 18 January 1900); 'An Old Offender', *Kenilworth Advertiser* (23 May 1891); 'Rowdies Beware', *BM* (7 February 1889); 'The Crusade Against Ruffianism', *BP* (16 April 1890);

ENDNOTES

'The Use of Buckled Belts' & 'The Digbeth Roughs' *BM* (9 & 15 April 1890); 1881 Census, TNA, Class RG 11, Piece 2989, Folio 59, p. 18 'Garden Robberies', *WH* (16 August 1888); 'A Brutal Assault', *BP* (14 November 1889); HO 140 (1 July 1898); WW1 Pension Ledgers and Index Cards, 1914–23 (28 July 1917).

173 'Unreliable Testimony', *BP* (22 May 1888); 'A Stabbing Affray', *BP* (3 April 1895); 'Birmingham Men Charged with Passing Bad Coin', *BM* (26 June 1896); 'Endangering a Man's Life', *BP* (4 April 1893); BCP, QS/B/20/114 (16 July 1913); 'Another Coining Case', BP (17 July 1913).

174 'The Chief Constable Says There is No Slogging', *BM* (22 April 1890); & 'Heavy Sentences on Sloggers', *BP* (16 April 1890).

175 'A Man's Skull Fractured' & 'A Brutal Assault', *BM* (24 March & 25 June 1890); 'The Highgate Slogging Gang', *BST* (10 May 1890); 'A Strike of "Supers"', *BP* (12 August 1890); 'Serious Charge of Assault', *BP* (28 May 1890); Born and Bred Brum, Letter, *BWP* (13 March 1936); Chinn, *The Real Story*, p. 85; 1891 Census, TNA, Class RG 12, Piece 2407, Folio 10, p. 16; 'Serious Charge of Unlawful Wounding', *BWP* (12 July 1902); 'A Forgiving Father-in-Law', *BM* (12 July 1902); & 1901 census, TNA, Class RG 13, Piece 2831, Folio 155, p. 24.

176 'The Leaders of a Slogging Gang', *BM* (5 September 1894).

177 *Daily News* (London) (17 April 1890); 'The Stipendiary's Caution to Roughs', *BP* (17 October 1888); & BCP, QS/B/20/34 (25. February 1887).

178 'The Way to Put Down Ruffianism', *BP* (6 October 1891); 'An Epidemic of Brutality', *BP* (3 May 1892); 'A Slogging Gang and Its "Captain"', *BG* (20 August 1892); & 'Storming a Shop', *BP* (14 October 1893).

179 Louise Mellor, 'Steven Knight Interview', https://peakyblinders.tv/exclusive/steven-knight-interview/ Accessed 27 October 2023; 'Ruffianism', *BP* (28 August 1894); 'Street Ruffianism' & 'Assaulting the Police' *BM* (28 June 1886 & 14 May 1887); 'Another Rough Severely Punished' & 'A Slogging Gang', *BP* (15 November 1888 & 24 July 1889); 'The Suppression of Slogging Gangs', *BWP* (27 July 1889); 'Disgraceful Assault on a Girl', *BWP* (9 November 1889); 'A Well-Merited Sentence', *BP* (19 April 1895); 'Unprovoked Assaults', *BP* (6 November 1895); (BCP, QS/B/20/72 & QS/B/20/138 (28 Oct 1907 & 21 March 1906).

180 'Ruffianism in Birmingham' & 'The Burglary at a Bordesley Public House', *BM* (5 April & 25 August 1899); 'Ladies in Park Street Gardens', *BP* (31 August 1899); 'A Remarkable Clue', *BM* (11 October 1899); 'The Most Lawless Part of Birmingham', *BWP* (3 March 1900).

181 'Stone-Throwing in the Street' & 'Cleveland Street v Weaman Street', *BP* (23 August 1892 & 2 August 1893); 'Street Riots Sheep Street versus Hall Street', *BM* (15 May 1872); 'Shocking Stabbing Affray in Aston' & 'The Stabbing Affray in Aston', *B&AC* (31 August & 5 October 1895); 'The Stabbing Affray in Aston' & 'The Park Lane Stabbing Case. Heavy Sentences,' *WH* (3 October & 12 December 1895); & 'Unlawful Wounding at Aston', BP (10 December 1895).

182 'A Brutal Affair', 'Slogging Gangs in Birmingham', 'Alleged Assault and Theft by a Boy' & 'Assaults on the Police', *BM* (5 June 1882, 3 July 1882, 20 February 1882, 30 April 1888); & 'Murderous Assault at Aston', *BP* (17 March 1893).

183 'The "Slogging Gangs" and How They Were Broken Up', *BWP* (10 February 1900); 'A Warning to Street Ruffians', *BP* (21 July 1886).

184 'The Aston Slogging Gang Again. A Reign of Terror', *BST* (21 August 1886); 'Street Rowdyism', *BP* (11 August 1886); & 'Roughs in the Street', *BP* (7 September 1886). The Nechells Gang was also known as the Rocky Lane Sloggers, 'Rocky Lane Sloggers at Birmingham', *BM* (31 May 1889).

185 'The Slogging Gang Again', *B&AC* (11 December 1886); 'Sunday Disorder in Aston', *BP* (9 July 1887); 'Unlawful Wounding', *Harborne Herald* (6 August 1887); & 'Assault on the Police', *BM* (25 May 1888).

186 'Capture of the "King of Sloggers"', 'The Slogging Gang Once More', & 'King of a Slogging Gang', *BM* (23 August 1888, 28 September 1886 & 21 December 1888); 'Unlawfully Wounding', *BP* (9 January 1889); 'A Slogging Husband', *B&AC* (9 July 1892); & Andrew Davies, *The Gangs of Manchester*, (2008) pp. 296–319.

187 'Fifty Years Ago', *BP* (3 July 1941); 'A Nechells Slogging Gang', *BM* (4 September 1888); 'Rowdyism at Ten Arches', *BP* (22 May 1900); 'Stone Throwing', *BM* (2 November 1885) – a band of thieves was previously called the Ten Arches Gang, *BM* (10 January 1883); 'The Drunken List', *B&AC* (8 October 1892); 'A Detective's Reminiscences. The Methods of

Birmingham's Slogging Gangs', *Gloucestershire Echo* (5 November 1904); & 'Hooliganism in Birmingham', *BM* (20 September 1899).

188   'Resumed Activity by the Aston Sloggers', *BM* (25 February 1889); 'Desperate Affray in Charles Henry Street' (17 May 1889); 'Brutal Treatment of a Boy' & 'An Ornament to the Slogging Gang', *BP* (5 June & 1 July 1889); 'More on the Slogging Gang', *BM* (29 June 1889); & BCP, QS/B/20/45 (29 June 1889).

189   1861 Census, TNA, Class RG 9, Piece 2146, Folio 88, p. 27; 1881 Census, TNA, Class RG11, Piece 3045, Folio 27, p. 8; 'Street Ruffianism in Birmingham', *BP* (24 June 1892); BCP, QS/B/20/63 (30 June 1892); & 'Outrage on a Youth', *Western Daily Press* (10 June 1892).

190   'Birmingham Police Court', *BP* (13 February 1893); 'His Eighteenth Assault', *B&AC* (20 December 1890); 'The Stipendiary and Assaults on Policemen', *BP* (21 April 1892); 'Slogging Gangs in Conflict', *BG* (31 October 1892); 'Wilful Damage', *BP* (27 June 1893); 'Notes and News', *BM* (13 April 1894); 'A Midnight Scene in New Summer Street', *BG* (26 October 1898); MEPO6 (25 October 1898); 'Fancied Some Chicken', *BM* (30 September 1904).

191   1891 Census, TNA, Class RG 11, Piece 2441, Folio 175, p. 175; 'Obscene Language', *WH (*1 August 1895); 'International Glove Contest at the Olympic Club Birmingham', *Sporting Life* (29 January 1898); 'The Olympic Club Case', *BM* (14 March 1898); HO 140 (14 March 1898); 'Disabled Constable. Savage Attack on a Birmingham Policeman', *BG* (3 January 1905); '"Bruiser" and Policeman', *BG* (20 December 1904); 'Crown-ed Heads', *ED* (15 October 1915); & 'A Rugged Battler', *Daily Herald* (30 July 1921).

192   'The "Slogging Gangs" and How They Were Broken Up', *BWP* (10 February 1900); 'Ex-Superintendent Walker', *The Coventry Herald and Free Press* (2 September 1905); 'A Troublesome Family', *BM* (8 June 1887); 'The "Sloggers"' Bank Holiday', *WH* (4 August 1887); & 'A Terror to the "Roughs"', *Leamington Spa Courier* (19 June 1931).

193   'A Reminiscence of the Slogging Gangs', *BM* (21 May 1900); 1881 Census, TNA, Class RG 11, Piece 3033, Folio 29, p. 49; 'Assault on a Woman' & 'Police and the Public', *BP* (29 July 1891 & 21 June 1898);

Yvonne Holder, Emails (1 November 2015 & 31 January 2016); 'Beaten with Belts', *BM* (8 January 1901); 'A Remarkable Career', *BM* (23 December 1898); & BCP, QS/B/20/135 (7 November 1905) & QS/B/20/136 (15 June 1905); MEPO6 (20 October 1902).

194   1871 Census, TNA, Class RG 10, Piece 3151, Folio 30, p. 7; 'The Slogging Gang', 'Assaults on the Police', *BM* (30 April 1886 & 12 August 1887); 'A Savage Attack on the Police', *WH* (28 March 1889); 'Assault', *BP* (4 September 1894); Chinn, *The Legacy*, pp. 17–20; 'A Gallant Act Rewarded', *WH* (4 October 1888); 'Bank Holiday Brawl', *WH* & 'Whit Monday Row at Aston', *BM* (8 June 1904); & MEPO6 (20 October 1902).

195   'Ten Arches Gang', *BP* (29 April 1909).

CHAPTER 4: BULLYING, ABUSIVE AND RACIST PEAKY BLINDERS

196   'Workman', Volunteer Attacked by Peaky Blinders, 'The Peaky at Bordesley Green', 'The Peakies Courtship', & 'The Murder Mystery', *BM* (21 July 1897, 19 February 1896, 7 January 1898, & 26 January & 28 October 1899).

197   George Gissing, *Eve's Ransom* (first published 1895, 1980 edn), p. 6; Bertram Hildick, 'The Peaky Blinders Were City Terrors', *BWM* (13 June 1954); & 1891 Census TNA, Class RG 12, Piece 2433, Folio 71, p. 18 & 1901 Census, TNA, Class RG 13, Piece 2886, Folio 169, p. 32.; & Arthur L. Matthison, *Less Paint, More Vanity* (1937), pp. 62–3.

198   J. R. C. 'Peaky Blinders', *Central Literary Magazine* vol. XIV, no. 2, (April 1879); p. 71, 'Terrorising Shopkeepers', *BM* (1 November 1902); Terry Proctor, Letter, Birmingham Lives Archive, Library of Birmingham (8 March 1996); '"Cadgers" and Shopkeepers', *BWP* (6 December 1902); & William Fisher, 'How I Beat the Peaky Blinders', *BWM* (19 December 1954).

199   Julie Tims, email (1 January 2024); 'Peaky Blinders', *Coventry Evening Telegraph* (30 December 1896); 'Terrorism of the Cheapside Slogging Gang', *BG* (25 June 1898); BCP, QS/B/20/118 (28 April 1898); 'The Use of the Knife in Birmingham', *BM* (26 December 1876); Rev. T. J. Bass, *Everyday in Blackest Birmingham. Facts no Fiction* (1898), pp. 8–9; &

ENDNOTES

'Unlawful Wounding' & 'A Caution to Street Roughs', *BP* (24 March 1877 & 18 October 1873).

200   1891 Census TNA, Class RG 12, Piece 2421, Folio 85, p. 4 & Piece 2418, Folio 12, p. 17; & 'News of the Day', *BWP* (24 April 1889).

201   'Street Ruffianism' & 'Heavy Sentences on Sloggers', *BP* (21 January 1890 & 6 April 1890); 'The Aston Slogging Gang', *BM* (21 January 1890); MEPO6 (12 June 1896); & 'Daring Burglaries', *WH* (5 July 1894).

202   'Street Ruffianism in Birmingham. A Man Killed in Summer Lane' & 'Notes and News' *BM* (28 April 1890) & 'The Summer Lane Manslaughter Case', & 'Local News and Jottings' (1 & 5 May 1890); 'The Porchester Street Affray', *B&AC* (9 August 1884); & 'More Street Ruffianism', 'The Fatal Affray in Summer Lane' & 'The Summer Lane Manslaughter', *BP* (28 April, 1 May & 11 August 1890); BCP, Qs/B/20/51 (2 August 1890); & 1881 Census, TNA, Class RG 11, Piece 3010, Folio 14, p. 22.

203   1891 Census, TNA, Class RG 12, Piece 2418, Folio 98, p. 16; 'Serious Charge of Stabbing', *BP* (29 August 1891); 'Heavy Sentence on a Birmingham Rough' & 'Assaulting a Landlady', *BP* (17 October 1891 & 18 May 1901); 'A Batch of Assault Cases' & 'A Blow With a Hammer', *BM* (22 July 1901 & 8 September 1902); & 'Corporation Street Warehouse Entered', *BP* (27 June 1906).

204   'Ruffianism in Birmingham. "Peaky" Outrages', (17 February 1902); 'Quarter Sessions', *BWP* (12 April 1902); MEPO 6 (3 April 1902); & 'Sensational Affair at Winson Green', *BM* (13 February 1899).

205   1871 Census, TNS, Class RG 10, Piece 3106, Folio 74, p. 29, 'Claims for Compensation in Birmingham', *The Manchester Courier and Lancashire Advertiser'* (27 June 1867); Serious Disturbance and Savage Assaults in New Canal Street', *BM* (19 August 1874); 'Shocking Assault on a Police Sergeant' & 'Violent Assaults', *BP* (21 January & 16 July 1878); 'Violent Assault on the Police', *BG* (24 August 1880); & 'Alleged Assault by an Italian', *BM* (7 July 1884).

206   'Three Dangerous Young Savages', *BWP* (7 July 1877); 1871 Census, TNA, Class RG 10, Piece 3106, Folio 63, p. 7 & Piece 3106, Folio 60, p. 1; & 1881 census, TNA, Class RG 11, Piece 2986, Folio 88, p. 22.

207   'Street Ruffianism' & 'Ruffianly Conduct at Aston', *WH* & *A&BC*
(17 & 19 September 1885); & 1881 Census, TNA, Class RG 11, Piece 3032,
Folio 20, p. 34.

208   'Ruffianly Revenge' & 'A Flogging Gang versus a Slogging Gang', *BG*
(17 & 31 October 1892).

209   'Moll, N. (2), Sense 2', *Oxford English Dictionary*, Oxford UP, March
2024, https://doi.org/10.1093/OED/1796392306; Donah, N., Sense 1.' *Oxford
English Dictionary*, Oxford UP, February 2024, https://doi.org/10.1093/
OED/3487717072; 'Donah, N., Sense 2.' *Oxford English Dictionary*, Oxford
UP, February 2024, https://doi.org/10.1093/OED/1016464449; & 'Love's
Young Dream', *Hull Daily Mail* (6 November 1896); & 'The World We Live
In', *Sheffield Weekly Telegraph* (4 January 1896).

210   'Table Talk', *BM* (26 November 1898); https://scalar.usc.edu/works/
anglo-american-music-theater-i/

211   'Tragic Death of a Birmingham Girl. A Lover Charged With
Manslaughter', 'The Tragic Death of a Birmingham Girl', & 'The Alleged
Manslaughter of a Girl', & 'The Manslaughter of a Sweetheart', *BM* (14, 16
& 17 November & 25 December 1898); 'The Summer Lane Fatal Kicking
Case' & 'Summary', *BG* (17 November & 16 December 1898); 1891 Census,
TNA, Class RG 12, Piece 2391, Folio 140, p. 22; British Army Service
Records WO 96, Militia Service Records 1806–1915, Box 106, Box Record
Number 36 (8 October 1897).

212   'Youth Charged with Murder', *Tamworth Herald* (19 November
1898); see Carl Chinn, *Poverty Amidst Prosperity. The Urban Poor
in England, 1834–1914* (first published 1985, 2006 edn), pp. 98–118;
Andrew Davies (2006) Youth, violence, and courtship in late-Victorian
Birmingham: The case of James Harper and Emily Pimm, The History
of the Family, 11:2, 107–120, DOI: 10.1016/ j.hisfam. 2006.07.00; 'The
"Peaky's" Courtship. A Phase of Birmingham Low Life', *BM* (19 November
1898).

213   Alexander Patterson, *Across the Bridges. Life in the South London
River-side* (1911), pp. 197–207. For a discussion on violence within
marriages see Carl Chinn, *They Worked All Their Lives. Women of the
Urban Poor, 1990–1919* (first published 1988, 2006 edn), pp. 141–42.

ENDNOTES

214   Library of Birmingham, Carl Chinn Collection MS 1902, Walter and William Chinn Interview (15 October 1979). Len Wells was a Militia man living nearby to my great-grandparents, British Army Service Records WO 96, Militia Service Records 1806–1915, Box 551, Box Record Number 127 (29 October 1901).

215   Bertram Hildick, 'The Peaky Blinders Were City Terrors', BWM (13 June 1954); 'My Bloke's a Peaky' (Roud 24185) Cecilia Costello, Old Fashioned Songs (no date); http://www.planetslade.com/broadside-ballads-peaky-blinder.html. Jon Wilks·Tradfolk 101 (8 March 2022); http://www.planetslade.com/broadside-ballads-peaky-blinder.html; J. R. C. 'Peaky Blinders', Central Literary Magazine vol. XIV, no. 2, (April 1879), p. 71; For a discussion of masculinity and hardness see Chinn, *The Legacy*, pp. 109–13; & 'A Slogging Gang', *Heywood Advertiser* (7 May 1897).

216   'Violent Assaults in Birmingham. A Peaky's Love Affairs', BM (18 August 1899); WWI Pension Record Cards and Ledgers, Pension Record Ledger, Reference Number 6/Mk/667 (5 March 1919) 'A Peaky's Courtship. Gross Brutality' & 'Another Peaky's Courtship', BM (31 August & 21 September 1899); 'A "Peaky's" Courtship', BM (10 January 1899); BCP, QS/B/20/135 (8 November 1905); Savage Assault on a Girl', 'Sidelights on Low Life. Birmingham "Peaky" Sent to Prison', & 'Birmingham Criminal's Appeal', BM (20 February & 26 May 1900 & 19 August 1910); 'The Three Graces', BST (6 May 1899); & 'A Brutal Ruffian', BWP (10 March 1900); 'Midnight Visitor', Ed (3 November 1903); & BCP, QS/B/20/122 (10 December 1903).

217   'Annoying the Salvation Army', A&BC (1 March 1884); 'Assaulting members of the Salvation Army', BM (24 December 1886); 'A Penitent', BP (31 December 1889); 'Assaulting the Salvation Army', BM (25 June 1888); 'Latest Epitome', *Globe* (London) (3 August 1887); 'Rowdyism at Balsall Heath', BP (14 February 1889); 'Disturbing the Salvation Army', BM (2 July 1891); 'Street Ruffianism', BP (3 July 1894); 'Birmingham Ruffianism', B&AC (7 July 1894); 'Assault with a Chopper', 'Two Months for Assaulting a Wife', BP (3 September 1895 & 27 March 1901).

218   Carl Chinn, 'The Peoples of Birmingham', in Carl Chinn and Malcolm Dick (eds), *Birmingham. The Workshop of the World* (2016) pp, 24–6; 1891 Census, TNA, Class RG 12, Piece 2375, Folio 32, p. 2; Piece 2375, Folio 31, p. 17, & Piece 2379, Folio 6, p. 10; 'Assaulting a German Jew', *B&AC* (13 February 1892); & 'The Attack on Foreigners', *BP* (13 February 1892).

219   'Birmingham', *Jewish World* (9 June 1899); 'Abusing Jews', *BP* (24 September 1895); 'A Gang of Freebooters in Birmingham', 'Jew Baiting in Florence Street', 'Notes and News', 'Serious Stabbing Affray', *BM* (2 August, 18 & 19 December 1899 & 24 October 1907); TNA, WO364, War Office: Soldiers' Documents from Pension Claims, First World War, Regimental Number 2991; 'Local Men Wounded', *BP* (1 May 1915); 'A Pickpocket Caught', *BWP* (17 May 1902); 'Stabbed in Hurst Street', *BG* (5 January 1904); 1911 Census, TNA, Class RG Piece 2831, Folio 155, p. 24; 'Conduct Befitting a Beast', *BP* (7 October 1914); TNA, WO 329, War Office and Air Ministry: Service Medal and Award Rolls, First World War, Regiment Number 3402; & TNA, 1939 Register, Line Number 11, Schedule Number 82, Sub Schedule Number 2, Enumeration District Qawk.

220   Chinn, *The Real Story*, pp. 237–42; Carl Chinn, '"We all Come from Round Sora": Italians in Birmingham, *c*.1821–1919', in Owen Ashton, Robert Fyson and Stephen Roberts (eds), *The Duty of Discontent. Essays for Dorothy Thompson* (1995), pp. 251–69; 'Wanton Mischief', *BP* (30 December 1878); 'Undesired Interference', *BM* (1 July 1885); Serious Affray in Bartholomew Street', *BP* (24 April 1886); MEPO6 (24 July 1891); Notes and News' & 'Murderous Assault Upon Italians', *BM* (24 April 1886 & 5 August 1891); 'Rowdyism in Garrison Lane', *BM* (10 July 1901); 'Murderous Assault upon Italians', *BM* (5 August 1891); 'The Assault on an Italian Organ Grinder', *BP* (13 May 1892); 'Birmingham Street Row', 'Trials of Prisoners' & 'Attack Upon An Italian', *BG* (8 August & 29 October 1907 & 16 March 1909).

221   Margaret Beale, Email (1 October 2014); Mr Beasley, Interview, Carl Chinn Bookmaking Archive, US39, Cadbury Research Library, University of Birmingham; 'Bromsgrove Street Row', *BM* (13 April 1908); 'Shots in a City Street', *BG* (22 June 1908); Acting Superintendent, 'Re Unlawful Assemblies in Watery Lane and District' (Handwritten MS 1909)

ENDNOTES

[West Midlands Police Museum]; 'Shooting Affray', *BG* (9 January 1909); 'Birmingham Vendetta', *BM* (30 January 1909); 'Jilted Lover's Revenge', *BP* (20 February 1900); Terence Lines, Email 25, February 2014); 'The Dartmouth Street Vendetta', *BG* & *ED* (3 & 5 May 1909); & Garrison Street Vendetta', *BG* (20 September, 29 November & 1 December 1910).

222 'Birmingham Stabbing Case' & 'Public-House Incident', *BM* (25 January & 21 March 1911); 'A Notorious Feud', *BG* (28 March 1912); A BIRMINGHAM VENDETTA: MAN SHOT IN THE HEAD IN A PUBLIC HOUSE. (1912/10/15/, 1912 Oct 15). *The Manchester Guardian* (1901–59) Retrieved from https://www.proquest.com/historical-newspapers/birmingham-vendetta/docview/475547901/se-2; 'A Prisoner's Threat', *BP* (5 April 1898); 'Birmingham Vendetta', *News of the World* (8 December 1912), 'Garrison Lane Vendetta', *BM* (7 December 1912); 'Sentence Reduced', *BG* (21 January 1913).

223 'The End of the Peaky Blinders', *Sheffield Independent* (28 June 1923); 1921 Census, TNA, RG 15, Piece 14250, Schedule 76, & Piece 14245; Schedule 70; 'Racecourse Pests', *Nottingham Evening Post* (3 September 1919); 'Roulette Swindle', *ED* (31 May 1928); 1939 England and Wales Register, TNA, Schedule 128, Sub Schedule 1, Enumeration District Qaxl & Schedule 45; Chinn, 'The Peoples of Birmingham', op. cit., pp. 28–9; & 'City Plans to Repel Tinker Incursion', *BP* (9 July 1963). Naming Irish Travellers as 'tinkers' is now regarded as offensive. Minority ethnic definitions are as given at https://travellermovement.org.uk/gypsy-roma-and-traveller-history-and-culture.

AFTERWORD: HISTORICAL REALITY

224 https://en.wikipedia.org/wiki/Peaky_Blinders#:~:text=for%20 a%20time.-,Notorious%20members, Harry%20Fowles%2C%20and%20 Stephen%20McNickle; https://www.findmypast.com/blog/discoveries/real-peaky-blinders

225 'False Pretences at Erdington', *BM* (5 August 1903); 'Alleged Aston Imposter', *ED* (31 July 1903); 'Preying Upon the Poor. One-Legged Rogue Sentenced in Birmingham', *BM* (18 October 1904).

226 'The Cycle Disappeared', *ED* (13 October 1904); 'A Bogus Collector', *BG* (6 March 1905); 1891 Census, TNA, Class RG 12, Piece 2416, Folio 106, p. 8; BCP, QS/B/20/109 (13 December 1901); 'Possession of Skeleton Keys', *ED* (10 Jul 1909); War Office: Soldiers' Documents, First World War 'Burnt Documents', WO363, Regimental Number 4938; Carl Chinn, Brum Undaunted. Birmingham During the Blitz (2005 edn), p. 166.

227 'Serious Aston Assaults', *BG* (17 July 1906); HO 140 (17 Oct 1899); 1921 Census, TNA, RG 15, RG 15, Piece 14315, Schedule 299; WWI Pension Record Cards and Ledgers, Pension Record Ledger, Reference 6/Mm/No.5474; War Office: Soldiers' Documents, First World War 'Burnt Documents', WO363, Regimental Number 62575; Ian Moseley, Email (13 May 2024).

228 'Slot Meters Rifled', *BG* (3 January 1907); BCP, Qs/B/20/67 (13 February 1907);'Scene in a Public-House', BM (28 August 1917); 'One Offence Follows Another', BP (17 October 1924); 'Man's Hands in Another's Pocket', Feats, *ED* (5 August 1938); 'Must Contribute Towards His Keep in Gaol', *BP* (2 June 1939); & Lucy Scott, Emails (19 July and 11 September 2023); Anglican Parish Records. Birmingham, England: Library of Birmingham, Deritend, St John and St Basil (23 July 1913); TNA, 1939 Register, Line Number 24, Schedule Number 55, Sub Schedule Number 1, Enumeration District Qbol; Chinn, *The Real Story*, pp. 5–9.